Preparing Pre-Service Teachers to Teach Computer Science: Models, Practices, and Policies

A Volume in
Research, Innovation & Methods in Educational Technology

Series Editors

Chrystalla Mouza
Nancy C. Lavigne

Research, Innovation & Methods
in Educational Technology

Series Editors

Chrystalla Mouza
University of Delaware

Nancy C. Lavigne
University of Delaware

BOOKS IN THE SERIES

Preparing Pre-Service Teachers to Teach Computer Science: Models, Practices, and Policies

Edited by

Chrystalla Mouza
Aman Yadav
Anne Ottenbreit-Leftwich

INFORMATION AGE PUBLISHING, INC.
Charlotte, NC • www.infoagepub.com

Library of Congress Cataloging-In-Publication Data

The CIP data for this book can be found on the Library of Congress website (loc.gov).

Paperback: 978-1-64802-456-6
Hardcover: 978-1-64802-457-3
E-Book: 978-1-64802-458-0

Copyright © 2021 Information Age Publishing Inc.

Printed in the United States of America

CONTENTS

PART I
PEDAGOGICAL PRACTICES FOR DEVELOPING AND ASSESSING PRE-SERVICE TEACHERS' KNOWLEDGE OF COMPUTER SCIENCE

DEDICATION

To our families for their support and patience during the preparation of this book

ACKNOWLEDGEMENTS

We greatly acknowledge the chapter authors for their contributions, hard work during multiple rounds of revisions, and commitment to the quality of their work.

We are very grateful to the Book Editorial Advisory Team for their constructive feedback and advise: Kevin Guidry (University of Delaware), Amy Hutchison (George Mason University), Diane O'Grady-Cunniff (University System of Maryland), and Colby Tofel-Grehl (Utah State University).

Finally, we like acknowledge the support of our colleagues at our respective institutions and the staff at Information Age Publishing.

INTRODUCTION

PREPARING PRE-SERVICE TEACHERS TO TEACH COMPUTER SCIENCE

Chrystalla Mouza, Aman Yadav,
and Anne Ottenbreit-Leftwich

COMPUTER SCIENCE EDUCATION IN
PRE-SERVICE TEACHER PREPARATION

In recent years, there has been increased interest in computer science (CS) education in primary and secondary classrooms across the globe, including the U.S., U.K, Finland, Israel, Estonia, and other countries (Angeli et al., 2016). One aspect of CS education that has gained momentum is computational thinking (CT), which has been recognized as a key mechanism for promoting CS education in K–12 settings (Yadav et al., 2018). CT combines skills that computer scientists draw upon to help learners make decisions or solve problems. Wing (2006) argued that CT is a fundamental skill for everybody and that "to reading, writing, and arithmetic, we should add computational thinking to every child's analytical ability" (p. 33). This focus on helping all students develop CT skills is also reflected in the latest National Educational Technology Standards for Students (ISTE, 2016) as well as

Preparing Pre-Service Teachers to Teach Computer Science: Models, Practices, and Policies, pages xiii–xxii.
xiii

content area standards, including Common Core State Standards in mathematics (CCSS, 2010) and the Next Generation Science standards (NGSS, 2013).

A key challenge in integrating CS across K–12 curricula is preparation and support for teachers as many lack a strong foundation in computing (DeLyser et al., 2018). While a number of efforts have focused on preparing practicing teachers to deliver CS curricula, pre-service education remains the sustainable path to a pipeline of well-prepared teachers (Guzdial, 2017). Yet relatively few efforts have prioritized new models, practices, and pedagogical approaches for pre-service teacher education in CS (DeLyser et al., 2018). The need to prepare pre-service teachers with the knowledge and skills needed to deliver CS is timely and urgent, especially due to the highly homogeneous population of K–12 students who engage with the field (Goode et al., 2020). This book extends current knowledge by presenting research-based strategies, pedagogical approaches, and policies that facilitate the preparation of pre-service teachers in the teaching of CS.

NEED AND IMPORTANCE OF THIS BOOK

Despite wide calls to make CS accessible to all students, there is wide variability across the U.S. and the world related to teacher preparation. In the U.S., for instance, few states require teacher certification pathways in CS (see also chapter 12) and few teacher education programs require pre-service teachers to develop knowledge and skills in CS (Delyser et al., 2018). In turn, as a field we lack comprehensive knowledge of evidence-based practices that help support pre-service teacher knowledge and practice of CS.

To date, few studies have examined pre-service teacher preparation in CS, making it difficult to extrapolate coherent lessons that can guide researchers, teacher educators, and practitioners seeking to develop the next generation of teachers. Of those, a number of studies focused on the preparation of secondary CS teachers who typically teach stand-alone CS courses (Hubwieser et al., 2013), while fewer focused on specific pedagogical strategies for the integration of CS content and pedagogy in teacher education coursework (e.g., McGinnis et al., 2020; Mouza et al., 2017). The scarcity of scholarly work at the intersection of CS and pre-service teacher preparation is problematic because CS education does not have the advantage of a long history in K–12 schools, similar to areas like mathematics and science. As Blikstein and Moghadam (2019) eloquently point out, professional societies for the teaching of mathematics and science have been around since 1920 and 1944, respectively. Yet the Computer Science Teacher Association (CSTA) was not launched until 2004. Professional organizations are important because they help identify qualities and standards for teaching within the discipline, while simultaneously disseminating research and best practices within their respective fields. Although substantial strides have been made by CSTA to support the development of standards and curricula, a demand remains for research and implementation guidelines specific to the preparation of pre-service teachers in CS.

Through this book we aim to bridge this gap at a critical juncture in the history of CS education, where efforts to scale are moving rapidly. These efforts, albeit timely and necessary, can also come at a cost if not implemented in a systematic and equitable manner (Margolis, 2017). The chapters in this book provide much needed guidance related to pedagogy, support, and policies around pre-service teacher education in CS. Such guidance is strongly needed because the success of both standards and curricula ultimately rely on effective implementation by teachers.

DESCRIPTION OF CHAPTERS

The book has been in preparation for two years. When we issued a call for chapters the response exceeded our expectations by far, demonstrating both the emerging vibrant community of scholars conducting work in this field, but also the need and desire for a cohesive volume that provides guidance on pre-service teacher preparation in CS. The chapters selected for this volume represent authors from different backgrounds and contexts as well as a variety of approaches ranging from theoretical to empirical investigations. Each chapter was first reviewed by the editors as well as peer-reviewed by an editorial board established for the book, consisting of researchers and educators with expertise in CS education: Kevin Guidry (University of Delaware), Amy Hutchison (George Mason University), Dianne O'Grady-Cunniff (University System of Maryland), and Colby Tofel-Grehl (Utah State University). Each chapter went through reviews and multiple stages of revisions prior to acceptance. The resulting book is divided into three sections that capture the work being done in the field. Those sections and the corresponding chapters are described below.

Part I: Pedagogical Practices for Developing and Assessing Pre-Service Teachers' Knowledge of Computer Science

As CS education becomes an integral part of the curriculum, an important question remains related to pre-service teachers' knowledge for teaching CS as well as their attitudes and beliefs towards the implementation of CS in their future classrooms. At the secondary level, some authors have already attempted to define the type and depth of knowledge needed to teach CS curricula. For instance, the German collaboration project aimed to identify competencies required to teach stand-alone CS courses (Hubwieser et al., 2013). Typically work in this area is useful in thinking about the knowledge and skills required to teach stand-alone CS curricula but does not address the needs of teachers who seek to integrate CS principles across content and curricula at the K–12 level.

The most significant framework used to conceptualize teacher knowledge is Shulman's tripartite scheme of content knowledge (CK), pedagogical knowledge (PK), and pedagogical content knowledge (PCK). The construct of PCK in particular has been widely studied in other fields and is used to differentiate knowledge of general pedagogical strategies that transcend subject matter from knowledge that is specific to each discipline. Yet Shulman's framework makes it clear that all three knowledge constructs are needed for effective teaching. In the field of CS, knowledge of computing (i.e., CK) alone is not enough. Rather, teachers' knowledge must be situated in an understanding of how people learn broadly (i.e., PK) and specifically in relation to CS (i.e., PCK). Further, the importance of teacher beliefs in the implementation of new technologies, curricula and policies has been widely documented in the literature (e.g., Ertmer & Ottenbreit-Leftwich, 2010; Mouza, 2009), and should be an important consideration in preparing pre-service teachers to teach CS. The chapters in this section address the use of general and content specific strategies for teaching CS, their attitudes and beliefs, and the development and assessment of teacher knowledge in relation to CS.

Chapter 1, Active Learning Techniques for Computing Education discusses active learning, a general pedagogical approach that emphasizes higher-order thinking, and its application in computing education. Active learning techniques are organized and categorized based on a framework that covers three key issues: (a) accountability and interdependence (solo, collaborative, or cooperative activities); (b) instructor effort in terms of guidance, preparation, and feedback (before, during, or after class); and (c) student engagement (active constructive, or interactive). Specific examples related to using these strategies are highlighted drawing from popular CS curricula available for teachers (e.g., Exploring Computer Science). The overall intent of the chapter is to provide teacher educators with a toolbox to support prospective teachers in using pedagogical strategies that support the design of CS lessons or lessons that integrate CS principles across K–12 curricula.

Chapter 2, Pre-Service Teachers' Perception, Confidence, and Experience of Computer Science Education presents an empirical investigation, which examines how CS education lessons influenced pre-service teachers' beliefs, confidence, and interest in teaching CS education in their future classrooms. Participants included 77 pre-service teachers who were introduced to the fundamental concepts of CS and programming in a stand-alone technology integration course. Using pre-and post-surveys, computational products, and course surveys, the authors examined changes in pre-service teachers' beliefs, confidence, and interest towards CS. Findings demonstrated that the course activities helped participants increase confidence and interest in teaching CS in their future classrooms. However, participants reported a lack of skills and understanding of CS concepts and tools even after the course, suggesting a need for additional preparation that better prepares pre-service teachers to implement CS curricula.

Chapter 3, Exploring Factors that Influence Pre-Service Teachers to Effectively Integrate Educational Robotics and Programming into Educational Practice also examines pre-service teachers' knowledge, attitudes, and perceptions focusing on one type of technology with promise for CS, namely educational robotics. Participants in the study completed coursework in both educational technology and educational robotics. Data were collected through questionnaires and focus groups with different cohorts of pre-service teachers. Findings indicated distinct needs in relation to educational robotics (e.g., using robotics platforms, developing educational activities, and acquiring experience in real-classrooms). Further, the authors found that pre-service teachers demonstrated positive attitudes towards robotics but expressed concerns related to their knowledge and skills in using robotics. Finally, results indicated that personal, professional and institutional factors influenced pre-service teachers' willingness to integrate robotics in their future educational practice.

Chapter 4, Eliciting Pedagogical Content Knowledge for Computer Science Teaching shifts attention from developing to eliciting teacher knowledge in CS. Specifically, the authors present specific methods (e.g., questionnaires) focusing on Shulman's construct of PCK aimed to capture and document PCK in relation to CS. They subsequently discuss examples of educators' responses in relation to CS concepts and share their reflections on the content and structure of those responses. The authors conclude with recommendations that help guide the use of PCK measures in teacher preparation programs and suggested avenues for further research, particularly approaches to eliciting pre-service teachers' PCK in practice.

Part II: Course Design Models for Preparing Pre-Service Teachers to Teach Computer Science

A critical step for successfully infusing CS into K–12 classrooms is to help pre-service teachers build an understanding of CS and its connection to their curricular context (Yadav et al., 2017). Elementary school pre-service teachers in particular lack knowledge and experience related to CS. Given the need to prepare for teaching all content areas they frequently have few opportunities to engage with CS coursework during their teacher education program. Another challenge facing elementary teachers is that effective practices for integrating CS into discipline-specific curricula are not well defined by standards (McGinnis et al., 2020). Weintrop et al. (2016) developed a taxonomy of CT practices for mathematics and science, but such work is only relevant for secondary teachers. Parallel work establishing direct connections and practices related to the application of CS across disciplines in elementary school settings is not widely available at this time.

One way to accomplish this goal is by developing CS modules that can be used in conjunction with methods courses in pre-service teacher preparation (Yadav et al., 2014). Examples of such modules, however, as well as research examining their impact on pre-service teachers' knowledge, beliefs and practices remain substantially under-developed. Similarly, examples of methods courses that help support pre-service teachers across the K–12 spectrum develop PCK related to CS are also lacking in the literature. This section features four chapters that address these gaps in the literature. They present CS modules that can be integrated in existing pre-service coursework, including entire teacher education curricula.

Further, they discuss stand-alone methods courses for helping pre-service K–12 teachers develop PCK in relation to CS.

Chapter 5, Creating Change Agents: A Teacher Preparation Model that Prepares All Teachers to Facilitate Computer Science Concepts presents a pilot teacher preparation model that integrates CS/CT throughout the undergraduate and graduate programs at The College of St. Scholastica. Through a tight collaboration between faculty in Education and CS, this model seeks to prepare all K–12 pre-service teachers with the knowledge and skills needed to teach CS through both interdisciplinary or stand-alone approaches. Key components of this model include a hybrid mini-course for faculty in education, scaffolded lessons in required education and content methods courses, and a field experience placement for pre-service teachers. Program outcomes address CT/CT content knowledge, curriculum and pedagogy as well as pre-service teachers' dispositions towards supporting CS learning for all students.

Chapter 6, Teaching Teachers: A Computer Science Methods Course describes a methods course at the University of Nebraska at Omaha focusing on CS teaching methods. The chapter begins by situating the work in the context of teacher licensure requirements in Nebraska as well as the teacher education pathway at the University towards teaching CS at all levels from kindergarten through AP Computer Science. Subsequently, the author offers a comprehensive description of the CS methods course, which includes five units: (a) curriculum & standards; (b) pedagogies; (c) assessment; (d) equity, access & differentiation; and (e) PCK and misconceptions. The chapter concludes with detailed descriptions and pre-service teacher sample work from three course assignments, including a CS autobiography, CS concept cartoons, and CT bins.

Chapter 7, Redesigning Educational Technology Coursework to Foster Pre-Service Teacher Learning of Computational Thinking in Content Area Instruction describes a pedagogical approach aimed at preparing pre-service teachers to integrate CT into K–8 education through the redesign of an educational technology course. The course focuses on the introduction of computing tools and pedagogies specific to incorporating CT concepts with content and pedagogy in K–12 settings. Using a total of 171 lesson plans developed by 57 pre-service teachers over the period of one semester, the authors identify specific CT concepts represented in pre-service teachers' work. Findings indicated that the concepts of data and problem decomposition were more frequently represented in participants' lesson designs. The authors conclude with implications and next steps for pre-service teacher preparation at the K–8 level.

Chapter 8, Preparing Secondary Education Mathematics Pre-Service Teachers for AP Computer Science Principles: A Two-Course Design Model, presents an interdisciplinary effort between secondary mathematics education and CS at the University of Alabama for preparing secondary mathematics pre-service teachers to teach Advanced Placement (AP) CS Principles. The authors present a two-course sequence and associated activities aimed at increasing the number of future educators without deep knowledge of CS content who are prepared to teach AP CSP courses. Through this effort, participants gain foundational knowledge of CS content followed by opportunities to develop lesson plans, examine the AP CSP curriculum framework in relation to national standards, engage in classroom observations at local schools, attend relevant conferences, and prepare for the certification exam in CS. The authors conclude with recommendations for adapting this model to other settings.

Part III: University and State Policies for Preparing Pre-Service Teachers to Teach Computer Science

In the last few years, state-level leaders have initiated efforts to elevate the role of CS in K–12 education. These efforts make it clear that state leaders increasingly recognize their role in supporting and sustaining CS teaching and learning. Similarly, higher education institutions have joined these efforts, creating pathways that allow the preparation and continuous development of teachers who have the knowledge and skills to teach CS in ways that reach all students. While several states have already proposed new policies to support expansion of CS teaching and learning, it is evident that both states and institutions of higher education need to adopt a broader vision of policy changes.

Several recommendations are proposed in the literature for building and sustaining a comprehensive policy framework for CS including: (a) creating a state plan, (b) defining CS, (c) allocating funding, (d) implementing clear certification pathways for CS teachers, (e) creating programs at institutions of higher education to offer CS to pre-service teachers, (f) establishing dedicated CS positions, (g) requiring that all secondary schools offer CS, (h) allowing CS to satisfy core graduation requirements, and (i) allowing CS to satisfy an admission requirement at institutions of higher education (Code.org & CSTA, 2018). The chapters in this section explicitly address two of these recommendations focusing on programs in higher education institutions, certification pathways as well as the manner in which states are responding to the demand for qualified teachers in CS. While no single solution exists to addressing the demand for CS teachers, chapters in this section provide innovative responses as well as examples from various U.S. states who have responded to the challenge.

Chapter 9, Using a Coaching Model to Support Computer Science Professional Development for Teacher Educators presents a pre-service program developed at the College of St. Scholastica which infused CS across the curriculum for all pre-service teachers. The authors focus on one aspect of the program, namely professional development and coaching for teacher educators as they developed, implemented and reflected on CS/CT lessons for pre-service teachers. Findings indicated that participants found coaching valuable in developing their own understanding of CS/CT content and pedagogy and were more confident in their ability to teach CS/CT integrated within their disciplinary specialty. The chapter highlights aspects of the coaching model, lessons learned, and key components for success.

Chapter 10, Increasing the Capacity of Schools of Education to Prepare Teachers to Teach Computer Science points to the need for more pre-service programs focusing on the preparation of teachers capable of teaching CS and the special role of the Schools of Education. Based on a summary from the HomeforCS report, the authors summarize the key elements necessary to enable schools of education to make an impact on CS education. These recommendations include: (a) moving K–12 computer science education into schools of education, (b) developing pedagogies for CS education teachers, (c) building education leadership for CS education, and (d) building strategic and innovative relationships with school districts.

Chapter 11, Understanding K–12 CS Education at the State Level builds on the work of the NSF-funded Expanding Computing Education Pathways (ECEP) Alliance, which includes teams of education and policy experts from 23 U.S. states and territories to examine state change around teacher preparation in CS education. The authors present the circumstances under which pre-service teacher preparation becomes a priority for state teams and the underlying conditions that need to be in place for such shift to occur. The authors conclude with recommendations on next steps for expanding understanding on how to scale pre-service CS teacher education.

Chapter 12, Teacher-Focused Policies to Broaden Participation in Computer Science provides an overview of state policies which govern pre-service teacher preparation programs, teacher licensure, and in-service teacher professional development across three exemplar states, including Arkansas, Maryland and Massachusetts. Based on lessons learned, the chapter concludes with innovative state recommendations which U.S. states can use to address CS teacher shortages.

NEXT STEPS

Without doubt, computing has become an integral part of daily life, transforming the way we work and learn. Ensuring that K–12 students have adequate opportunities to become creators and not just users of computing innovations is more important than ever. Foundational CS knowledge is critical for personal, civic and career efficacy (Stanton et al., 2017). Further, there is a desperate need for a more diverse and inclusive participation in CS, which can drive both social and economic innovation. To ensure the promise of the CS for All movement, however, it is essential that we shift attention to the preparation of pre-service teachers, including the development of new courses, new pathways, and new policies that support teacher learning. The chapters in this book have begun to address these critical challenges in pre-service teacher education, providing examples of coursework that weaves CS principles with content and pedagogy, innovative pedagogies for helping prospective teachers teach CS, and policies that support CS teacher preparation.

Nonetheless, much work still remains to be done in this area. In particular, we identify three important lines of future work. First, in order to integrate CS into pre-service teacher preparation programs, all teacher educators must also develop foundational knowledge and skills (see Chapter 10). Without a fundamental understanding and recognition of the importance of CS within specific disciplines, CS will remain isolated from disciplinary content and pedagogy. Second, although all efforts presented in this book are noteworthy, it is important to point out that few have followed pre-service teachers in the field, or better, their future classrooms, to examine the manner in which they apply new learning into practice. Future studies need to adopt longitudinal designs examining the role and impact of pre-service teacher preparation on both knowledge and practices. Third, future studies need to pay closer attention to the ways in which the size, geographic location, and target pre-service population of higher education institutions influence CS integration efforts and pre-service teacher outcomes. This is important because most work to date has focused on individual courses alone or boutique teacher education programs. As a result, there is a need to build a more cohesive understanding of these efforts across teacher education contexts.

REFERENCES

Angeli, C., Voogt, J., Fluck, A., Webb, M., Cox, M., Malyn-Smith, J., & Zagami, J. (2016). A K–6 computational thinking curriculum framework: Implications for teacher knowledge. *Educational Technology & Society, 19*(3), 47–57.

Blikstein, P., & & Moghadam, S. P. (2019). Computing education: Literature review and voices from the field. In S. A. Fincher & A. V. Robins (Eds.),*The Cambridge handbook of computing education research* (pp. 56–78). Cambridge University Press.

Code.org, & CSTA. (2018). *2018 State of computer science education.* https://advocacy.code.org/

Common Core State Standards in Mathematics. (2010). National Governors Association Center for Best Practices & Council of Chief State School Officers.

DeLyser, L. A., Goode, J., Guzdial, M., Kafai, Y., & Yadav, A. (2018). *Priming the computer science teacher pump: Integrating computer science education into schools of education.* CSforAll.

Ertmer, P. A., & Ottenbreit-Leftwich, A. T. (2010). Teacher technology change: How knowledge, beliefs, and culture intersect. *Journal of Research on Technology in Education, 42*(3), 221–251.

Goode, J., Skorodinsky, M., Hubbard, J., & Hook, J. (2020) Computer science for equity: Teacher education, agency, and statewide reform. *Front. Educ. 4*, 162. doi: 10.3389/feduc.2019.00162

Guzdial, M. (2017, April). Phone interview with Paulo Blikstein.

Hubwieser, P., Magenheim, J., Mühling, A., & Ruf, A. (2013, August). Towards a conceptualization of pedagogical content knowledge for computer science. *Proceedings of the ninth annual international ACM conference on international computing education research* (pp. 1–8). ACM. https://doi.org/10.1145/2493394.2493395

ISTE. (2016). *National educational technology standards for students.* Retrieved https://www.iste.org/standards/for-students

Margolis, J. (2017). *Stuck in the shallow end: Education, race, and computing*. MIT Press.

McGinnis, J. R., Hestness, E., Mills, K., Ketelhut, D. J., Cabrera, L., & Jeong, H. (2020). Preservice science teachers' beliefs about computational thinking following a curricular module within an elementary science methods course. *Contemporary Issues in Technology and Teacher Education, 20*(1). https://citejournal.org/volume-20/issue-1-20/science/preservice-science-teachers-beliefs-about-computational-thinking-following-a-curricular-module-within-an-elementary-science-methods-course

Mouza, C. (2009). Does research-based professional development make a difference? A longitudinal investigation of teacher learning in technology integration. *Teachers College Record, 111*(5), 1195–1241

Mouza, C., Yang, H., Pan, Y.-C., Yilmaz Ozden, S., & Pollock, L. (2017). Resetting educational technology coursework for pre-service teachers: A computational thinking approach to the development of technological pedagogical content knowledge (TPACK). *Australasian Journal of Educational Technology, 33*(3), 61–76. https://doi.org/10.14742/ajet.3521

NGSS Lead States. (2013). *Next generation science standards: For states, by states*. The National Academies Press.

Stanton, J., Goldsmith, L., Adrion, R. W., Dunton, S., Hendrickson, K. A., Peterfreund, A., … (2017). *State of the states landscape report: State-level policies supporting equitable K–12 computer science education*. EDC.

Weintrop, D., Beheshti, E., Horn, M., Orton, K., Jona, K., Trouille, L., & Wilensky, U. (2016). Defining computational thinking for mathematics and science classrooms. *Journal of Science Education and Technology, 25*, 127–147.

Wing, J. M. (2006). Computational thinking. *Communications of the ACM, 49*(3), 33–35. https://doi.org/10.1145/1118178.1118215

Yadav, A., Krist, C., Good, J., & Caeli, E. (2018). Computational thinking in elementary classrooms: Measuring teacher understanding of computational ideas for teaching science. *Computer Science Education, 28*(4), 371–400.

Yadav, A., Mayfield, C., Zhou, N., Hambrusch, S., & Korb, J. T. (2014). Computational thinking in elementary and secondary teacher education. *ACM Transactions on Computing Education, 14*(1), Article 5. https://doi.org/10.1145/2576872

Yadav, A., Stephenson, C., & Hong, H. (2017). Computational thinking for teacher education. *Communications of the ACM, 80*(4), 55–62. https://doi.org/10.1145/2994591

PART I

PEDAGOGICAL PRACTICES FOR DEVELOPING AND
ASSESSING PRE-SERVICE TEACHERS' KNOWLEDGE OF
COMPUTER SCIENCE

CHAPTER 1

ACTIVE LEARNING TECHNIQUES FOR COMPUTING EDUCATION

Cazembe Kennedy, Eileen T. Kraemer, and Lisa C. Benson

Active learning is a pedagogical approach that emphasizes higher-order thinking and encourages students to analyze, synthesize, and evaluate rather than to solely passively listen to lectures. This chapter categorizes, describes, and provides examples of various active learning techniques in a computing education research context. The techniques have varying types of student accountability and interdependence (solo, collaborative, or cooperative activities), instructor effort in terms of guidance, preparation, and feedback (before, during, or after the class session), and student engagement (active, constructive, or interactive), with different benefits and resource requirements. From commonly used techniques such as pair programming to those less frequently used in a computer science context such as jigsaw or fishbowl, this chapter provides computer science teachers with a toolbox of methods for actively engaging students in their learning process. This chapter describes active learning techniques commonly used in the computer science context and proposes how other active learning techniques could be adapted for this context. The materials in this chapter will empower preservice teachers to design lessons with these techniques in mind and to incorporate the techniques into current classroom practices.

Preparing Pre-Service Teachers to Teach Computer Science: Models, Practices and Policies, pages 3–28.

Keywords: Active Learning; Pedagogy; STEM Education; Computing Education; Accountability; Interdependence; Engagement

INTRODUCTION

The prospect of moving away from classes that are primarily lecture-based and toward a more learner-based approach has generated excitement and discussion in the computer science (CS) education community. As market demand for workers with CS expertise has risen, so has the desire for a broad and diverse group of workers to be educated to meet this need. This has driven efforts for more students to engage with CS content and for CS education to be conducted in more inclusive ways. In recent years, many projects have been funded through the United States Department of Education, the National Science Foundation, and other entities to explore how to achieve these goals. Approaches that deeply involve students in their own learning processes offer the prospect of increased engagement and interest by a broader student population than has traditionally been seen in CS classrooms.

Active learning is a pedagogical approach that emphasizes higher-order thinking and encourages students to analyze, synthesize, and evaluate. Felder and Brent (2009) define active learning as "short course-related individual or small-group activities that all students in a class are called upon to do, alternating with instructor-led intervals in which student responses are processed and new information is presented" (p. 5). Researchers in science, technology, engineering, and mathematics (STEM) education have identified benefits that can be gained from active learning such as increased retention in the course for all students (Felder et al., 1998; Seymour & Hewitt, 1997), increased engagement and improved retention of content, and reductions in the achievement gap between ethnic groups (Haak et al., 2011; Lorenzo et al., 2006) and between men and women (Rivard & Straw, 2000; Seymour & Hewitt, 1997) when compared to traditional lecturing (Prince, 2004). Research in CS education supports the use of collaborative and cooperative learning techniques in the classroom (Prince, 2004) and shows that active learning has benefits for broadening participation in computing (Olson & Riordan, 2012; Tobias & Lin, 1991).

Despite these results, many instructors hesitate to incorporate active learning into their CS courses because of fears that less content would be taught, pre-class preparation time would be higher, control of the classroom would have to be given up, or course evaluations from students would suffer (McConnell, 1996). Felder and Brent (2016) dispute these claims, stating that teachers can do short activities that will not take too much class time away from content or prepare lecture notes in handout form to allow students to read through them and use active learning activities to drive the points home. Felder and Brent also claim that preparation time can be as little or as much as the teacher makes it. Some techniques are as simple as having students work in pairs or small groups to discuss questions that instructors already ask during their lecture. Further, preparation demands lessen over time as instructors become more familiar with the activities and integrate them into their courses.

We view active learning techniques as important and useful tools in an instructor's pedagogical toolkit. This chapter provides a review of various active learning techniques that can be used in CS classrooms. Teachers can integrate these techniques into their repertoire over time as they build experience and confidence with the techniques, the course content, and their own abilities as well as the abilities, performance, and reactions of their students.

We do not seek to rank the techniques, but rather to describe and categorize them to support teachers in selecting those that are appropriate for their local context and course content. The categories we employ capture differences among the techniques in terms of: (a) student accountability and interdependence (i.e., solo, collaborative or cooperative activities); (b) instructor effort in terms of guidance, preparation, and feedback (i.e., before, during, or after the class session); and (c) student engagement (i.e., active, constructive, or interactive), with varying benefits and resource requirements.

We have chosen these categories as they address a wide breadth of what active learning techniques can offer and they address instructors' logistical and pedagogical concerns in selecting new classroom techniques. Many, such as collaborative and cooperative, as well as the active, constructive, and interactive categories have definitions in research. We present our definitions of these terms as well as others we have used in this chapter in the **key concepts and terms** section. From commonly used techniques such as pair programming to those less frequently used in a CS context such as jigsaw, we aim to provide a toolkit of methods that educators can use to actively engage students in their learning process.

Our guiding question is: *How can active learning techniques be used in a CS context?* To explore this question, we draw on exemplars from CS curricula, particularly high school courses such as Exploring Computer Science (ECS) and Advanced Placement Computer Science Principles (AP CSP), and studies conducted at the undergraduate level, generally in introductory CS courses. We describe each technique, discuss the benefits documented in the literature, classify the techniques using the categories mentioned above, provide examples, and finally provide an overall discussion. We expect that these materials will empower both in-service and pre-service teachers as they design lessons that engage students through active participation in the classroom.

BACKGROUND

Our understanding of learning is informed by a constructivist epistemology, which asserts that students actively engage with their environments and that learning happens as students extend and refine their knowledge frameworks (Doolittle, 2014). In this view, learning is considered a process of active discovery and teachers act as facilitators, providing the necessary resources and guiding learners as they attempt to integrate new knowledge with old and modify the old to accommodate the new. Active learning techniques may employ elements of discovery learning (Bruner, 1961), or include collaborative work as supported by theories of social constructivism (Bandura & Walters, 1977), which emphasize the role of language and culture in cognitive development (Vygotsky, 1978).

Research shows that active learning techniques are beneficial (Prince, 2004). A meta-analysis of the literature on active learning in STEM courses reported increases of about 6% on examination scores and further increases on test scores of conceptual understanding (Freeman et al., 2014). This meta-analysis also found a lower average failure rate in courses that used active learning (21.8% versus 33.8%). Similarly, Graham et al. (2013) developed a persistence framework showing active learning to be a key element for increasing persistence of college students in STEM.

A number of factors support the benefits observed with active learning, including reduced cognitive load and working memory (Sweller, 1988; Sweller et al., 2019; Valcke, 2002), retrieval practice (Karpicke & Blunt, 2011), and increased attention (Prince, 2004). In a typical lecture, students encounter new information, which enters working memory. Faced with a steady stream of new information in a content-heavy lecture and given the limited capacity of working memory, students may experience cognitive load, or difficulty in processing and storing much of the information (Sweller et al., 2019). Engaging students in short activities in classes can reduce their cognitive load. Further, activities that require students to use recently presented information provide an opportunity to rehearse the information and examine how it relates to what they already know (Zimmerman & Martinez-Pons, 1988). In this way, active learning activities may serve as productive breaks.

One factor contributing to the effectiveness of active learning activities is that they require students to recall and use recently acquired information. Research shows that such *retrieval practice* (Karpicke & Blunt, 2011), also known as *test-enhanced learning* (Pyc et al., 2014), is associated with improved retention and transferability. Additional benefits have been documented if the activities are challenging, are spaced out over time, or are accompanied by timely feedback (Brown et al., 2011).

Finally, student attention is essential for learning. However, studies have shown that student attention in a standard lecture peaks at about 10 minutes into the lecture and then falls off (Bligh, 1998; Stuart & Rutherford, 1978). Lectures that contain short breaks in which students engage in activities show increased attention at the time of the activities (Middendorf & Kalish, 1996). In this way teachers may "rescue" the attention level from plummeting by interspersing lecture with course-related activities.

Key Concepts and Terms

To facilitate our discussion of active learning techniques and their potential benefits and appropriateness or applicability to a CS context, we introduce three dimensions along which these techniques may vary: (a) student accountability and interdependence, (b) instructor effort, and (c) student engagement.

Student Accountability and Interdependence

Student accountability and interdependence captures dimensions around student effort and work products, including how students are evaluated, whether that evaluation is informal or formal, how students interact with one another, and the extent to which students rely on one another in completing their work. This can range from students working alone (*solo*), to sharing information (*collaborative*), to relying on others in their group to perform specific tasks or provide unique information (*cooperative*). Consistent with Gokhale (1995), we define collaborative techniques as those that place the accountability on the group as a whole, requiring all members to work on the same problem. In our definition of cooperative techniques, on the other hand, individual group members take responsibility for some part of the assignment and then the group as a whole must combine these elements to solve the overall problem (Slavin, 1988). Without all of the individual pieces, the assignment cannot be fully completed. In these group activities, instructors can decide whether grades will be assigned individually or whether all members of the group will receive the same grade. Thus, accountability and interdependence may be intertwined as a student's efforts on a collaborative or cooperative project may impact not only their own grades but those of their peers. To simplify discussion, we use the term *accountability* to capture both accountability and interdependence.

Instructor Effort

Instructor effort captures what a teacher does (i.e., what technique is implemented), the timing of implementation, and the effort involved in implementing a given technique. It includes teacher efforts prior to the lesson, during the lesson, and after the lesson following completion of student work. For some techniques, instructor effort may be weighted heavily toward preparation of materials before the class session. Efforts during class may consist largely of monitoring student interactions and re-directing their attention as needed. For other techniques, the teacher's effort may be focused on setting up and guiding the activity while it is occurring. Finally, for other techniques, teacher's effort occurs after the class session and involves evaluating student-created artifacts and providing feedback. We categorize active learning techniques based on where the majority of teacher's effort is expected (before, during, or after), and discuss elements of instructor effort that occur during other time periods. In cases where effort is equally divided between time periods, we apply multiple labels. To simplify the discussion, we use the term *effort* to capture teacher effort in preparation before the lesson, guidance during the lesson, or feedback after the lesson.

Student Engagement

Student engagement captures what students do: the types of tasks students are asked to perform and the depth of their involvement. For this category we look to Chi's (2009) well-defined active-constructive-interactive framework to categorize active learning techniques. Chi describes *active* as "doing something physically," which can incorporate things such as gazing, underlining or highlighting, repeating information, etc. (p. 77). These activities can activate existing knowledge, assimilate, encode, or store new information, or search existing knowledge. Constructive is described as "producing outputs that contain ideas that go beyond the presented information" (Chi, 2009, p. 77). In constructive activities students may explain or elaborate, justify, construct a concept map, etc. The cognitive processes involved include inferring new knowledge, integrating new information with existing knowledge, organizing own knowledge for coherence, repairing own faulty knowledge, or restructuring own knowledge. Chi describes interactive as "dialoguing substantively on the same topic, and not ignoring a partner's contributions (p. 77).

Interactive activities may include revising errors iteratively, responding to scaffolding, arguing, defending, confronting or challenging, or building on a partner's constructed knowledge. Cognitive processes include the creation of processes that incorporate a partner's contributions. To simplify the discussion, we use the term *engagement* to capture what students do and whether the activities are active, constructive or interactive.

To provide examples of active learning techniques in CS curricula we refer to two of the most commonly used high school level curricula: Exploring Computer Science (ECS) (Goode & Chapman, 2018) and the Advanced Placement Computer Science Principles (AP CSP) curriculum (College Board, 2017). We also include several examples from undergraduate curricula. For the AP CSP curriculum, we rely most heavily on the version provided by the UTeach group at the University of Texas (Beth & Moreland, 2017).

EXEMPLARS

General Purpose Active Learning Techniques

General-purpose techniques include activities such as asking students to recall material from a prior class, answer a question, draw a diagram, predict the next step in a process, or summarize a reading or lecture (Felder & Brent, 2016). Students may be asked to work individually, in pairs, or small groups.

Think-Pair-Share

Think-pair-share (TPS) is a general purpose active learning technique that combines individual and group learning. The instructor issues a prompt/question and allows a short amount of time for students to provide an individual written/coded response (Felder & Brent, 2009). Students then discuss briefly with a partner. Working in pairs gives students the opportunity to reconcile and improve their solutions. Finally, the instructor calls on a few individuals or pairs to share responses with the class. Felder and Brent (2009) indicate that this activity takes a little more time than a simple group activity, but leads to greater learning because it also includes individual thinking.

Azlina (2010) claims the TPS technique can enhance students' oral communication skills as they have time to think and then the opportunity to discuss their ideas with one another. Kothiyal et al. (2013) measured levels of engagement during the three phases of Think-Pair-Share using direct observation of student behaviors such as writing in a notebook, reading notes, and responding to teachers' questions. Reports showed that students were either fully or mostly engaged between 70% and 95% of the time during the Think phase depending on the problem, and between 75% and 90% of the time in the Pair and Share phases. Examining the effects of TPS on student achievement, Bamiro (2015) focused on chemistry students' achievement under three conditions: (a) a control group; (b) a group being taught through guided discovery, in which "the teacher guides the students in their learning task by asking them thought-provoking questions that would assist them to generate their own correct ideas of the subject matter"; and (c) a group being taught using Think-Pair-Share strategies. Using a validated chemistry achievement test, TPS was found to have the greater effect, just ahead of guided discovery when comparing post-test results to the control group.

The ECS curriculum makes frequent use of TPS, often in combination with journaling. In Unit 1, for instance, students work in pairs to fill out a Communications Methods chart that offers various means to communicate with someone (texting, email, Twitter, etc.) and situations where information needs to be communicated. The student pairs fill out two columns: one with the method they would choose to communicate the information and the other with why they would choose that method. Students are then polled to see which communication methods were most commonly chosen for the various situations. Finally, a few pairs are selected to discuss the reasons they chose a method.

In terms of engagement the activity in this example is *interactive*. Students first participate in an active step for the Think phase, and then work interactively in the Pair phase to construct knowledge to understand and apply selected concepts. During the Share phase, they either present information or take in information presented from peers. The instructor is required to put in *effort* both before and during the class. The teacher must develop adequate prompts or concepts to have students think about and prepare the lecture with these prompts in mind, and can then let students work with their partner until it is time to share. The teacher must manage the time of the activity, ensure students are in proper groups, and facilitate a discussion after students have been paired. Finally, in terms of accountability, this activity is *collaborative*. Students share information but do not rely on one another to provide unique skills or information. This is typically an informal activity and generally does not produce an artifact that is graded.

In summary, Think-Pair-Share requires no special resources on the part of the teacher. In larger classrooms, it may be useful to have students write down their work on the various phases and then collect the artifacts, not for the purpose of grading, but to examine and gain a better view of where the class stands on particular topics. Kothiyal's (2013) findings on engagement suggest that this technique could be incorporated in CS classrooms as a way of getting students more involved in their learning process.

Peer Instruction

Peer instruction (PI) is an activity where the class session is divided into multiple short presentations that each focus on one concept (Crouch & Mazur, 2001). Following a presentation, students are given 1–2 minutes to individually answer a related conceptual question ("ConcepTest"). The answers can be reported informally by having students raise their hands or hold up cards or more formally using personal response systems, such as clickers that log the results. Students then discuss their answers in small groups for 2–4 minutes and try to come to agreement. Individual student answers may have changed because of the discussions. The teacher then calls the class together and asks the same question again, polls the students for their answers, explains the correct answer, and moves on. The *ConcepTests* themselves are not graded, but some credit is given for participating consistently over the semester. A further incentive to participate is that midterm and final exams typically include a significant number of *ConcepTest*-like questions.

Prior research indicates that scores on a standardized assessment in an introductory physics course improved dramatically in a class that used PI, as did performance on traditional quantitative problems (Crouch & Mazur, 2001), independent of the instructor teaching the material. Student reactions were generally positive to PI, although there was some resistance to being taught in a nontraditional manner. Similar findings in terms of knowledge-building were reported in a later study on PI, particularly for students with less background knowledge (Lasry et al., 2008).

PI was utilized at the University of New Orleans for Cybersecurity courses by Ahmed and Roussev (2018). The research team developed 280 PI questions for three courses, one of which was close to a standard lecture format while the other two were hands-on classes. The group developed the questions by first finding a *concept identification*, or identifying a target concept. They then introduced *concept triggers,* such as having students compare and contrast or providing answer choices with common misconceptions to stimulate the thought process of students. The final step in preparing questions was determining how to present the questions to students to properly facilitate understanding. In bringing PI into the course, the researchers found that students adapted quickly to the format, found it useful, and highly recommended the approach be extended to a variety of subjects.

In terms of engagement, this activity is *interactive*. Students first actively think about the answer to a question and must commit to a response (Active). They then work in small groups and are asked to defend their answers and convince others or be convinced by others as to the right answer, allowing students to have their knowledge and viewpoints challenged.

The instructor effort for this activity is required *prior* to the course. Specifically, the instructor must have multiple conceptual questions prepared for class. The questions should be designed to probe at potential misconceptions. The instructor or TAs may circulate around during class to help respond to group concerns. The instructor must also have an explanation of the correct answers. Finally, in terms of accountability this activity is *collaborative*. Students share information but do not rely on one another to provide unique skills or information. This activity is typically not graded.

In summary, PI appears to be highly applicable to many aspects of computer science. For example, asking students to predict the output of a print statement involving a function call could be used to explore their understanding of parameter passing.

Jigsaw/Jigsaw II

Jigsaw/Jigsaw II is a technique in which each member of a group of four attempts to become a subject matter expert in 1 of 4 areas selected from current course material (Keyser, 2000). Each member teaches their subject matter to other team members. This may include a second phase in which students consult with members of other teams who were assigned the same topic. Team members are then tested on all topics. A related technique, Student Teams-Achievement Divisions (STAD), has students of different academic abilities assigned to 4–5 member teams (Slavin, 1978) and students are assigned a subject to teach to other group members. They are then tested individually, but can earn recognition based on how well their team members have progressed in their achievements.

STAD and jigsaw have benefits similar to those of cooperative learning. Students immerse themselves in an active learning technique in which they are accountable to learn specific parts of a topic and provide the information to their group. This gives the students a reason to motivate one another to ensure that everyone in the group is able to learn the material. These techniques can also help ensure that all teammates follow their responsibilities so that neither they nor their peers lose points.

The version of jigsaw used in the ECS curriculum largely applies the concept of "divide and conquer." For example, in one ECS activity, teams of students are asked to learn one of three Web 2.0 applications and each group is assigned a different application. Each group then prepares a presentation on the application for the rest of the class. In terms of engagement, the students are tasked to learn about things individually (i.e., *constructive*) and have a responsibility to bring that knowledge back to the rest of the group. This allows students to put pressure on one another to ensure that learning is occurring (i.e., *interactive*). Specifically, students must achieve a level of understanding such that they can explain and teach a concept to other students. If students, however, choose to learn only their piece and teach it without allowing for other team members to discuss perspectives and question parts of the instruction, this activity would fall into the constructive category more so than interactive.

In this activity the instructor is required to put in effort *prior* to the course. In addition to selecting appropriate concepts in the curriculum for the student team members to learn, the teacher must also decide how to form teams and must be available during class to redirect students as needed and answer questions. Finally, in terms of accountability the activity requires *cooperative* learning. Students work in groups with specific roles for each group member. Responsibility lies with each individual to ensure that the whole group has all of the necessary information.

These techniques give students the opportunity to teach and motivate themselves and one another. Students in the group may be able to help explain concepts that they were not tasked to learn by offering a different perspective. The success of the group is dependent on the success of the individuals. This can be problematic if some students are less motivated than others. The benefit is that, in addition to the teacher, the students can push one another to learn and excel. STAD has the same benefits as jigsaw with the additional feature that testing is done individually. STAD often uses semester-long teams and provides students with practice in working together, which is common in industry CS positions.

Role Playing/Simulations/Games

Role Playing/Simulations/Games are techniques that have students and/or faculty perform specific roles in order to demonstrate concepts. Simulations and games typically include guiding principles, specific rules, and structured relationships (Van Amburgh et al., 2007). Games may vary from things like Jeopardy to crossword puzzles and be played individually, in small groups, or by the whole class. The benefits of these techniques can vary, but in general they revolve around increased student engagement. Students having opportunities to act out roles using blocks of code and see simulated versions of what is happening inside of a computer can provide necessary and useful context to the concepts being taught during class.

Unit 4 of ECS uses role playing to demonstrate the concept of broadcasting events as seen in the Scratch programming environment (Resnick et al., 2009). Students take on the roles of characters in Scratch and props may be used if the resources are available. The characters demonstrate various Scratch functions and actions such as Say (have a line that a character says), Show (character comes on stage), and Hide (character disappears off stage), and these actions are triggered by an event such as the clicking of a particular color flag. The script can also experiment with things such as changing the background of the scene or changing the costume of a character.

In terms of engagement, this activity is *constructive* or *interactive*. Students must use concepts learned and skills acquired in order to apply them to a simulation or game that is designed for the class. If students are tasked to do this individually, this would be constructive. If they work in small groups, this would be interactive. The activity requires that the instructor puts in effort *before* and *during* class. Specifically, the teacher must select games that are appropriate for course material or design the formatting/layout of the game. The teacher must also play the role of authority figure who determines what is right or wrong when playing games or engaging with simulations. In terms of accountability, the activity requires *cooperative* learning. Students help each other learn and understand by taking on specific roles in a role-playing scenario, simulation, or game.

In summary, these activities can be an interesting and engaging technique in the classroom, allowing students to learn while they feel that they are playing. Games can also bring out the competitive nature of students, which can increase interest for some but may discourage others. The key to this technique is that it is most useful when students already have a basis of knowledge that they can apply in the context of the game or simulation. Later in this section, we describe CS Unplugged activities, which are a CS-specific version of simulation/role play.

Know-Want-Learn Charts

Know-Want-Learn (KWL) charts ask students before the lesson to write down what they *know*, what they *want* to know, and later to write down what they *learned*. The goal of these graphic charts is to help students organize information before, during, and after a unit or lesson to introduce students to a new topic, activate prior knowledge, share unit objectives, and monitor student learning. Though reports of benefits are not available for this technique, we believe it can act as a benchmark for students to gauge their own learning and strive to improve as the course/semester continues.

The UTeach CSP curriculum provides a template for KWL charts and recommends the use of a KWL for each unit. Students maintain individual KWL charts and the teacher periodically asks students to share ideas and questions from their individual charts for inclusion in a group chart. Students are reminded to update their KWL chart throughout the unit.

In terms of engagement, students take an *active* role in deciding what they want to learn and in reactivating their prior knowledge in determining what they already know. The instructor must put in effort *during* and *after* class. Specifically, the instructor may poll the students for items from their individual charts to include in the group chart and may read student charts to gain an understanding of students' prior knowledge and learning goals. Regarding accountability, this activity can be *solo* and *collaborative*. The individual students are responsible for filling out their charts and a chart representing the entire class may also be created. In summary, this technique sets clear goals for students, and makes them a central part of what they learn. KWL charts offer a quick and easy way to let students hold themselves accountable for their learning.

One Minute Papers

One minute papers are designed to allow students to focus attention on a single important term, name, or concept from a particular lesson (Stead, 2005). They are typically assigned at the end of a class, and students are asked to briefly answer two questions, which are generally: (a) What was the most important thing you learned in class today? and (b) What question is unanswered? Students are given about a minute to complete the papers. The instructor later reads the papers and responds to them either at the next class or on an individual basis. The goals are to organize student thinking and assess student comprehension. This activity can be varied in ways such as making the assignment collaborative, or allowing the responses to be anonymous. The assignment may be graded or ungraded. This activity can be a useful learning tool, especially in large lectures where instructors do not typically have the opportunity to interact with each student. It is also a good way for instructors to obtain instant and detailed feedback from students. Related to one-minute papers are journal activities, short writing assignments that may occur at any point in the lesson and typically employ a lesson-specific prompt. An important goal of journaling is to focus "the attention of students on how they know what they know and how their knowledge connects to larger ideas, other domains, and the world beyond the classroom" (Council et al., 1996, p. 36).

Almer et al. (1998) found that one-minute papers were a valuable means of obtaining timely feedback about students' understanding of course material. The authors also found that the comments written in the papers provided useful feedback on students' perceptions of their learning experience and on teaching style. A statistically significant difference on subsequent essay quizzes was found with the use of one-minute papers. Further, performance increases did not depend on the student's ability level or instructor. Studies on the effect on multiple-choice tests, however, have been mixed; while some researchers documented benefits, others did not. Nonetheless, teacher analysis of student journals can provide a basis for making instructional adjustments and can provide insight into the design of learning activities "that build from student experience, culture, and prior understandings" (Council et al., 1996).

Both ECS and AP CSP make extensive use of journaling, one-minute papers, and other short writing tasks. The ECS curriculum guide recommends incorporating strategies such as journaling into as many lessons as possible and provides specific journal prompts to be used in the lessons that make up the curriculum. The journal entries are sometimes discussed as a class and other times used to facilitate future activities within the unit. Example prompts for a student journal entry in the ECS curriculum include "List at least three ways in which you currently use the internet" and "What do you think about when you hear the word data? Where can it be found? Where does it come from?"

These activities require *active* engagement. Students are forced to think about the lecture or prior experiences and try to explain their understanding of a concept. The instructor must put in effort both *before* and *after* the course. The instructor must select appropriate prompts, but the majority of teacher effort is in reviewing the responses. This could be especially time consuming in a large classes. Further, these activities are usually conducted *solo*. Students must be active but on their own.

In summary, one-minute papers and journaling offer a way to quickly and easily gather qualitative data on how the class is going and what topics might be causing issues. As with KWL charts, they can help students organize their thinking and activate prior knowledge. They have the benefit of working with nearly any topic and are not resource intensive. Instructors, however, need to be willing to analyze the papers and commit to making instructional adjustments based on student responses.

Projects and Presentations

Projects and presentations are popular active learning techniques in CS curricula. The ECS course employs projects and presentations as an integral component of the overall curriculum. It frequently has students work together, often in pairs or small groups on topics related to the curriculum. In contrast, the UTeach CSP curriculum uses a project-based learning (PBL) model: each unit is driven by a project, beginning with a challenge and ending with student presentations of an artifact that showcases a solution to the challenge. The projects are collaborative, open-ended, and have milestones. That is, smaller pieces of the project are assigned as specific tasks throughout the unit rather than having a single, large deliverable at the end. These projects serve as a vehicle for teaching the knowledge and skills that students need to learn and serve as the framework for the curriculum and instruction.

Projects and presentations, particularly those that employ cooperative learning can help to maintain student interest and guide students to discover the desired information (Johnson & Johnson, 1984). Studies of PBL, as seen in the UTeach CSP curriculum, show that it can promote student learning: in a review of 20 studies of PBL, strong support was found for social studies and science but more limited support has been demonstrated for mathematics and literacy (Kingston, 2018).

One project in the ECS curriculum is the Computer Buying Project. Students are divided into groups and tasked with researching various specifications of a computer with the intent to purchase one. The groups must select an interview they had conducted with a family member on important elements for buying a computer and based on the selected interview, give the interviewee four options for a computer to buy and advice as to why that computer would make sense based on the preferences of the person interviewed. Another ECS example is a "Privacy Activity" in which students break into groups, are assigned a privacy-related scenario and then prepare a presentation on that scenario. The final presentations are cooperative in that each group is responsible for answering a particular question and teaching it to the class. In the UTeach CSP curriculum, a project forms the basis for each unit, such as a password generator project, a Scratch programming project, and an image filter project.

Projects and presentations are typically *interactive*, are performed in small groups, and require students to build on prior knowledge and the knowledge gained through the assignment. The instructor must put in effort *before/during class*. Specifically, instructor effort is primarily in setting up the project, preparing a rubric and directing the student groups as they work along in class. In terms of accountability, these activities are *collaborative*. The groups are responsible as a whole for completing the projects and generally work together to complete the various parts.

In summary, projects may range from small tasks designed to engage student interest and provide opportunities to apply learning in practice to fully-fledged projects that guide curriculum and instruction as in the UTeach CSP. The benefits of project-based learning have been demonstrated in areas such as science and social studies and are a topic of current research in CS education.

Process Oriented Guided Inquiry Learning (POGIL)

Process Oriented Guided Inquiry Learning (POGIL) is a technique that allows students to learn through activities rather than lectures (Hu & Kussmaul, 2012). Activities are specifically designed and scaffolded to facilitate guided learning and are typically performed in groups of 3–4 students (Moog, 2014). Learning benefits of POGIL have included higher grades (more As and Bs) (McKnight, 2011) and lower fail rates at both small and large colleges (Straumanis & Simons, 2006). Students also expressed preference for POGIL compared to traditional learning (Hanson & Wolfskill, 2000). Finally, POGIL has shown that students can turn in more code, including code that is more clean and efficient compared to traditionally taught programming courses (Hu & Shepherd, 2013).

Since 2005, Hu and others have co-taught an upper level scientific computing course using the POGIL method (Hu & Shepherd, 2013). POGIL has not yet been utilized in AP CSP or ECS, although ECS already has an inquiry-based curriculum. In terms of engagement, POGIL exercises are *interactive* and focus on students constructing their own knowledge in small groups. The instructor effort is generally *before*, in preparing the activities that engage student in the guided process. In terms of accountability, although students are in groups of 3 to

4, individuals are not expected to learn pieces on their own and then present that knowledge with their group, so this technique would be *collaborative*.

CS-Specific Active Learning Techniques

In addition to the general-purpose active learning techniques described in the previous subsection, numerous active learning techniques exist that are either specific to CS or have CS-specific variations.

Pair Programming

Pair programming, one of the most widely known active learning techniques for CS, is defined as "a style of programming in which two programmers work side by side at one computer, continually collaborating on the same design, algorithm, code, or test" (Williams & Kessler, 2002, p. 3). Students engaged in pair programming share a single workstation but take on different roles. The student at the keyboard is the *driver*. The other student, the *navigator*, is also actively involved in the programming task but focuses more on overall direction. The students periodically (every 30 minutes) swap roles. Williams and Kessler (2000) provide an accessible guide to the use of pair programming in the classroom.

There are a number of documented benefits to pair programming, including: improvements in course pass rates and retention rates in introductory CS, higher rates of retention in the CS major, improvements in the quality of programs, and student programmers' confidence and enjoyment in their work (Braught et al., 2011; Williams et al., 2003). Other studies have shown that pair programming may improve retention for female students and for students with less prior programming experience, and may reduce student need for instructor assistance while engaged in programming tasks (Li et al., 2013). Nagappan et al. (2003) reported that students benefited by having their questions answered immediately by a partner while also having a peer help them identify minor errors, thus allowing them to focus on understanding conceptual knowledge. In both the ECS curriculum and the AP CSP curriculum, students are frequently asked to work in pairs on both programming and non-programming tasks. In Unit 2 (Programming) of the UTeach AP CSP curriculum, students are directed to work using the pair programming methodology and the reading *All I Really Need to Know about Pair Programming I Learned in Kindergarten* (Williams & Kessler, 2000) is assigned for homework.

Pair programming engages students in *interactive* activities as they work to create and understand code. They are actively involved in helping one another while coding. In terms of effort, the instructor must select appropriate problems for the students to solve *before class*. The instructor must also assign students to pairs. For example, the instructor may group students of similar demonstrated abilities to the same pair, which is supported in the literature (Thomas et al., 2003), or may allow students to choose partners. The instructor will circulate through the classroom to help pairs who are having trouble. During these activities students engage in *cooperative* learning. Students contribute their own ideas and help their partners to refine their thinking.

In summary, pair programming is a technique that is supported by both the cognitive and social constructivist theories of learning. Students must use their knowledge and experiences to problem solve while also working together to potentially exchange different viewpoints and come to better solutions. Pair programming is a technique that can engage students in both design and coding tasks of CS course work. This activity is a staple in the CS active learning community, requires instructor planning in terms of team formation, and can reduce the load on instructor time by having students engage with and answer questions for one another.

Live Coding

Paxton (2002) defines live coding as "the process of designing and implementing a [coding] project in front of class during lecture period" (p. 52). This technique has been examined pedagogically in instructor-led form (Gaspar & Langevin, 2007; Paxton, 2002) or, to get students more actively involved, student-led form (Gaspar & Langevin, 2007). The student-led version traditionally utilizes a wireless keyboard and has one student working to implement a coding assignment. It allows the instructor to observe and share with the class how a student is thinking when working to solve a coding problem.

Paxton (2002) found that students in a live coding group performed statistically better on a final coding project than a control group, and performed at least equally as well on other metrics (assignments, exams, overall grades). Gaspar and Langevin (2007) found with a small sample size that when asked Likert-scale questions about live coding experiences, students found both instructor-led and student-led live coding more useful than seeing the final solutions directly on a screen. However, all students found student-led live coding more useful than instructor-led live coding.

When the ECS curriculum begins to introduce programming, students are tasked with many small programming assignments (creating a map route, creating a movie storyboard, etc.). Generally, teachers are asked to show solutions or have students present their solutions to a programming assignment. Teachers typically create their solutions from a blank document, and allow students to see the process of putting the code blocks together in a cohesive way that completes the programming activity.

Live coding focuses on *active* engagement. Students observe others in the process of implementing code and learn the process through examples. In terms of effort, the teacher must prepare appropriate code walkthroughs or examples to show the students *before class* begins. Finally, in terms of accountability, live coding is *collaborative*. Students learn about how to program through discussion of live examples with either their instructors or peers.

In summary, live coding allows students to learn about programming through doing—they see the code and potential mistakes in real time as opposed to learning concepts through lecture and then having to experiment with using those concepts. For teaching, it is a useful tool to help students visualize code firsthand.

Design Review

A design review is a technique in which students evaluate the design of code or of artifacts such as user interfaces or web pages. Students may be asked to identify examples of good or bad design and describe why they are good or bad. Day and Foley (2006) conducted an experiment in which a web lecture intervention was used in an undergraduate Human-Computer Interaction (HCI) course. In the study, two classes were taught. One class was given web-based lectures to watch prior to class and then in-class time was used to do engaging activities based on course material. The other was a control group that was taught in a standard way. The experimental section outperformed the control on all assignments and tests, and improvement on final exam scores trended positively. A specific CS active learning activity used in this study was called *Hall of Fame/Shame*, in which students were asked to find an example of a really great and a really bad interface design, then present and explain the reasons they were good or bad. Day and Foley found that the experimental group had significantly higher final course grades than the control group, even when accounting for the semester project, which could not be graded blindly.

ECS uses a technique similar to a design review, allowing students to constructively comment on each others' work. The activity showcases a product of some form (e.g., storyboard for a website) that students have created. The students are then asked to examine a subset of the total products created in a poster session-like format, writing down comments, questions, or feedback on post-it notes and sticking them to the posters of their peers. These activities are spread throughout various units, with names such as *Gallery Walk* (showing designs of website), *Arcade Walk* (showing video games students have programmed), and other types of *Walks*.

Design review is *constructive* in that it asks students to evaluate a piece of work. This requires a higher level of understanding than just knowing the basic concept and allows the students to construct their own knowledge/opinion on a design. In terms of effort, the instructor must put in effort both *before* and *after*. The instructor must do prep work to find interesting code or artifacts that will help students learn through evaluation. Assessment of the assignments after they've been presented also involves significant instructor effort. Finally, in terms of accountability, this is a technique that students can perform *solo* once they are shown how to do it.

In summary, this technique is particularly useful in CS because of the emphasis not only on operational aspects, but also on the quality of design of code and artifacts. In an introductory CS course, the concept could easily be used in lessons on formatting and code readability. This would allow students to experience examples of good/bad code, and the expectation would be that fewer mistakes would be made after engaging in the activity.

Scaffolding With Code

Scaffolding with code focuses on the idea of building on parts to make a whole (Van Gorp & Grissom, 2001). In this technique, students are given code that solves a problem. Students work in small groups to insert comments that explain how the code works. Alternatively, students may be given blocks of comments and asked to generate the associated code. Van Gorp and Grissom (2001) performed a study with an introductory CS course using a variety of active learning techniques, one of those being scaffolding with code. In this study, they found a slightly positive correlation of final exam grades and the frequency of constructive activities.

The general idea of scaffolding is used throughout the ECS curriculum. For example, a lesson has students build small parts of a website with HTML (starting with a title and body, then add paragraphs and headings, etc.). In the AP CSP curriculum, scaffolding with code is used as students work with block-based code and are given only a portion of the necessary blocks to complete a certain function.

This technique is focused on understanding code and algorithms in interactive ways with less emphasis on developing the algorithm. It looks at mapping from comments to code or code to comments. Students *interact* to come to an agreement on how to explain code with comments or how to translate comments into code. The instructor provides code or comments that are clear enough for students to either annotate the code with comments or write code based on the comments. The instructor or TA (Teaching Assistant) must circulate around *during class* to help when questions arise, therefore effort is needed both before and during class. In terms of accountability, the work is *collaborative*. Students work together looking at the same code snippets to solve a common problem.

In summary, students have the option to work together and aid one another in solving the programming problem posed. Scaffolding with code is a relatively simple approach but it can help beginning programmers, like training wheels on a bicycle, until they are ready to ride on their own. The preparation time on the part of the instructor is greater than some of the other techniques. Allowing students to start understanding the concepts behind programming in a piece-by-piece manner has support in the literature (Van Gorp & Grissom, 2001) and allows students to build their knowledge up and have a place to fall back on if they get stuck at some point as opposed to having to start again from scratch.

CS Unplugged

CS Unplugged is a collection of activities designed to demonstrate CS concepts to K–12 students in a fun and engaging way without using computers (Bell et al., 2012). Activities are often physical and kinesthetic: students move around and manipulate physical objects such as cards or strings or buttons. CS topics addressed by CS Unplugged (unplugged) activities include binary numbers, error detection and correction, searching, and sorting. Materials for these lessons may be freely downloaded from the CS Unplugged website (Computer Science Unplugged, 2017).

CS Unplugged materials were originally developed for outreach settings such as camps, workshops, and after-school programs with the goals of affecting student views of computing and computer scientists and encouraging participants to study CS or pursue a career in computing. Increasingly, unplugged activities are being applied in the context of regular classroom instruction and are included in both the ECS and AP CSP curricula.

While unplugged activities are well known and quite popular, studies of the effects on student views, attitudes, and intentions have concluded that unplugged activities "start a process of changing the students' views, but that this process is partial" and found also that students had difficulty in making connections between unplugged activities and concepts in CS (Taub et al., 2009) and between unplugged activities and future careers (Taub et al., 2012). Older students may find unplugged activities less appealing than do younger students. Studies of unplugged activities with high school students found disinterest from both students, who may view themselves as "experienced programmers" and as too mature for this style of activity (Feaster et al., 2011), and from teachers, who cited concerns about the kinesthetic aspect, effectiveness, and age appropriateness (Thies & Vahrenhold, 2016).

An open question is whether unplugged activities are appropriate for regular classroom instruction as opposed to outreach activities and if so, how these activities must be structured and supported to ensure that desired learning objectives are met. An analysis of the unplugged activities according to Bloom's taxonomy of educational objectives for cognitive and knowledge domains found that their classification "explains and supports" the success of unplugged for outreach purposes (no cognitive inhibition threshold is reached by participants). Nonetheless, the analysis indicated that the use of unplugged in an unmodified form as stand-alone material for teaching concepts at a secondary level is "limited" because the learning objectives of unplugged activities neither provide comprehensive representation of the field nor do they cover the cognitive processes and types of knowledge that are needed in this context (Thies & Vahrenhold, 2012).

For example, in a study of middle school students, unplugged was compared to the use of think-pair-share on the learning of factual, procedural, and conceptual knowledge (Thies & Vahrenhold, 2013) and no significant difference was found between the groups. Some researchers have proposed to compensate for the lack of content hierarchy and assessment material in unplugged by encapsulating unplugged activities in formalized lesson plans (Rodriguez et al., 2016; Thies & Vahrenhold, 2016). Rodriguez, et al. (2016) isolated specific factors key to successful implementation, including priming activities, individual practice, vocabulary worksheets, and relevant tie-ins to real world contexts.

ECS and AP CSP make broad use of CS Unplugged activities including the Binary Count, the Dots activity, the Lightest and Heaviest activity, the Muddy City activity, the parity bit trick, etc. The engagement, effort, and accountability categorizations vary widely for CS Unplugged Activities. CS Unplugged Activities can be active, constructive, or interactive with effort before, during, or after the task and accountability ranging from solo to collaborative or cooperative.

In summary, by promoting student interaction with physical representations of data and processes, unplugged activities incorporate active learning into CS education. Students take ownership of their learning and personalize it as they interact with the environment. The hands-on, kinesthetic component exploits multi-channel input and the visual and verbal cues provided should allow students to benefit from richer cognitive networks and content acquisition (Clark & Paivio, 1991). While unplugged activities capitalize on learning theory with an active, collaborative, and constructivist environment, students need appropriate guidance for content knowledge schema acquisition. Age appropriateness remains a concern for teachers who express hesitation to implement detailed physical representations of data or to employ kinesthetic methods (Feaster et al., 2011; Thies & Vahrenhold, 2016).

Programming Projects

For many CS courses, programming projects are a key component of student activity. These may either be individual or small group assignments, with the goal of writing code that performs some functionality specified by the instructor. Programming projects generally extend beyond a single class or lab session, and are completed by students largely outside of class over the course of multiple weeks. Programming projects receive many of the same benefits as general purpose active learning. By contextualizing a problem and potentially getting to work with others to solve it, these projects can help improve retention and increase student interest and engagement with content.

In introductory CS courses, a programming project that has anecdotally been seen at multiple high schools and universities is having students design a calculator program. The program can take in multiple integers or another form of variable type and perform calculations based on what the user requests. A brief version of this programming project was used in a study of student thinking while engaged in programming (Kennedy & Kraemer, 2019). Stanford's CS department has a website filled with "Nifty Assignments" that have been submitted by CS instructors in the CS education community (Parlante et al., 2007). ECS and AP CSP utilize programming projects throughout the curriculum as discussed in the projects and presentations section.

In terms of engagement, these activities are *constructive* or *interactive* depending on whether the projects are assigned as individual or as group activities.

Having students work in groups would give them the opportunity to construct their own knowledge and then share that knowledge with other group members so that they can build knowledge together. The instructor typically puts in effort both *before* and *after* class. These projects require significant forethought to plan out assignments that will be useful in ensuring students understand the target concepts. Significant effort is associated with providing feedback as students go through the process and grading the projects when they are finally turned in. Similar to engagement, accountability depends on whether the activity is individual. If the projects are in pairs or groups, students will generally work together to solve the problem. It is possible that groups decide to divide and conquer project parts, which would make the technique *cooperative* assuming they ensured their fellow group members understood the parts they worked on, but the usual accountability would be *collaborative*. In summary, programming projects are an integral part of many CS curricula. They provide students the opportunity to apply the concepts from their classwork and homework assignments.

NEXT STEPS

As noted earlier, teachers may hesitate to adopt active learning techniques. We recommend starting with techniques that are easy to implement and that can be used in many class sessions such as journal entries/one-minute papers, Know-Want-Learn Charts, or think-pair-share. Integrating these types of techniques regularly into the classroom will allow teachers the chance to refine them and determine how they best can be incorporated into lesson plans. Use of one of the more involved techniques, such as design reviews/walks and programming or mini-projects (potentially combined with jigsaw/STAD), needs to be carefully planned and would probably be used less frequently than other techniques (one or two per unit potentially). These techniques work towards a goal and require more preparation time as well as more effort from students, but can offer great benefits. It is important that teachers planning to use these techniques keep in mind that they depend on local context and available resources. Teachers may wish to introduce techniques incrementally with increasing comfort levels and experiences, refine for their local context, and evaluate their impact and their refinements. Techniques that are successful with one class may not work as well with another class of students. Thus, teachers may wish to remain flexible and adapt their strategies to meet the needs of the current students.

Multiple studies have shown that active learning benefits students (Freeman et al., 2014; Graham et al., 2013; Prince, 2004). However, we know of no guidelines for the ideal amount of active learning versus standard lecturing, recommendations for sequencing the introduction of active learning techniques, nor best practices in the selection of particular techniques for specific concepts. All of these questions are open for exploration by the CS education research community.

Our recommendation is to incorporate these techniques into pre-service curricula, so that instructors learn how to use the techniques during their teacher preparation program. A multi-day workshop could be developed to give pre-service teachers a crash course in these active learning techniques, their benefits, and how best to incorporate them into lesson planning. A more convenient dissemination method would be to develop online resources that assist pre-service teacher learning and decision-making as they determine the CS active learning techniques that are the best fit for them. We also suggest that professors model these techniques in their university classrooms to connect the way CS concepts are taught at the high school level and at the college level. Professors using these techniques in their college courses open up opportunities for research on the benefits, drawbacks, and effectiveness of active learning techniques.

Additionally, there is a need to explore relationships between active learning and the formation of CS identity. With research suggesting that active learning benefits center around engagement, and engagement having an impact on self-efficacy and identity, it is certainly possible that active learning helps students to identify more with being computer scientists. A key element here is to ensure that techniques used in the classroom can be related to the actual field and type of work that computer scientists perform as opposed to having students merely engage in interesting activities but without making explicit connections between those activities and the CS in practice.

REFERENCES

Ahmed, I., & Roussev, V. (2018). Peer instruction teaching methodology for cybersecurity education. *IEEE Security & Privacy, 16*(4), 88–91.

Almer, E. D., Jones, K., & Moeckel, C. L. (1998). The impact of one-minute papers on learning in an introductory accounting course. *Issues in Accounting Education, 13*(3), 485.

Azlina, N. N. (2010). Cetls: supporting collaborative activities among students and teachers through the use of think-pair-share techniques. *International Journal of Computer Science Issues (IJCSI), 7*(5), 18.

Bamiro, A. O. (2015). Effects of guided discovery and think-pair-share strategies on secondary school students' achievement in chemistry. *Sage Open, 5*(1), 1–7.

Bandura, A., & Walters, R. H. (1977). *Social learning theory*. Prentice-Hall.

Bell, T., Rosamond, F., & Casey, N. (2012). Computer science unplugged and related projects in math and computer science popularization. In *The multivariate algorithmic revolution and beyond* (pp. 398–456). Springer.

Beth, B., & Moreland, A. (2017). UTeach CS principles: broadening participation through K–12 computer science education and teacher professional learning and support. In *Proceedings of the 2017 ACM SIGCSE technical symposium on computer science education* (pp. 733–733). ACM.

Bligh, D. A. (1998). *What's the use of lectures?* Intellect books.

Board, T. C. (2017). *AP computer science principles: Course and exam description*. Author.

Braught, G., Wahls, T., & Eby, L. M. (2011). The case for pair programming in the computer science classroom. *ACM Transactions on Computing Education (TOCE), 11*(1), 2.

Brown, P. C., Roediger, H. L., & McDaniel, M. A. (2014). *Make it stick.* Harvard University Press.

Bruner, J. S. (1961). The act of discovery. *Harvard Educational Review, 31,* 21–32.

Chi, M. T. (2009). Active-constructive-interactive: a conceptual framework for differentiating learning activities. *Topics in cognitive science, 1*(1), 73–105.

Clark, J. M., & Paivio, A. (1991). Dual coding theory and education. *Educational psychology review, 3*(3), 149–210.

Computer Science Unplugged. (2017). Retrieved May 11, 2019 from: https://csunplugged. org/en/

Crouch, C. H., & Mazur, E. (2001). Peer instruction: ten years of experience and results. *American Journal of Physics, 69*(9), 970–977.

Day, J. A., & Foley, J. D. (2006). Evaluating a web lecture intervention in a human-computer interaction course. *IEEE Transactions on education, 49*(4), 420–431.

Doolittle, P. E. (2014). Complex constructivism: A theoretical model of complexity and cognition. *International Journal of Teaching and Learning in Higher Education, 26*(3), 485–498.

Feaster, Y., Segars, L., Wahba, S. K., & Hallstrom, J. O. (2011). Teaching CS unplugged in the high school (with limited success). In *Proceedings of the 16th annual joint conference on innovation and technology in computer science education* (pp. 248–252). ACM.

Felder, R. M., & Brent, R. (2009). Active learning: An introduction. *ASQ Higher Education Brief, 2,* 4–9.

Felder, R. M., & Brent, R. (2016). *Teaching and learning stem: A practical guide.* John Wiley & Sons.

Felder, R. M., Felder, G. N., & Dietz, E. J. (1998). A longitudinal study of engineering student performance and retention. v. comparisons with traditionally-taught students. *Journal of Engineering Education, 87*(4), 469–480.

Freeman, S., Eddy, S. L., McDonough, M., Smith, M. K., Okoroafor, N., Jordt, H., & Wenderoth, M. P. (2014). Active learning increases student performance in science, engineering, and mathematics. *Proceedings of the National Academy of Sciences, 111*(23), 8410–8415.

Gaspar, A., & Langevin, S. (2007). *Active learning in introductory programming courses through student-led "live coding" and test-driven pair programming.* Paper presented at International Conference on Education and Information Systems, Technologies and Applications, Orlando, FL.

Gokhale, A. A. (1995). Collaborative learning enhances critical thinking. *Journal of Technology Education, 7,* 22–30.

Goode, J., & Chapman, G. (2018). *Exploring computer science.* http://www.exploringcs. org/curriculum

Graham, M. J., Frederick, J., Byars-Winston, A., Hunter, A.-B., & Handelsman, J. (2013). Increasing persistence of college students in stem. *Science, 341*(6153), 1455–1456.

Haak, D. C., HilleRisLambers, J., Pitre, E., & Freeman, S. (2011). Increased structure and active learning reduce the achievement gap in introductory biology. *Science, 332*(6034), 1213–1216.

Hanson, D., & Wolfskill, T. (2000). Process workshops-a new model for instruction. *Journal of Chemical Education, 77*(1), 120.

Hu, H. H., & Kussmaul, C. (2012). Promoting student-centered learning with Pogil. In *Proceedings of the 43rd ACM Technical Symposium on Computer Science Education* (pp. 579–580). ACM.

Hu, H. H., & Shepherd, T. D. (2013). Using POGIL to help students learn to program. *ACM Transactions on Computing Education (TOCE)*, *13*(3), 1–23.

Johnson, D. W., & Johnson, R. T. (1984). *The impact of cooperative, competitive, and individualistic experiences on minority individuals' educational and career success.* Minnesota University of Minneapolis Cooperative Learning Center.

Karpicke, J. D., & Blunt, J. R. (2011). Retrieval practice produces more learning than elaborative studying with concept mapping. *Science, 331*(6018), 772–775.

Kennedy, C., & Kraemer, E. T. (2019). Qualitative observations of student reasoning: Coding in the wild. In *Proceedings of the 2019 ACM Conference on Innovation and Technology in Computer Science Education (ITiCSE)* (pp. 224–230). ACM.

Keyser, M. W. (2000). Active learning and cooperative learning: understanding the difference and using both styles effectively. *Research Strategies, 17*(1), 35–44.

Kingston, S. (2018). Project based learning & student achievement: What does the research tell us? *PBL Evidence Matters, 1*(1), 1–11.

Kothiyal, A., Majumdar, R., Murthy, S., & Iyer, S. (2013). Effect of think-pair-share in a large cs1 class: 83% sustained engagement. In *Proceedings of the Ninth Annual International ACM Conference on International Computing Education Research (ICER)* (pp. 137–144). ACM.

Lasry, N., Mazur, E., & Watkins, J. (2008). Peer instruction: From Harvard to the two-year college. *American Journal of Physics, 76*(11), 1066–1069.

Li, Z., Plaue, C., & Kraemer, E. (2013). A spirit of camaraderie: The impact of pair programming on retention. In *Proceeding of the IEEE 26th Conference on Software Engineering Education and Training* (pp. 209–218).

Lorenzo, M., Crouch, C. H., & Mazur, E. (2006). Reducing the gender gap in the physics classroom. *American Journal of Physics, 74*(2), 118–122.

McConnell, J. J. (1996). Active learning and its use in computer science. *ACM SIGCSE Bulletin, 28*(SI), 52–54.

McKnight, G. (2011). *Effectiveness of POGIL.* https://pogil.org/about-pogil/effectiveness-of-pogil

Middendorf, J., & Kalish, A. (1996). The "change-up" in lectures. *TRC Newsletter, 8*(1), 1–5.

Moog, R. (2014). *Process oriented guided inquiry learning.* Washington University Libraries.

Nagappan, N., Williams, L., Ferzli, M., Wiebe, E., Yang, K., Miller, C., & Balik, S. (2003). Improving the cs1 experience with pair programming. *ACM SIGCSE Bulletin, 35*(1), 359–362.

National Research Council. (1996). *National science education standards.* National Academies Press.

Olson, S., & Riordan, D. G. (2012). *Engage to excel: Producing one million additional college graduates with degrees in science, technology, engineering, and mathematics. Report to the President.* Executive Office of the President.

Parlante, N., Cigas, J., Shiflet, A. B., Sooriamurthi, R., Clancy, M., Noonan, B., & Reed, D. (2007). Nifty assignments. In *Proceedings of the 38th SIGCSE Technical Symposium on Computer Science Education* (pp. 497–498).

Paxton, J. (2002). Live programming as a lecture technique. *Journal of Computing Sciences in Colleges*, *18*(2), 51–56.

Prince, M. (2004). Does active learning work? a review of the research. *Journal of Engineering Education (JEE)*, *93*(3), 223–231.

Pyc, M. A., Agarwal, P. K., & Roediger III, H. L. (2014). Test-enhanced learning. In V. A. Benassi, C. E. Overson, & C. M. Hakala (Eds.), *Applying science of learning in education: Infusing psychological science into the curriculum* (pp. 194–205). Society for the Teaching of Psychology.

Resnick, M., Maloney, J., Monroy-Hernández, A., Rusk, N., Eastmond, E., Brennan, K., Silverman, B., Millner, A., Rosenbaum, E., Silver, J., & Kafai, Y. (2009). Scratch: Programming for all. *Communications of ACM*, *52*(11), 60–67.

Rivard, L. P., & Straw, S. B. (2000). The effect of talk and writing on learning science: An exploratory study. *Science Education*, *84*(5), 566–593.

Rodriguez, B., Rader, C., & Camp, T. (2016). Using student performance to assess cs unplugged activities in a classroom environment. In *Proceedings of the 2016 ACM Conference on Innovation and Technology in Computer Science Education (ITiCSE)* (pp. 95–100). ACM.

Roediger III, H. L., & Butler, A. C. (2011). The critical role of retrieval practice in long-term retention. *Trends in Cognitive Sciences*, *15*(1), 20–27.

Seymour, E., & Hewitt, N. M. (1997). *Talking about leaving: Why undergraduates leave the sciences*. Westview Press.

Slavin, R. E. (1978). Student teams and achievement divisions. *Journal of Research and Development in Education*, *12*(1), 39–49.

Slavin, R. E. (1988). Cooperative learning and student achievement. *Educational Leadership*, *46*(2), 31–33.

Stead, D. R. (2005). A review of the one-minute paper. *Active Learning in Higher Education*, *6*(2), 118–131.

Straumanis, A., & Simons, E. (2006). Assessment of student learning in POGIL organic chemistry. In *Abstracts of papers of the American Chemical Society* (Vol. 231). American Chemical Society.

Stuart, J., & Rutherford, R. (1978). Medical student concentration during lectures. *The Lancet*, *312*(8088), 514–516.

Sweller, J. (1988). Cognitive load during problem solving: effects on learning. *Cognitive science, 12*(2), 257–285.

Sweller, J., van Merrienboer, J. J., & Paas, F. (2019). Cognitive architecture and instructional design: 20 years later. *Educational Psychology Review*, 1–32.

Taub, R., Armoni, M., & Ben-Ari, M. (2012). Cs unplugged and middle-school students' views, attitudes, and intentions regarding cs. *ACM Transactions on Computing Education (TOCE)*, *12*(2), 8.

Taub, R., Ben-Ari, M., & Armoni, M. (2009). The effect of cs unplugged on middle-school students' views of cs. *ACM SIGCSE Bulletin*, *41*(3), 99–103.

Thies, R., & Vahrenhold, J. (2012). Reflections on outreach programs in cs classes: Learning objectives for unplugged activities. In *Proceedings of the 43rd ACM Technical Symposium on Computer Science Education (SIGCSE)* (pp. 487–492). ACM.

Thies, R., & Vahrenhold, J. (2013). On plugging unplugged into cs classes. In *Proceeding of the 44th ACM Technical Symposium on Computer Science Education* (SIGCSE) (pp. 365–370). ACM.

Thies, R., & Vahrenhold, J. (2016). Back to school: computer science unplugged in the wild. In *Proceedings of the 2016 ACM Conference on Innovation and Technology in Computer Science Education (ITiCSE)* (pp. 118–123). ACM.

Thomas, L., Ratclife, M., & Robertson, A. (2003). Code warriors and code-a-phobes: A study in attitude and pair programming. *ACM SIGCSE Bulletin, 35*(1), 363–367.

Tobias, S. (1991). *They're not dumb, they're different.* (Vol. 101). Research Corporation.

Valcke, M. (2002). Cognitive load: Updating the theory? *Learning and Instruction, 12*(1), 147–154.

Van Amburgh, J. A., Devlin, J. W., Kirwin, J. L., & Qualters, D. M. (2007). A tool for measuring active learning in the classroom. *American Journal of Pharmaceutical Education, 71*(5), 85.

Van Gorp, M. J., & Grissom, S. (2001). An empirical evaluation of using constructive classroom activities to teach introductory programming. *Computer Science Education, 11*(3), 247–260.

Vygotsky, L. (1978). Interaction between learning and development. *Readings on the Development of Children, 23*(3), 34–41.

Williams, L. A., & Kessler, R. R. (2000). All I really need to know about pair programming I learned in kindergarten. *Communications of the ACM, 43*(5), 108–114.

Williams, L., & Kessler, R. (2002). *Pair programming illuminated.* Addison-Wesley Longman Publishing Co., Inc.

Williams, L., McDowell, C., Nagappan, N., Fernald, J., & Werner, L. (2003). Building pair programming knowledge through a family of experiments. In *2003 International Symposium on Empirical Software Engineering, 2003. ISESE 2003 Proceedings.* (pp. 143–152). IEEE.

Zimmerman, B. J., & Martinez-Pons, M. (1988). Construct validation of a strategy model of student self-regulated learning. *Journal of Educational Psychology, 80*(3), 284.

CHAPTER 2

PRE-SERVICE TEACHERS' BELIEFS, CONFIDENCE, AND INTEREST IN COMPUTER SCIENCE EDUCATION

Jung Won Hur

The purpose of this study was to examine how computer science (CS) education lessons affected pre-service teachers' beliefs, confidence, and interest in teaching CS education in their future classrooms. A total of 77 pre-service teachers were introduced to the fundamental concepts of CS and programming tools (e.g., Scratch and Ozobot) in a stand-alone technology integration course. In order to examine changes in pre-service teachers' beliefs, confidence, and interest, pre- and post-surveys, Scratch assignments, and students' reflections were collected. The findings demonstrated that the course activities helped participants increase confidence and interest in teaching CS in their future classrooms. However, participants reported a lack of skills and understanding of CS concepts and tools even after several CS education classes, suggesting a need to provide more CS lessons to pre-service teachers to help them be better prepared to teach CS in their future classrooms.

Preparing Pre-Service Teachers to Teach Computer Science: Models, Practices, and Policies, pages 29–48.

29

Keywords: Computer Science Education, Computational Thinking, Self-Efficacy, Pre-service Teachers, Teacher Beliefs

INTRODUCTION

Computer science (CS) education has become an important focus in the field of education worldwide (Hubwieser et al., 2015). Heintz et al., (2016) reported that 17 out of 21 European countries have introduced or are in the process of introducing CS education in schools. In the U.S., 34 states have K–12 CS standards, and 5 additional states are in the process of developing their own state standards (State of Computer Science Education, 2019). CS education advocates have highlighted the importance of integrating CS education into K–12 schools to help students develop computational thinking skills. According to Wing (2008), "Computational thinking is taking an approach to solving problems, designing systems and understanding human behaviour that draws on concepts fundamental to computing" (p. 3717). Computational thinking is an analytical thinking skill that includes problem solutions that can be represented as algorithms and computational steps (Aho, 2012). The core idea of computational thinking is to think like a computer scientist when confronted with a problem (Grover & Pea, 2013).

A number of educators and non-profit educational organizations have promoted CS education in K–12 schools to expose students at an early age to help them develop computational thinking skills (Yadav et al., 2017). Parents also expressed a strong interest in providing their child with CS education (Google & Gallup, 2015). In order to assist states and schools with the development of CS curriculum and standards, a group of computer scientists, educators, and engineers collectively developed the *K–12 Computer Science Framework* based on the vision of providing all K–12 students with opportunities to engage in the fundamental concepts and practices of CS (K–12 Computer Science Framework Steering Committee, 2016). The framework includes five core concepts (what students should know) and seven core practices (what students should do). The core concepts cover major content in the field of CS and include: (a) computing systems, (b) networks and the Internet, (c) data and analysis, (d) algorithms and programing, and (e) impacts of computing. The core practices represent the behaviors that students need to demonstrate while engaging with the core concepts. These include: (a) fostering an inclusive culture, (b) collaborating around computing, (c) recognizing and defining computational problems, (d) developing and using abstractions, (e) creating computational artifacts, (f) testing and refining computational artifacts, and (g) communicating about computing.

While there has been a growing interest in teaching CS in K–12 classrooms, integrating this into core academic subjects creates several challenges, including a shortage of qualified educators who can teach CS concepts and practices effectively (Menekse, 2015). Future teachers should be able to demonstrate confidence in their skills and knowledge to guide student learning of CS. Yadav et al. (2017)

argued, "We need to prepare new teachers who are able to incorporate computational thinking skills into their discipline and teaching practice so they can guide their students to use computational thinking strategies" (p. 58). One feasible way to educate future teachers about core concepts and practices of CS is to introduce computational thinking skills in an existing technology integration course (Mouza et al., 2017). In addition to introducing various emerging technology tools for classroom teaching, the course can help future teachers think computationally and explore ways to promote students' use of such skills.

This study examined pre-service teachers' beliefs, confidence, and interest in teaching CS education in their future classrooms before and after they were engaged in various CS education activities in a stand-alone technology integration course. The state of Alabama became the 15th state to adopt CS education standards in K–12 schools (Alabama Today, 2018). Along with the states of Rhode Island and Tennessee, Alabama's standards are combined with digital literacy guidelines to reflect the state's vision of providing students with a solid foundation of digital fluency, computational practices, and ethical and responsible application of technology to solve problems (Alabama Course of Study, 2018; State of Computer Science Education, 2018). All Alabama K–12 school teachers are expected to incorporate CS concepts and practices in their subject areas by the 2022–2023 academic year (Nusbaum, 2019). In order to help future Alabama teachers gain knowledge and confidence in teaching CS in their classrooms, I taught fundamental concepts of CS in my technology integration course and introduced several programming tools, such as Scratch and Ozobot. This chapter reports changes in the participants' beliefs, confidence, and interest in teaching CS after pre-service teachers had been engaged in various CS activities.

BACKGROUND

Pre-Service Teachers' Self-Efficacy, Pedagogical Beliefs, and CS Education

Bandura et al. (1987) defined self-efficacy as belief in one's ability to successfully accomplish a task and produce positive outcomes in a given condition. People take part in an action, interpret the outcomes of their behavior, and use the interpretation to create beliefs about their abilities to engage in subsequent actions in a similar domain (Pajares & Valiante, 1997). Unless people believe that their action will lead to the desired outcomes, they have little motivation to act. Self-efficacy belief influences aspirations for goal commitment, motivation to act, and persistence of efforts and engagements in the event of setbacks (Bandura et al., 1996). Self-efficacy is more than feeling confident (e.g., "I can read."); it is a very specific and situational judgment of one's capabilities (Linnenbrink & Pintrich, 2003). For instance, self-efficacy in the field of CS might be expressed as "I can program my robot to move faster and win this game."

People who demonstrate a high level of self-efficacy tend to try new activities and not fear difficult tasks (Pajares & Valiante, 1997). They set challenging goals for themselves, sustain their efforts even when they do not meet goals, and quickly recover their self-confidence after failures. They attribute a failure to a lack of effort, knowledge, and skills rather than blaming others or outside environments (Bandura, 1994). Self-efficacy also affects individuals' behaviors, thinking patterns, and emotional reactions (Pajares, 1996). People with low self-efficacy view difficult tasks as personal threats and present weak commitment to the goals they selected to pursue (Tahmassian & Moghadam, 2011). They tend to consider problems to be more difficult than they really are and become stressed and depressed in such situations (Bandura, 1994).

Scholars have found that self-efficacy is a predominant factor affecting students' decisions to choose a career or major in science, technology, engineering or math (STEM) (Alexander et al., 2010). Students are more likely to pursue a STEM career if they believe that they will be likely to succeed in the program (Lamb et al., 2017). Likewise, teachers are more likely to teach CS if they feel that they can successfully teach students the core concepts and practices of CS. "Teachers with a strong sense of self-efficacy are more open to new ideas and they are more willing to experiment with new methods at the same time offering students new and different learning opportunities" (Paraskeva et al., 2008, p. 1084). Ertmer and Ottenbreit-Leftwich (2010) claimed that providing time and effort to help pre-service teachers develop knowledge and skills to utilize technology is important to help them gain confidence in technology integration.

Another factor that can affect pre-service teachers' CS teaching is their pedagogical beliefs. Over the past several decades, many scholars have examined factors affecting technology use in K–12 classrooms, reporting several enablers and barriers (e.g., Hur et al., 2016; Inan & Lowther, 2010). One critical factor that was commonly identified was teachers' pedagogical beliefs concerning technology use. Ertmer (2005) explained the differences between beliefs and knowledge by citing definitions used by Calderhead (1996). Ertmer (2005) said, "Whereas beliefs generally refer to suppositions, commitments, and ideologies, knowledge refers to factual propositions and understandings" (p. 28). Thus, when learning a new concept, one can accept it as true or not. For instance, after pre-service teachers learn a block-based programming language such as Scratch and review how the program is being used in K–12 classrooms, pre-service teachers may still believe that incorporating Scratch activities is not useful for their students, making no further effort to integrate it into their teaching.

Studies have indicated that those teachers who perceive technology use as beneficial for student learning are more likely to integrate technology in the classroom by overcoming challenges (Ertmer & Ottenbreit-Leftwich, 2013). This implies the importance of examining pre-service teachers' beliefs in CS education in classrooms. If pre-service teachers view CS education as useful for student learning, they will be more apt to actively learn and teach CS in their future classrooms. They could be willing to find solutions for possible challenges of teaching CS education, such as a lack of time and lack of instructional support. Thus, understanding pre-service teachers' beliefs in CS education is important to promote CS education in K–12 schools.

CS Teaching Strategies and Educating Computational Thinking Skills

A number of educators have examined issues and strategies of teaching and learning CS for the past three decades, but most of this research has focused on computer programming education for undergraduate students (Grover & Pea, 2013). While several non-profit organizations (e.g., Code.org) have created instructional resources and guidelines for K–12 teachers, not much research has been conducted on a K–12 classroom level. Thus, limited information on teaching CS is available for K–12 school teachers.

Researchers have shared instructional tips for teaching computer programming for undergraduate students. For instance, Brown and Wilson (2018) shared ten tips, including encouraging peer instruction, using live coding, promoting pair programming, and incorporating authentic tasks. Scholars have also suggested promoting peer assessment, as it provides students with opportunities to review the assessment rubric thoroughly and help students learn from their peers (Wang et al., 2017). Another study introduced a studio format in which lectures, recitations, and lab activities are combined for teaching and learning computer programming (Barak et al., 2007). The studio format was intended to increase interaction among students and with their instructors when reviewing course projects and class exercises.

A small number of studies have introduced computational thinking skills in a teacher education course. Mouza et al. (2017) incorporated computational thinking skills in an existing technology integration course when teaching various tools, such as interactive whiteboard, internet research, and concept mapping. For instance, after pre-service teachers learned the use of concept mapping software, they developed a lesson integrating this into a teaching subject, such as applying the idea of decomposition (i.e., breaking down a complex problem into smaller parts) to solving a math problem. The researchers measured participants' understanding of computational thinking, knowledge, and beliefs and reported a statistically significant increase between the pre- and post-surveys.

Yadav et al., (2014) reported the findings from teaching a one-week module (two 50-minute classes) on computational thinking skills. In the first class, the researchers defined computational thinking and explained five key concepts (i.e., problem identification and decomposition, abstraction, logical thinking, algorithms, and debugging) by integrating everyday problem-solving examples. In the second class, students learned how computational thinking can be integrated into subject teaching and the benefits of its integration into K–12 classrooms. The researchers examined students' understanding of computational thinking and reported that those who took the computational thinking module (i.e., the experiment group) were able to define computational thinking skills in a more sophisticated manner than those in the control group. Additionally, those students who took the computational thinking module were better able to explain how computational thinking skills can be integrated into their future classrooms.

While computational thinking involves more than computer programming, learning computer programming is an effective way to promote computational thinking skills. Providing students with opportunities to engage in computer programming activities can help them become technology creators, not simply technology consumers (Mouza et al., 2017). Several researchers taught programming languages in a teacher education program and explored pre-service teachers' experiences and perceptions. For instance, Dağ (2019) taught three different computer programming languages—Scratch, Small Basic, and Alice— for a semester and reported that pre-service teachers gained knowledge about teaching CS at the K–12 level and shared positive perceptions on coding education.

Purpose of the Study

In order to properly guide pre-service teachers' learning and teaching of CS, teacher educators should understand how pre-service teachers perceptions on CS education and their ability to learn and teach CS in their future classrooms. In addition, promoting pre-service teachers' confidence in teaching CS is critical to help them successfully teach CS. Participants in this study were engaged in various CS activities, and changes of beliefs, confidence, and interest were measured. The following two research questions guided the study:

- What are pre-service teachers' perceptions about their ability to learn and teach CS?
- What is the influence of the engagement in CS learning on pre-service teachers' beliefs, confidence, and interest in teaching CS education in K–12 classrooms?

METHOD

Participants

Participants included 77 pre-service teachers attending a college of education in Alabama; most were either sophomores (n = 34) or juniors (n = 40). There were two seniors and one freshman. Approximately 92% of the students (n = 71) were female. In terms of ethnicity, there were 71 white, 3 black, and 3 Asian students. Regarding participants' majors, 50 students were majoring in elementary education, and 15 students were majoring in early childhood education. Six students were majoring in special education, and the other six students were majoring in secondary education (five in social studies and one in language arts). About 25% of the students (n = 19) indicated that they had had prior CS learning experiences. However, six students indicated that their CS experience involved learning the use of Microsoft products, while another group of six had learned website development using Weebly or Wix, presenting participants' limited exposure to the field of CS. Only three students specifically talked about computer programming experience, such as learning Scratch.

Data Collection

In order to answer the two research questions, four different datasets were collected. First, a pre-survey asked 19 questions, including five items related to demographics. The survey questions examined participants' prior CS education experiences (e.g., "Have you ever engaged in any CS activities, such as using programming to create software, apps, games, websites or electronics?"), their beliefs regarding teaching CS education in K–12 classrooms (e.g., "What do you think about Alabama's effort to promote CS education in K–12 classrooms?"), and their perceived confidence in teaching CS in their future classrooms (e.g., "How confident are you that you could teach CS if you want to?"). To measure participants' beliefs in teaching CS, five items from the survey by Google and Gallup (2015) were included (e.g., "It is a good idea to try to incorporate CS education into other subjects at school"; and "Most students should be required to take a CS course"). Participants were asked to respond to each item using a five-point Likert scale ranging from 1 (strongly disagree) to 5 (strongly agree). The reliability test indicated good internal consistency of the items; Cronbach's alpha was .869. Another item examined participants' perceptions on CS in comparison to other subjects: "Do you think offering opportunities to learn CS is more important, just as important or less important to a student's future success than other elective courses like art, music and foreign languages?" This item came from the Google and Gallup (2015) survey as well.

The pre-survey also asked participants to indicate their familiarity with five CS-related tools (i.e., Code.org, CS Unplugged, Scratch, Scratch Jr. and Ozobot) on a five-level scale rating from 1 (I do not know what it is) to 5 (I am quite familiar with this tool). Five questions were open-ended, asking students to describe their prior answer. For instance, participants were asked to indicate their level of interest in teaching CS (1: not interested, 2: somewhat interested, 3: very interested) and then were asked to describe the reasons for their selection.

The post-survey assessment consisted of 13 items, including 3 open-ended questions. Most questions were the same as the pre-survey, examining participants' perceived beliefs and confidence in teaching CS in K–12 schools. The post-survey also asked participants to indicate their intention to teach the aforementioned five CS related tools on a three-level scale (1: I won't teach it, 2: I might teach it, 3: I would love to teach it).

Third, all students were asked to complete the Scratch project. I used one of the design scenarios (e.g., Underwater Conversation) available at http://scratched. gse.harvard.edu/ct/assessing.html. The example included two bugs (i.e., two dialogues appear at the same time, not one by one; a third sprite needs to appear after the end of the dialogue). Students were asked to (a) fix the bugs, (b) add more backdrops (i.e., background pages), and (c) extend stories by adding several animation features (e.g., gliding, scoring points). Finally, students were required to submit a reflection. The reflection template consisted of ten guiding questions, including the following:

- Defining CS education (e.g., "If someone who does not have any CS education experience asked you, "What is CS education about?", what would you tell him or her?);
- Reflecting on the debugging and remix process (e.g., "Please describe what you did in Scratch to complete this project. For instance, if you made your character disappear, explain how you did it. Also, if you added a game component, explain how you did it. Explain at least three elements.");
- Sharing beliefs in CS education (e.g., "What do you think about the emphasis on CS education in K–12 schools? Is it beneficial or not? What made you think so?"); and
- Explaining their interest in teaching CS in their future classrooms (e.g., "Let's imagine your future school is looking for volunteers who would introduce the basics of CS to students or other teachers. Are you willing to volunteer to share the lessons that you learned in this class with others? Why or why not?").

Procedure

Participants were asked to complete the anonymous pre-survey before CS resources were introduced. Throughout the semester, I used about 20 % of course time to teach and learn CS concepts and practices. I taught CS unplugged lessons from the CS Unplugged website (e.g., binary numbers, sorting algorithms) and from the Code.org site (e.g., loop). Students reviewed various Scratch tutorials available at the website (https://scratch.mit.edu/projects/editor/?tutorial=all) and practiced a different tutorial in each class. After participants had become familiar with various Scratch programming environments, they were introduced to Scratch Jr., comparing the two tools and discussing how they might use Scratch and Scratch Jr. in their future classrooms. They also explored Ozobot and Ozoblocky. They first learned lesson activities available on the Ozobot education website (e.g., president's parade, multiplication table practice) and programmed their Ozobot using Ozoblocky. Toward the end of the semester, students were asked to complete a Scratch assignment and reflect on their programming experiences. In the last week of the semester, students were invited to fill out the anonymous post-survey.

Data Analysis

Descriptive analysis was performed on the pre- and post-surveys (Field, 2013). No identifying information was collected from the pre- and post-surveys, and thus it was not possible to perform the paired-t test. Only the mean scores were compared between the pre- and post-surveys. In order to analyze the qualitative data, I first carefully reviewed participants' open-ended answers. I identified common codes (e.g., future job, lack of experience) while reading students' answers and applied the common codes to all data while I examined the data second time. Then, I divided the answers into three groups: supporting CS education, not supporting CS education, and neutral opinion. In each group, I examined the main reasons for the support or lack of support. After I analyzed the pre-survey data, I reviewed students' reflections and identified emerging codes. Particular attention was paid to those students who specifically expressed that their beliefs, confidence, or interest in CS education had changed during the course. I compared the emerging codes with the pre-survey findings and investigated how students' reflections were similar to or different from the pre-survey data. The findings of qualitative data analysis were compared with the pre- and post-survey quantitative data, reviewing the frequency of willingness to support CS education, a level of confidence, and a level of interest.

I reviewed each student's Scratch assignment in terms of bug correction, the addition of a backdrop as well as an animation feature, and its overall logic. The Scratch activity was a 10 point assignment (out of 150 total grade), and students received 7 points if they were able to correct the bugs. As they included extra component, such as a backdrop with a few dialogues or animations, they received additional points. While reviewing the assignment, I also examined each student's reflection in order to understand his or her actual programming experience (e.g., what was difficult) and their overall perceptions of developing a story using Scratch. The reflection was a 15 point assignment and was graded based on the depth of reflection, details of the programing experience, clear expression of personal opinions, and required components. These two assignments were worth 16 % of their total grade for the course.

RESULTS AND DISCUSSION

Previous studies examining factors affecting teachers' adoption of technology in classrooms revealed interconnected relationships among different factors (Inan & Lowther, 2010). Internal factors (e.g., teacher beliefs, self-efficacy) and external factors (e.g., professional development, appropriate budget) directly and/or indirectly affect teachers' adoption of technology (Hur et al., 2016). The analysis of the data in this study also presented interconnections of beliefs, confidence, and interest in teaching CS. While participants generally believed that providing CS education in K–12 classroom is important, they were somewhat hesitant to teach this in their future classrooms due to their limited knowledge and confidence. The findings also indicated that while the course activities helped participants increase knowledge and confidence in teaching CS, participants still reported a lack of skills and understanding, suggesting a need to provide more CS lessons to pre-service teachers. Detailed findings are summarized below.

Beliefs on Teaching CS in K–12 classrooms

Participants' general beliefs on CS education in K–12 schools were measured through pre and post-surveys as well as reflections. Responses in general demonstrated that participants shared positive views on teaching CS in K–12 classrooms. The mean scores of all items in both the pre- and post-surveys ranged from 3.26 to 4.12 (see Table 2.1).

The item, "it is a good idea to try to incorporate computer science education into other subjects at school," received highest mean scores both for the pre- and post-surveys, Pre-M = 4.08 (SD = .823) and Post-M = 4.12 (SD = .897). A student expressed in his pre-survey why he supported CS education: "Everything in the world today is done on computers, and our job as educators is to prepare students for the real world. In today's world that means we need to give at least a basic education in computer sciences" (Junior, Social Studies major, Male). Another student also expressed her support of CS education by sharing future job benefits:

> I totally support the idea of incorporating more computer science in the classroom because technology is only improving and so many people today are getting more knowledgeable about different technological resources which could spark in interest in many students that could potentially lead to a career (Sophomore, Elementary Education major, Female).

The item that received lowest mean scores was "students should receive computer science education at a young age: Pre-M = 3.42 (SD = 1.03) and Post-M =

TABLE 2.1. Participants' Beliefs in Teaching CS in K–12 Classrooms

Survey Items	Pre-Mean (SD)	Post-Mean (SD)
It is a good idea to try to incorporate computer science education into other subjects at school.	4.08 (.823)	4.12 (.897)
Most students should be required to take a computer science course.	3.42 (1.094)	3.92 (.968)
Promoting computer science related knowledge and skills is beneficial for students.	4.10 (.754)	4.25 (.741)
Students should receive computer science education at a young age.	3.42 (1.030)	3.86 (1.032)
I believe offering computer science education is important in my future classroom.	3.69 (1.042)	3.99 (1.007)

3.86 (SD = 1.03). According to the pre-survey, students had concerns about excessive reliance on technology especially for young leaners and were hesitant to provide young leaners with CS education. A student explained in her pre-survey:

> I think that technology is beneficial for the classroom, but this sounds like it is being overemphasized and will cause too much screen time for kids. I think that kids can learn a lot through playing and experience without having to bring in tons of technology, and therefore I don't think that computer science is foundational for elementary school kids (Freshman, Elementary Education major, Female).

Another student also shared her concern of too much technology use for young leaners. She expressed, "I think that at a young age, there are much more important things for children to learn than computer skills. I do think they are necessary, but not when a child is in elementary school" (Sophomore, Elementary Education major, Female). The responses to the survey item examining participants' perceptions on CS in comparison with other elective courses (e.g., art, music) indicated that over 60% students believe that offering a CS education experience is as important as teaching other courses, while about 30% students believed that it is less important.

While students had concerns about teaching CS to young leaners, they generally believed the importance of teaching CS particularly for older students. A student presented, "I think as you get older and ready to go into a job field or to college, it is essential to have a good background knowledge of the computer science subject" (Junior, Social Studies major, Male). Another student made a similar comment: "I do not think that it should be taught starting at the Kindergarten age. I think that it should come into the curriculum around 4th grade" (Junior, Early Childhood Education major, Female).

The post-survey results demonstrated increased positive beliefs, implying that the engagement in CS education helped participants perceive CS education in K–12 classrooms more positively (See Table 2.1). Participants reflected on their K–12 technology experiences and discussed the usefulness of CS education. A student discussed this in her reflection:

> I personally did not have this computer science education opportunity during my K–12 years of school. However, now that I have been exposed to it, I definitely feel as if my generation missed out on this great, new opportunity. There are many positive lessons that come out of this computer science education. Computational thinking skills, step-by-step algorithm exposure, and even Internet/ social networking safety are all great takeaways from this computer science education (Sophomore, Elementary Education major, Female).

Another student also claimed a missed opportunity by expressing, "I wish that I had been taught this when I was younger because now that I know about it, I feel like it is too late to pursue it as a career" (Junior, Elementary Education major, Female).

While participants' reflections presented positive views on the emphasis of CS education in K–12 classrooms, there was a group of students who presented some concerns about the new mandatory requirement and technology reliance in their reflections. One student claimed the following:

> I think it is beneficial but not dire. It is helpful but it is not do or die. I feel this way because I had it in school, and I think I would be doing just was as well if I hadn't. I don't feel as if it is a super important area for me to be familiar (Junior, Special Education major, Female).

Another student expressed her concerns of technology reliance. She suggested the following:

> I think if we only focus on technology it may take away from normal pen and paper education that is also still so important in life today. Everyone should know how to use technology and be educated in computer science but we should not be completely reliant on it (Sophomore, Early childhood Education major, Female).

Confidence in Learning and Teaching CS

Students' perceived familiarity with CS education resources was examined via pre- and post-surveys. The pre-survey indicated that over 85%–93% of participants did not know the five CS education resources that were taught in the course (see Table 2.2). After various CS lessons, participants indicated improved confidence; 70%–95% participants expressed that they felt fairly confident or very confident in using the five resources in their future classrooms (see Table 2.2). Participants' assignments also demonstrated their improved skills in computer programming using Scratch. Before the course, over 90% of participants reported that they did not know the program at all. After they explored the tool for over a month, however, all of them were able to demonstrate their skills to create a short story by using different blocks (e.g., event, condition) in Scratch. While students' skills were varied, they were able to at least correct all the identified bugs (e.g., show/hide a sprite) and add their own dialogues and a backdrop to expand the story. The post-survey presented that over 52% of students indicated that they felt very confident in using Scratch in their future classrooms, while over 42% of participants expressed that they feel fairy confident.

As participants felt comfortable using different CS tools, their confidence in learning and teaching CS also increased. The pre-survey results of confidence in *learning* CS was Pre-M = 3.71 (SD = 1.164), and confidence in *teaching* CS was Pre-M = 3.31 (SD = 1.128). The post-survey results of confidence in *learning* CS was increased to Post-M = 4.21 (SD = 0.804), and confidence in *teaching* CS was increased to Post-M = 3.84 (SD = .811). The analysis of reflections revealed that while the CS lessons helped participants feel confident in teaching CS in their future classrooms, they still reported a lack of knowledge and skills. A student wrote in her reflection:

TABLE 2.2. Participants' Perceived Confidence in CS Education Resources Before and After CS Lessons

CS Resources Survey Item	Code.org		CS Unplugged		Scratch		Scratch Jr.		Ozobot	
	Pre (%)	Post (%)	Pre (%)	Post (%)	Pre (%)	Post (%)	Pre (%)	Post (%)	Pre (%)	Post (%)
I do not know what it is	85.7	1.4	96.1	1.4	90.9	0	93.5	0	92.2	0
I have limited knowledge/skills in using this tool.	13.0	27.4	3.9	17.8	6.5	5.5	5.2	4.1	6.5	5.5
I am fairly confident in using this tool in my class.	0	47.9	0	50.7	1.3	42.5	0	41.1	0	32.9
I am very confident in using this tool in my class.	1.3	23.3	0	30.1	1.3	52.1	1.3	54.8	1.3	61.6

I think in some ways I am prepared for teaching computer science in my future classroom, but I feel that I definitely have more to study and learn. I am excited for the things I have learned so far, but I think that it will take more practice to not only know how to do these computer science activities but to teach someone how to do them.... I think some skills I am lacking is overall technology specific questions students may ask. Why does something work the way it does, why it is like this, etc.? I want to be able to answer these questions, and I think that my skill set is not quite where it needs to be (Sophomore, Elementary Education major, Female).

Another student also expressed his lack of skills. He described the following:

I feel like I have improved a lot on my computer science knowledge since beginning this class, but I still do not feel prepared to teach a class on it. I would need to learn more about what the most important activities to incorporate into the lessons are and how computer science would be used in the real world (Junior, Social Studies major, Male).

Interest in Teaching CS Education

The analysis of pre- and post-surveys demonstrated that after the lessons, the number of participants who were not interested in teaching CS was reduced, while the number of participants who were interested in teaching CS was increased (See Figure 2.1). About 11 % of participants expressed their lack of interest in teaching CS before taking the CS lessons. As discussed before, participants had a concern about excessive reliance on technology, one of reasons for not want-

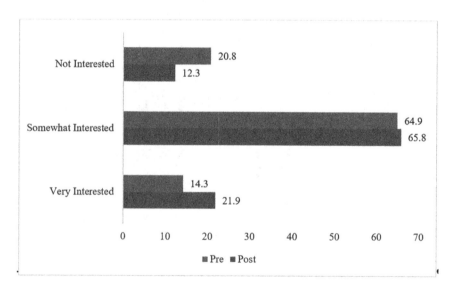

FIGURE 2.1.   Changes of Interest in Teaching Computer Science Education

ing to teach CS in their future classrooms. Over 60% students indicated that they were somewhat interested in teaching CS. Several students particularly explained that their lack of understanding was a main reason why they were unsure whether they would want to teach CS in their future classrooms. A student wrote in the pre-survey, "As of right now, I do not know enough about computer science to be interested in teaching it in my future classroom. I want to use technology in my future classroom but I do not believe I am equipped with teaching it" (Junior, Elementary Education major, Female). Another student expressed, "I am a little interested but I would be more interested if I was confident in my own abilities to learn the subject matter of computer science" (Junior, Elementary Education major, Female).

The analysis of post-survey and reflections demonstrated participants' increased interest in teaching CS. The percentage of students who were not interested in teaching CS was reduced to 12% from 21% previously. The percentage of students who were interested in teaching CS was increased to 22% from 14%. Table 2.3 presents participants' interest in utilizing resources that they learned in the class. Participants particularly enjoyed using Ozobot, and 63% of participants indicated that they would love to teach Ozobot in their future classrooms. A large group of students in the course wanted to teach K–4 students, and approximately 47% of students indicated that they would like to teach Scratch Jr. in their future classrooms. Because most students did not know the five resources at all before taking the course, the pre-survey did not ask their intention to teach these tools. Thus, pre- and post-survey comparison on the intention of using the tools for CS education was not performed.

The analysis of reflections also revealed students' increased interest in teaching CS after they learned CS lessons. A student wrote in her reflection, "I have enjoyed the things I have learned in this class, and I am looking forward to using them in my classes someday after I graduate" (Sophomore, Early Childhood Education major, Female). Some students explained how they would apply what they learned in the course to their future teaching. A student discussed the following:

> I have learned many helpful tips and techniques and would like to incorporate them in my future classroom. I plan to begin teaching this subject by teaching computer science without the computer and then start guiding the students towards reaching

TABLE 2.3. Interest in Teaching CS Resources in Future Classrooms

	Code.org	CS Un- plugged	Scratch	Scratch Jr.	Ozobot
I won't teach it	15.1%	12.3%	21.9%	12.3%	8.2%
I might teach	57.5%	52.1%	42.5%	41.1%	28.8%
I would love to teach it	27.4%	35.6%	35.6%	46.6%	63%

the goal of managing, editing, and creating a program on Scratch or Scratch Jr. (Junior, Elementary Education major, Female).

Similar to previous research (e.g., Dağ, 2019; Google & Gallup, 2015), the current study found that pre-service teachers in general had positive views on CS education. In this study, many pre-service teachers agreed with the importance of teaching CS in K–12 classrooms and were excited to learn about the basics of CS and teach it in their classrooms. Teachers' beliefs influence how they behave in the classroom and how they overcome teaching challenges (Bender et al., 2016). Participants' positive beliefs may suggest that more teachers would be willing to teach CS in their future K–12 classrooms as long as appropriate trainings and resources are available for new teachers.

While the results presented that CS learning experiences in the technology integration course helped participants feel somewhat confident in integrating CS teaching tools (e.g., Scratch, Ozobot, code.org), many of them indicated a need for additional training to boost their confidence. In addition, teaching both digital literacy skills and computational thinking skills in one technology course confused participants as to exactly what was involved in CS education. According to the analysis of participants' reflections, even after engaging in CS education activities, participants still defined CS education as utilizing different digital technologies to support learning. The findings suggest a need to offer additional CS education courses in teacher education programs. Having both a traditional technology integration course and a CS education course would help pre-service teachers be better prepared to teach both digital literacy skills and computational thinking skills in their future classrooms. Additionally, Ertmer and Ottenbreit-Leftwich (2010) explained that pre-service teachers' confidence in using technology can be improved when they observe the usefulness of technology to facilitate students' success. Likewise, providing pre-service teachers with opportunities to observe how K–12 students are engaged in various CS activities could help them not only feel that they could guide their student learning but develop a positive belief in the benefits of CS lessons for students.

NEXT STEP

Teacher education programs should make a significant effort to foster CS education in K–12 classrooms. To do so, I illustrate several important areas that teacher educators should focus on as well as future research ideas. First, developing lessons on promoting pre-service teachers' computational thinking skills is important. While there are a number of lessons available on coding education, only limited resources are available on integrating computational thinking into a subject. K–4 level teachers would likely want to integrate CS into their subject teaching rather than teaching a stand-alone CS course. To assist these teachers, lesson plans and resources that foster young leaners' computational thinking in subject teaching should be developed and shared with teacher educators and practicing teachers.

Next, providing faculty who teach technology integration courses with opportunities to learn effective ways to teach CS education and the latest CS education resources is important. While some education faculty have strong knowledge and skills in CS, not every education faculty (including adjunct faculty and graduate students) who teach a technology integration course have a background in CS education. Teaching CS is more than simply introducing education resources or teaching the basics of programming. Education faculty should develop a solid understanding of CS principles and practices as well as pedagogical content knowledge in CS education to confidently guide pre-service and in-service teachers' CS learning. To do so, online and off-line learning opportunities for faculty need to be provided, and best practices and teaching resources need to be shared.

In addition to the faculty who teach a technology integration course, teacher education programs should help all faculty better understand CS education. Due to the lack of previous experience, I found that the education faculty had a very limited understanding of CS education. Similar to what pre-service teachers thought about CS education in this study, some faculty with whom I have communicated shared the idea of CS education as teaching Microsoft products. In order to promote CS education for pre-service teachers, education faculty, particularly administrators and methods course faculty, should have a clear idea of what CS education is about and why we need to provide pre-service teachers with this new learning experience. Promoting collaboration with faculty who teach methods courses would be particularly important in helping pre-service teachers incorporate activities promoting computational thinking skills in their subject teaching.

More research should examine pre-service teachers' CS knowledge and skills in-depth and identify areas that need additional support. In this study, I only examined the assignment requirements (e.g., whether they were able to debug, extend the story, add animation features, etc.) but did not measure the quality of the Scratch programs. To measure quality, researchers could use Dr. Scratch (http://www.drscratch.org/), a free web application that evaluates a person's computational thinking skills including abstraction, logical thinking, user interactivity and data representation (Moreno-León & Robles, 2015). Once a user supplies the Scratch URL, Dr. Scratch will provide feedback on the user's Scratch project, presenting sub-scores as well as overall scores for computational thinking.

While this study examined pre-service teachers' beliefs on and confidence in teaching computer science education, I did not use a specific instrument to measure participants' improved computer programing self-efficacy. Recently, Tsai et al., (2019) developed the Computer Programming Self-Efficacy Scale (CPSES), which examines five subscales: logical thinking, algorithm, debug, control, and cooperation. Utilizing this kind of instrument can help researchers better understand how CS trainings helped teachers develop self-efficacy in computer programming.

REFERENCES

Aho, A. V. (2012). Computation and computational thinking. *The Computer Journal, 55*(7), 832–835.

Alabama Course of Study. (2018). *Digital literacy and computer science.* https://www.alsde.edu/sec/sct/COS/Final%202018%20Digital%20Literacy%20and%20Computer%20Science%20COS%5B5206%5D.pdf

Alabama Today. (2018, March 15). *Alabama becomes early adopter of new computer science standards.* http://altoday.com/archives/22028-alabama-becomes-early-adopter-of-new-computer-science-standards

Alexander, P. M., Holmner, M., Lotriet, H. H., Matthee, M. C., Pieterse, H. V., Naidoo, S., Twinomurinzi, H., & Jordan, D. (2010). Factors affecting career choice: Comparison between students from computer and other disciplines, *Journal of Science Education and Technology, 20*(3), 300–315.

Bandura, A. (1994). Self-efficacy. In V. S. Ramachaudran (Ed.), *Encyclopedia of human behavior* (Vol. 4, pp. 71–81). Academic Press.

Bandura, A., Barbaranelli, C., Caprara, G. V., & Pastorelli, C. (1996). Multifaceted impact of self-efficacy beliefs on academic functioning. *Child Development, 67*(3),1206–1222.

Bandura, A., O'Leary, A., Taylor, C. B., Gauthier, J., & Gossard, D. (1987). Perceived self-efficacy and pain control: Opioid and nonopioid mechanisms. *Journal of Personality and Social Psychology, 53*(3), 563–571.

Barak, M., Harward, J., Kocur, G., & Lerman, S. (2007). Transforming an introductory programming course: From lectures to active learning via wireless laptops. *Journal of Science Education and Technology, 16*(4), 325–336.

Bender, E., Schaper, N., Caspersen, M. E., Margartitis, M., & Hubwieser, P. (2016). Identifying and formulating teachers' beliefs and motivational orientations for computer science teacher education. *Studies in Higher Education, 41*(11), 1958–1973.

Brown, N. C. C., & Wilson, G. (2018). Ten quick tips for teaching programming. *PLOS Computational Biology, 14*(4), 1–8.

Calderhead, J. (1996). Teachers: Beliefs and knowledge. In D. Berliner & R. Calfee (Eds.), *Handbook of research on educational psychology* (pp. 709–725). Macmillan.

Dağ, F. (2019). Prepare pre-service teachers to teach computer programming skills at K–12 level: Experiences in a course. *Journal of Computer in Education, 6*(2), 277–313.

Ertmer, P. A. (2005). Teacher pedagogical beliefs: The final frontier in our quest for technology integration? *Educational Technology Research and Development, 53*(4), 25–40.

Ertmer, P. A., & Ottenbreit-Leftwich, A. T. (2010). Teacher technology change: How knowledge, confidence, beliefs, and culture intersect. *Journal of Research on Technology in Education, 42*(3), 255–284.

Ertmer, P. A., & Ottenbreit-Leftwich, A. (2013). Removing obstacles to the pedagogical changes required by Jonassen's vision of authentic technology-enabled learning. *Computers & Education, 64*(1), 175–182.

Field, A. (2013). *Discovering statistics using SPSS* (4th ed). Sage Publication.

Google & Gallup. (2015). *Searching for computer science: Access and barriers in U.S. K–12 education.* https://services.google.com/fh/files/misc/searching-for-computer-science_report.pdf

Grover, S., & Pea, R. (2013). Computational thinking in K–12: A review of the state of the field. *Educational Researcher, 42*(1), 38–43.

Heintz, F., Mannila, L., & Färnqvist, T. (2016). A review of models for introducing computational thinking, computer science and computing in K–12 education. In *2016 I.E. Frontiers in Education Conference* (FIE) *Proceedings* (pp. 1–9). https://www.ida.liu.se/divisions/aiics/publications/FIE-2016-Review-Models-Introducing.pdf

Hubwieser, P., Armoni, M., & Giannakos, M. N. (2015). How to implement rigorous computer science education in K–12 schools? Some answers and many questions. *ACM Transactions on Computing Education, 15*(2), 1–12.

Hur, J., Shannon, D., & Wolf, S. (2016). An investigation of relationships between internal and external factors affecting technology integration in classroom. *Journal of Digital Learning in Teacher Education, 32*(3), 105–114.

Inan, F., & Lowther, D. (2010). Factors affecting technology integration in K–12 classrooms: A path model. *Educational Technology Research and Development, 58*(2), 137–154.

K–12 Computer Science Framework Steering Committee. (2016). *K–12 Computer Science Framework.* http://www.k12cs.org.

Lamb, R., Annetta, L., Vallett, D., Firestone, J., Schmitter-Edgecombe, M., Heather, W., Deviller, N., & Hoston, D. (2017). Psychosocial factors impacting STEM career selection in Computer Science and Engineering. *Journal of Educational Research, 111*(4), 446–458.

Linnenbrink, E. A., & Pintrich, P. R. (2003). The role of self-efficacy beliefs in student engagement and learning in the classroom. *Reading & Writing Quarterly: Overcoming Learning Difficulties, 19*(2), 119–137.

Menekse, M. (2015). Computer science teacher professional development in the United States: A review of studies published between 2004 and 2014. *Computer Science Education, 25*(4), 325–350.

Moreno-León, J., & Robles, G. (2015). Dr. Scratch: A web tool to automatically evaluate scratch projects. *In Proceedings of WiPSCE'15 of workshop in primary and secondary computing education* (pp. 132–133). Association for Computing Machinery.

Mouza, C., Yang, H., Pan, Y.-C., Ozden, S., & Pollock, L. (2017). Resetting educational technology coursework for pre-service teachers: A computational thinking approach to the development of technological pedagogical content knowledge (TPACK). *Australasian Journal of Educational Technology, 33*(3), 61–76.

Nusbaum, L. (2019, August 1). *All K–12 public schools will need to offer computer science courses in 3 years.* https://www.waff.com/2019/08/02/all-k-public-schools-will-need-offer-computer-science-courses-years/

Pajares, F. (1996). Self-efficacy beliefs in academic settings. *Review of Educational Research, 66*(4), 543–578.

Pajares, F., & Valiante, G. (1997). Influence of writing self-efficacy beliefs on the writing performance of upper elementary students. *Journal of Educational Research, 90*(6), 353–360.

Paraskeva, F., Bouta, H., & Papagianni, A. (2008). Individual characteristics and computer self-efficacy in secondary education teachers to integrate technology in educational practice. *Computers & Education, 50*, 1084–1091.

State of Computer Science Education. (2018). *Policy and implementation.* https://code.org/files/2018_state_of_cs.pdf

State of Computer Science Education. (2019). *Equity and diversity*. https://advocacy.code.org/2019_state_of_cs.pdf

Tahmassian, K., & Moghadam,N. J. (2011). Relationship between self-efficacy and symptoms of anxiety, depression, worry and social avoidance in a normal sample of students. *Iranian Journal of Psychiatry and Behavioral Sciences, 5*(2), 91–98.

Tsai, M., Wang, C., & Hsu, P. (2019). Developing the computer programming self-efficacy scale for computer literacy education. *Journal of Educational Computing Research, 56*(8), 1345–1360.

Wang, X.-M., Hwang, G.-J., Liang, Z.-Y., & Wang, H.-Y. (2017). Enhancing students' computer programming performances, critical thinking awareness and attitudes towards programming: An online peer-assessment attempt. *Educational Technology & Society, 20*(4), 58–68.

Wing, J. (2008). Computational thinking and thinking about computing. *Philosophical Transactions of the Royal Society A,366*(1881), 3717–3725.

Yadav, A., Mayfield, C., Zhou, N., Hambrusch, S., & Korb, J. T. (2014). Computational thinking in elementary and secondary teacher education. *ACM Transactions on Computing Education, 14*(1), 5:1–16.

Yadav, A., Stephenson, C., & Hong, H. (2017). Computational thinking for teacher education. *Communications of the ACM, 80*(4), 55–62.

CHAPTER 3

EXPLORING FACTORS THAT INFLUENCE PRESERVICE TEACHER INTEGRATION OF EDUCATIONAL ROBOTICS AND PROGRAMMING IN EDUCATIONAL PRACTICE

Nikleia Eteokleous and Raphaela Neophytou

Given the extensive use of educational robotics in various school systems around the globe, this work investigates preservice teachers' knowledge as well as attitudes and perceptions towards the integration of educational robotics in classroom teaching. The study employed a mixed method approach, collecting data from questionnaires and focus groups from 40 preservice teachers. The results of the study present the factors influencing preservice teachers' willingness to integrate robotics in their future educational practice, their attitudes and perceptions of preservice teachers on robotics integration into the educational process and finally the level of preservice teachers' knowledge and skills of educational robotics. Finally, the study provides an action plan for professional development, workshops and support for teachers in

Preparing Pre-Service Teachers to Teach Computer Science: Models, Practices, and Policies,
pages 49–67.
49

order to effectively integrate educational robotics as a cognitive-learning tool as well as discusses implications for various stakeholders (e.g. universities, policymakers).

Keywords: Preservice Teachers, Educational Robotics Integration, Factors, Profile, Attitudes, Professional Development Training

INTRODUCTION

There has been a great deal of research over the last 30 years on the integration of technology in education, including teachers' perceptions and attitudes towards technology, factors influencing technology integration, technology use etc. (Eteokleous, 2008; Fullan, 2008; Hermans et al., 2008). Understanding teachers' perceptions of technology is important because they could guide decision-making among stakeholders, such as researchers and policymakers regarding technology integration in educational practice (e.g. pre-service teachers' education, teachers' professional development etc.). However, there is limited research (e.g., Chalmers et al., 2012; Kim et al., 2015) investigating the attitudes and perceptions of pre- and in-service teachers about a particular form of technology, namely educational robotics, and the factors that influence their integration in education practice. Educational robotics have potential for helping students develop innovative ideas, disruptive thinking, and higher order learning skills (e.g., Ma & Williams, 2013; Mataric, 2004; Talaiver & Bowen, 2010). As a result, it is important to explore teacher attitudes in regards to the integration of educational robotics within educational practices. The success of educational innovation or change depends to a large extent on what teachers think, what teachers do, and what attitudes they have (Fullan, 2008; Hermans et al., 2008).

In this work, we sought to investigate preservice teachers' knowledge as well as attitudes and perceptions towards the integration of educational robotics in classroom teaching. Specifically, we examine the following questions:

1.   What are preservice teachers' knowledge and skills of educational robotics?
2.   What are the attitudes and perceptions of preservice teachers towards the integration of robotics into their future educational practices?
3.   To what degree is educational background and professional development important to preservice teachers willingness to integrate robotics into their future educational practices?

BACKGROUND

Educational Robotics

The use of robotics in education has gained global momentum due to positive effects in the teaching of science, technology, engineering and mathematics (STEM) (Andjic et al., 2015; Bers, & Portsmore, 2005; Bers et al., 2013; Chalmers, 2013; Chalmers, 2017; Ortiz et al., 2015). Existing studies have shown that through the use of robotics students are actively engaged, they collaborate, and contribute on meaningful learning outcomes (Chen, & Chang, 2008; Eteokleous & Ktoridou, 2014; Malec, 2001; Petre & Price, 2004; Rogers, 2012; Williams et al., 2007). Further, existing studies have demonstrated that robotics integration can promote the development of students' higher-order thinking skills such as application, synthesis, evaluation, problem solving, decision-making, and scientific investigation (Bers et al., 2002; Chambers & Carbonaro, 2003; Khanlari, 2013; Miglino et al., 1999; Mikropoulos & Bellou, 2013; Papert, 1980; Resnick, 2003; Talaiver & Bowen, 2010; Williams et al., 2010). Previous studies, however, illustrated that to transform and improve the educational environment, robotics activities need to be appropriately designed and henceforth implemented in the educational practice (Bauerle, & Gallagher, 2003; Benitti, 2012; Papert, 1993; Williams et al., 2010).

Robotics education mainly follows the constructionist educational approach developed by Papert (Alimisis, 2013; Eguchi, 2010; Papert, 1980). Constructionist learning is based on the idea that individuals learn better when they are engaged in building and manipulating artefacts that are significant to them (Eguchi, 2010). In robotics, the materials used (e.g. building blogs/bricks, sensors, gears, and motors) are perceived as toys by the students, and the educational activities designed using the aforementioned materials focus on solving a problem, identifying a solution, and explaining various phenomena by connecting theory to practice (Chambers & Carbonaro, 2003; Williams et al., 2010).

Integration of Robotics in Educational Practice

There are two lines of thought around the integration of robotics in the educational practice: (1) as a subject matter, and (2) as a learning and cognitive tool. The first line of thought suggests that robotics should be introduced within the school curriculum as a subject matter, such as Mathematics, English, Literature, Computers (Eteokleous, et al., 2013; Malec, 2001). Yet Eteokleous and colleagues suggested that when robotics was integrated as a subject matter meaning as an autonomous entity (teaching about robotics), there was limited educational potential and value.

The second line of thought suggests that robotics integration in educational practice should be used as a tool that enhances student learning experience and supports the achievement of specific learning goals (Eteokleous et al., 2013; Jonassen, 1999; Miller et al., 2008). Ward et al., 2012). Prior work indicates that when robotics is integrated as a cognitive-learning tool within a well-designed learning environment, its full potential is exploited by students (Eteokleous et al., 2013). The integration of robotics as a cognitive-learning tool does not aim at helping students learn how to use a particular robotics package and its programming software (learn about robotics and programming). Rather, robotics is used as a tool within a specific educational context (learn with robotics and programming). In other words, robotics can be employed as a tool to teach and deliver concepts within various subjects at the K–12 levels such as mathematics (Whitehead, 2010), engineering (Craig, 2014), science (Vollstedt, 2005), physics, biology, and psychology (Bers et al., 2002; Craig, 2014; Eguchi, 2007; Eteokleous et al., 2013).

Both lines of thought influenced the current study, yet greater emphasis was given to the integration of robotics as a cognitive-learning tool. While preservice teachers in this work were given an opportunity to learn how to use a robotics package and its programming software, emphasis was placed on using the robotics package as a tool within a specific educational context to achieve learning objectives (Bers et al., 2002; Craig, 2014; Eguchi, 2007; Eteokleous et al., 2013; Vollstedt, 2005; Whitehead, 2010).

Factors Influencing Technology Integration

Research into the use of technology by teachers recognizes a complex pattern of interrelated factors that are key determinants of the successful implementation of technology in education (Drent & Meelissen, 2008). Various factors influencing the integration of ICT into education have been grouped into different categorizations, as shown on Table 3.1.

Over the past decade, in particular, the relationship between teachers' pedagogical beliefs and the use of technology has been extensively examined (Ertmer & Ottenbreit-Leftwich, 2010; Prestridge, 2012; Sang et al., 2009). Some studies have suggested that teachers' attitudes towards technology (teachers' beliefs) and the perceived level of readiness for technology use (teacher readiness) are the two most important factors of whether or not teachers will integrate technology (Ames, 2016; Shiomi et al., 2015). A literature review by Azarfam and Jabbari (2012) revealed that some teachers have a negative stance towards technology and are not comfortable with its use. Further, some teachers decide to use technology primarily to respond to external policies and social pressure and not because they believe in the role and importance of technology in education (Azarfam, & Jabbari, 2012). Since teacher perceptions of new technologies play a key role in their classroom use, research suggests that professional development focusing on altering those perceptions may be important (Looi et al., 2008).

Technology Acceptance Model

Teachers' involvement is important for the implementation and success of any innovation, thus the investigation of their perceptions and attitudes towards tech-

TABLE 3.1. Factors That Influence Teachers in ICT Integration

Categorizing Factors Based on the Literature	Authors
Technology tools, teacher, environment and professional development due to the requirements of teaching.	Buabeng-Andoh (2012)
School factors: Leadership support, technical support) and initiative factors (technological and pedagogical support)	Carano, Liu & Hedrick (2014) Wadmany & Levin (2004).
Direct and Indirect Factors: the level of support, professional development and technological access. The level of teacher education and didactic experience are examples of indirect factors.	Ames (2016)
First and second order factors. First-rate factors are those factors that are not directly related to the teacher, such as the lack of technological equipment. Second-order actors have to do with "obstacles" directly related to teachers, such as the lack of teachers' knowledge and skills.	Hew & Brush (2007) Spektor-Levy & Granot-Gilat (2012) Ertmer & Ottenbreit-Leftwich (2013)
Personal factors to which the demographic characteristics of the subjects fall—age, gender, educational background.	Buabeng-Andoh (2012)
Institutional factors—the school environment (accessibility to technology, management support and the environment.	Eickelmann (2011) Almekhlafi & Almeqdadi (2010)
External factors such as access to appropriate equipment or training opportunities and on internal factors such as the concern about the advantages of technology and their personal attitude towards technological innovations.	Azarfam & Jabbari (2012).

nology integration is critical (Mitra, 1998; Rozell & Gardner, 2000). For example, various studies showed that positive attitudes towards technology integration predispose the users in real technology use while negative attitudes lead to avoidance of technology use (Mitra, 1998; Rozell & Gardner, 2000). The Technological Acceptance Model (TAM) was specifically designed to explain individual technology acceptance decisions across a wide range of organizational contexts, computer technologies, and user populations (e.g., Davis, 1989; Venkatesh & Davis, 2000). TAM postulates that two particular beliefs, perceived usefulness, and perceived ease of use, are of primary relevance for computer acceptance behaviours.

Some studies (TAM; Davis, 1989) suggested that teachers' perception in regards to the usefulness of new technologies is direclty related to the intention of use and indirectly with the ease of use (Mitra, 1998; Rozell & Gardner, 2000). According to the model, user perceptions regarding the usefulness and ease of use constitute decisive factors for using technology in classroom (Holden & Karsh, 2010; Ma et al., 2005; McFarland, & Hamilton, 2006). In this work we use the TAM model as a lens for uncovering preservice teachers' educational robotics acceptance.

Robotics Integration in Education

Recent studies have examined factors that influence pre- and in-service teachers' integration of robotics in the educational practice as well as their beliefs, attitudes and approaches towards robotics. For example, Kim et al. (2015) studied preservice teachers STEM engagement, learning and teaching through robotics in an elementary teacher program of study. They found that robotics positively influenced preservice teachers' STEM engagement. Further, robotics as a tool influenced preservice teachers interest, enjoyment, and emotional engagement in STEM, which in turn positively influenced their behavioral and cognitive engagement in STEM.

Along the same lines, Chalmers (2017) studied about 150 teachers who participated in a university robotics-based education outreach program aimed at building teachers' confidence and capacity while encouraging students' interest in STEM. Chalmers highlighted that teachers reported benefits after participating and partnering with the university outreach program. The benefits can be summarized in the following: "…the development of their robot building and programming skills; the sharing of ideas for STEM activities to engage their students; and the on-going support provided by the outreach program" (p. 17). Therefore, Chalmers argues that hands-on trainings and courses could help preservice teachers build knowledge and confidence in implementing engaging robotics-based STEM activities.

In 2012, Chalmers and colleagues examined the implementation of technology activities by 30 fourth year preservice teachers (enrolled in a technology education curriculum unit) with 22 primary school students from a school in a low socio-economic area. The study examined the value of a robotics-based school engagement experience for preservice teachers. By the completion of the unit and based on the experience and knowledge gained, the study analyzed their perceived abilities and confidence to design and implement engaging technology activities. The results of this study suggested that engagement with robotics increased preservice teachers' confidence and helped them develop positive attitudes towards technology. The authors argued that the confidence gained by preservice teachers during the engagement with the robots would also assist them in the development and implementation of other technology activities in their future classrooms. Furthermore, preservice teachers' engagement and experiences with the robots, helped the, develop knowledge for implementing engaging technology activities and strategies to motivate students.

In another study, Kucuk and Sisman (2018) collected data from 15 preservice teachers via semi-structured interviews aiming to identify their experiences in a learning robotics design and programming course. Three main themes were revealed from the data analysis: course process, professional development and teaching children. Based on the aforementioned themes, the study suggested that courses related to robotics and programming within preservice teachers' program of study could be extremely influential and beneficial. The preservice teachers reported that robotics programming courses positively influenced their attitudes towards programming and improved their programming skills. Additionally, participants indicated that they had opportunities to learn by doing, they had fun, they enjoyed the robotics and programming activities, and developed positive attitudes towards robotics and programming.

Sisman and Kucuk (2019) further examined 30 preservice teachers' perceptions and experiences in an educational robotics course. Specifically, they examined the levels of satisfaction, motivation, enjoyment, collaboration, and challenge of the preservice teachers enrolled in the course. A post activity survey, observation, and interview were used as data collection tools. Their findings revealed high levels of satisfaction, motivation, enjoyment, and collaboration. Further, results showed that the robotics activities developed an edutainment learning environment and that preservice teachers were highly engaged with robotics, showing no difficulty in completing the activities. Preservice teachers were motivated by the fact that they would be teaching what they had learned about the science of robotics to their future students.

CONTEXT OF THE STUDY

The study took place in a private university in Europe. Participants were preservice teachers enrolled in a Primary Education (grades 1–6) program of study (undergraduate degree). Within the program of study the students were required to attend three courses in relation to technology: (1) Computer Applications, (2) Educational Technology, and (3) Educational Robotics and Programing. The last one was recently added to the program of study as part of the program update in order to respond to the needs of a 21st century education. Computer Applications is not part of the program of study at this time, but all participants in their junior and senior year of student completed the course. A total of 60 preservice teachers enrolled in the program, however only 40 participated in the current study.

Participants

A total of 40 preservice teachers participated in the study. Of those, 74% were females, and 26% were males. In terms of age, 47% of the participants were 20 or 21 years old. In regards to year of study, 28% were in their 3rd and 4th year, 16% in their 2nd year, and 15% in their 1st year. None of the preservice teachers owned an educational robotics package. Of the participants, 74% completed a Computer Application course during their program of study at the university and in high school (secondary education). All of the participants completed the Educational Technology course (required course) during their program of study at the university. None of them attended any additional courses related to educational technology integration. The participants rated their Computer Application course as satisfactory (31%), and very satisfactory (25%) and the Educational technology course as satisfactory (34%), and very satisfactory (19%).

TABLE 3.2. Data Collection Methods and Sample Description

Data Collection Methods	Participants
Electronic questionnaires (purposive sampling)	40 preservice teachers
Group Interviews (voluntarily)	12 preservice teachers
Computer Application Course (required college course)	40 preservice teachers
Educational Technology Course (required college course)	40 preservice teachers
Robotics and Programming Course (This is required course that was recently included in the program of study)	8 preservice teachers
Attended professional development training by the Robotics Academy	12 preservice teachers (4 of them also attended the Robotics and Programming Course)
Group Interviews of those attended the training	All who attended the professional development course—12 preservice teachers

Only 20% of the participants (8 preservice teachers) attended an Educational Robotics and Programming course. It had been recently added in the Program of Study of Primary Education in the Fall of 2018. They rated the Educational Robotics and Programming Course as satisfactory (29%), and very satisfactory (21%). Additionally, 30% of the participants (12 preservice teachers) voluntarily attended the series of professional development offered by the Robotics Academy. The Robotics Academy is an educational-research unit that promotes and conducts research in the area of robotics education that has operated in the university for the past 6 years (http://akrob.frederick.ac.cy, https://www.facebook.com/AkadimiaRompotikis). For more information see Table 3.2.

Methods and Data Collection

A mixed method approach was employed, using both quantitative and qualitative data (Creswell, 2014). Two data sources were used: questionnaires and focus groups. The study research design process included four distinct steps: (1) completion of a questionnaire, (2) focus groups with preservice teachers, (3) robotics and programming professional development, and (4) focus groups with the preservice teachers who attended the professional development training. The data collection took place during Spring, Summer and Fall of 2018.

The questionnaire used in this study was developed by the authors and pilot tested prior to the study. The 60 item questionnaire includes 4 parts: (1) demographics; (2) intrinsic and extrinsic factors (e.g., digital literacy, stress, robotophobia, skills and knowledge of robotics packages and platforms, equipment, technical support, preparation); (3) attitudes and perceptions towards educational robotics; and (4) professional development (e.g., courses, training and workshops attended, content, satisfaction rate, and experience).

The 60 item questionnaire was developed based on other research studies (literature review), as well as existing research scales and questionnaires. It consisted of open/closed ended items. Specifically, items from five different existing questionnaires were used: (1) the Greek Computer Attitudes Scale (Roussos, 2007); (2) the Computer Attitude Scale (Nickell & Pinto, 1986); (3) Computer Anxiety Rating Scale—CARS (Heinssen et al., 1987); (4) the Teacher questionnaire— MASTER EN (Teachers Inspiring Life Long Learning, n.d.) and (5) the Teacher Questionnaire on the use of Information and Communication Technology (ICT, 21st Digital Class, 2015). Sample items included the following: (1) digital literacy, (2) technophobia/robotophobia, (3) knowledge and skills regarding educational robotics, (5) technological support (6) preparation time, (7) professional development, (8) preservice teachers attitudes and beliefs.

Purposive (or selective) sampling was employed (Kvale, 1996) to select 40 preservice teachers enrolled in a Primary Education program of study (undergraduate degree) offered by a Department of Educational Sciences in a private university in Europe. The questionnaire was delivered electronically via the learning management platform to all preservice teachers enrolled in the Primary Education program of study. Preservice teachers were given one week to complete the questionnaire. All 40 preservice teacher completed the questionnaire at the end of their courses.

The qualitative component was addressed via two focus groups. Semi-structured focus groups with 12 teachers who agreed to participate were organized. The preservice teachers were organized in two focus groups (6 participants per group) based on a number of parameters addressed in the questionnaire, such as: year of study, digital literacy, and experience with robotics and programming. The semi-structured interview protocol included questions to further clarify issues and gain in-depth understanding on the parameters examined through the questionnaire. Sample questions of the interview protocol included the following: experience with technology, experience with robotics and programming, attitudes and beliefs with regards to robotics and programming integration, and factors that influence the integration of robotics in educational settings.

During the interviews, preservice teachers were informed that a 16 hour Educational Robotics and Programming professional development course would be offered by the Robotics Academy, an academy affiliated with the University. A total of 12 preservice teachers chose to enroll. After the completion of the professional development, focus groups were scheduled with all the attendees (12 preservice teachers). The purpose of the second focus group was to evaluate and identify the importance and necessity of professional development specific to robotics for future teachers (see Table 3.2).

Data Analysis

Data from participants' questionnaires were analyzed quantitatively. Specifically, analysis included descriptive statistics (frequencies, percentages, means, and standard deviations). The qualitative data was analyzed using the constant comparison method (Maykut & Morehouse, 1994). A comparison coding scheme was developed by the authors in order to categorize the emergent themes and facilitate the data analysis. The authors compared the data collected among the 12 preservice teachers who participated in focus groups.

RESULTS AND DISCUSSION

The data analysis from the quantitative and qualitative data collection methods were integrated for the results' presentation and discussion purposes.

Level of Preservice Teachers' Knowledge and Skills of Educational Robotics

Results from the questionnaire indicated that the majority (88%) of preservice teachers considered themselves informed about educational robotics and programming. However, results indicated that their knowledge and skills in regards to educational robotics and programming varied. For example, some participants (32%) reported that they can develop programming exercises for their students based on a robotics model, where other participants (23%) reported very basic level of robotics knowledge by only being able to use the preprogrammed robots (i.e. Bee-Bot, Robot-Mouse).

The results of the questionnaire identified three distinct areas of need for preservice teachers needed to integrate robotics and programming in the educational practice: (1) acquiring knowledge and skills in robotics and programming (learn how to use different educational robotics packages and visual programming platforms); (2) developing educational materials (activities) in order to integrate robotics in programming in their educational practice as cognitive-learning tools; and (3) gaining practice in real-classroom environments. In regards to the first need preservice teachers (82%) noted that besides the course within their programs of study additional (future, beyond the university program of study) professional development would be necessary in order to keep them updated and informed with new developments in the field (Kucuk & Sisman, 2018). In regards to the second need, results indicated that only 40% of the preservice teachers (16 preservice teachers) felt comfortable in developing appropriate educational material in regards to robotics and programming. Those were primarily the preservice teachers who attended the Robotics and Programming Course as well as professional development training offered by the Robotics Academy. Finally, results clearly indicated a need for practice in classrooms. Specifically, none of the preservice teachers had the opportunity to experience educational robotics within a classroom and preservice teachers described this as a great disadvantage and an extremely influential factor in deciding to integrate robotics in their teaching and learning practice in the future.

The preservice teachers who either decided on their own to attend the professional development courses offered by the Robotics Academy and/or also attended the university course reported having a higher-lever of knowledge and skills related to robotics. Those teachers felt more comfortable in employing educational robotics, however they felt that practicing the knowledge and skills gained in a real-classroom environment was necessary. These results point to the importance of providing preservice teachers with opportunities to experience robotics and programming during their program of study. Although participants were asked through the series of professional development courses to develop educational materials related to robotics and programming and conduct micro-teaching within the robotics academy courses, they were not provided with authentic classroom experiences.

Furthermore, some preservice teachers (28%) indicated that they were not interested in attending advanced programming courses since they believed that it was not necessary at the elementary school level to have this level of knowledge and skills in regards to robotics. Specifically, only 3 of the preservice teachers who attended the training provided by the Robotics Academy reported that they would consider attending more advanced courses as a professional development course, but not during their university program of study.

Attitudes and Perceptions of Preservice Teachers on Robotics Integration into the Educational Process

To examine the attitudes and perceptions of preservice teachers on robotics integration into the educational process, data was gathered from the questionnaire and focus groups. Findings from the questionnaires revealed three different groups of participants. The first group of preservice teachers expressed positive attitudes towards robotics and were receptive to the new challenges. Those preservice teachers were convinced for the necessity, usefulness, and value of educational robotics. For example, one preservice teacher during the focus groups stated:

> …we need to provide to our students, future citizens, new ways of learning and thinking. I believe that educational robotics can help them develop specific thinking processes of solving a problem. It does not mean that all kids are becoming engineers and computer scientists. But with robotics they can develop thinking processes of solving problems.

They also described not being scared and willing to give robotics integration a try.

The second group of preservice teachers appeared to be extremely hesitant. They articulated concerns that were derived from their own restricted digital literacy levels, and their negative perceptions towards the necessity and value of robotics integration in the teaching practice. For example, one preservice teacher during focus groups stated:

> ...I am not sure If robotics need to be integrated within the school curriculum. This course should be as an extracurricular activity having instructors who have also advanced technical skills. How am I supposed to solve a technical problem that may appear when using a robotics package in class? How would I deal with my students when such a problem appears?

The third group blended these two perspectives. This third group of preservice teachers embraced educational robotics integration, however they expressed numerous concerns. For example, one preservice teacher stated:

> ...I really liked the idea of educational robotics. I do believe that it has educational value for the students, but I do not feel ready to integrate them in class. I need continuous professional development and support and maybe a mentor.

These preservice teachers described feeling ready and willing to try to integrate robotics in their classroom practices, while expressing concerns related to their lack of basic knowledge and skills.

Factors Influencing Preservice Teachers Willingness to Integrate Robotics in their Future Educational Practice

Based on the results of the questionnaires, the study suggests that there were three categories of factors that influenced preservice teachers' willingness to integrate robotics in their future educational practices: personal, professional, and institutional. Special emphasis was given by the preservice teachers to their educational background, studies, experience, and continuous professional development and support. These results align with previous studies related to technology integration (e.g. Cox et al., 1999; Eteokleous, 2008; Gerick, & Eickelmann, 2014; Hermans et al., 2008; Mumtaz, 2000; Player-Koro, 2012).

Most preservice teachers (75%) did not express negative attitudes in relation to robotics integration in their future educational practice. Even though their reported skills and knowledge in regards to robotics varied, the majority of them reported not being able to extensively use them in educational practice. For example, one preservice teacher suggested that she did not feel confident enough to successfully address any technical challenges that may appear in a robotics lesson. They described that this was due, in part, to the absence of practice during their studies. Further, some of the preservice teachers expressed concern that in the future they may be pressured to include educational robotics in their classroom practices and adjust to this high-tech setting. A preservice teacher commented on the fact that the Ministry of Education is taking measures towards the integration of new and emerging technologies in the elementary classroom practices. More than half of the preservice teachers who participated in the questionnaires (24 preservice

TABLE 3.3. Four Categories of Preservice Teachers Perceptions Based on the TAM Model.

A/A	Four Categories of Preservice Teachers Perceptions	Quotes From Preservice Teachers Focus Groups Sessions
1.	Usefulness of use	"As a future teacher my job performance would be measured based on the successful completion of my tasks, meaning to achieve the learning goals set for my students. In selected cases robotics integration facilitates and promotes the achievement of the learning goals. I realized the aforementioned through the professional development training that I participated."
2.	Ease of use	"Less effort will be needed in order to explain particular concepts to students, such as right, left, forward and backwards, as well as west, east, south and north with robotics."
3.	Teachers' readiness	"As preservice teachers we need to be pedagogically and technologically prepared in order to be able to integrate robotics in the teaching and learning practice. We will feel more comfortable and confident if we design, develop and deliver lessons were robotics are integrated within classroom practices, experience and realize their educational value and get constructive feedback from our instructors, tutors."
4.	Value and usefulness for the students	"Changes in students' attitudes and behaviors will make me realize that educational robotics are valuable and useful to be integrated as learning tools within the educational practice."

teachers) agreed that it was necessary to integrate educational robotics in their classroom practices because it is important to motivate and engage their students as well as deliver lessons aligned with their interests.

Twenty percent of preservice teachers' expressed skepticism about robotics in the classroom, raising concerns such as: not sufficient number of packages, giving more emphasis on the technology part than the pedagogical one, and K–12 students' digital literacy level. This skepticism seemed to emerge from two factors: (1) the level of their knowledge and skills, and (2) their concerns on the educational value and usefulness of educational robotics for students. Using the TAM, it is revealed that preservice teachers' perceptions were classified into four categories: (1) usefulness of use, (2) ease of use, (3) readiness, and (4) value and usefulness for the students (Mitra, 1998; Rozell & Gardner, 2000) (see Table 3.3).

NEXT STEPS

This study sought to explore the factors that influence preservice teachers' integration of educational robotics as a cognitive-learning tool into their future educational practice. Therefore, we provided an action plan for professional development, workshops and support for preservice teachers in order to effectively integrate educational robotics as a cognitive-learning tool as well as discuss implications for various stakeholders (e.g. universities, policymakers).

Results suggest that preservice teachers may be in a transformational phase in regards to integrating technology and overall innovative practices. Results also indicate that preservice teachers are interested in more innovative practices that are outside of typically norms and the boundaries of their comfort zone. Further, results revealed positive views towards robotics but needs for continuous support, guidance and training. Once off solutions (i.e., 16 hour professional development and/ or a course at their program of study undergraduate or graduate course) are the beginning of such effort and are not of great help and value if they do not continue. Specifically, preservice teachers need to have continuous professional development training and a mentor to guide and support them in their practice.

It is important that preservice teachers experience educational robotics integration in the educational practice because they will have the opportunity to design develop and deliver lessons where robotics are integrated as learning tools (Sisman & Kucuk, 2019). Additionally, it is important that constructive feedback is given to preservice teachers during robotics integration in the educational practice. To achieve this, preservice teachers need to further develop their robotics and programming literacy level and recognize the importance of their integration in the educational practice. Various suggestions are given below in order to prepare preservice teachers to face the challenge of robotics integration in the educational practice.

First, special attention should be given by higher education institutions and specifically by Schools of Education in regards to preservice teachers' development of appropriate knowledge and skills through theory and practice. We recommend that preservice teachers should be required to complete required courses related to Educational Robotics and Programming. Related elective courses may also be included in the program of study in order to give the opportunity to those interested to further examine the educational robotics integration. Future preservice teachers need to experience educational robotics and programming during their teaching practice because they will have the opportunity to realize its educational value and usefulness and understand the changes in students' attitudes and behaviors. Further, in this work we found that preservice teachers desired practical school-based experiences. Therefore, practicum experiences should be part of these courses in order to provide preservice teachers the opportunity to relate theory to practice, apply the knowledge and skills gained within the courses, and acquire experiences in real-classroom environments. Establishing partnerships with local schools may increase the opportunity to further practice educational robotics and programming integration as well as develop educational materials.

Second, schools of education may also need to alter their philosophy and approach towards new developments in the education field and specifically to the educational technology field. In order for Schools of Education to appropriately prepare future educators, we need to develop the mechanisms that will allow future teachers to be more open (and not closed systems) and adjust to the needs of the society and economy. Finally, there is a need to develop an educational policy to guide educational robotics and programming integration at all levels (primary, secondary and higher) of the educational system and all types of institutions (i.e., public and private).

The study exemplified the necessity to further examine and define the appropriate learning environments and settings for preservice teachers to be able to employ new technologies (i.e., educational robotics, augmented reality, tinkering, DIY technology tools, and programming) within schools. The preservice teachers should be provided with those opportunities and experiences that will adequately prepare them for the rapid-changing, high-tech, globalized society. Teachers are one of the most influential factors to employ new and emerging technologies in the teaching practice, thus their preparation is of vital importance to ensure we can promote and achieve educational robotics integration in schools.

REFERENCES

Alimisis, D. (2013). Educational robotics: Open questions and new challenges. *Themes in Science and Technology Education, 6*(1), 63–71.

Almekhlafi, A. G., & Almeqdadi, F. A. (2010). Teachers' perceptions of technology integration in the United Arab Emirates school classrooms. *Journal of Educational Technology & Society, 13*(1), 165.

Ames, C. W. (2016). *Teacher perceptions of factors influencing technology integration in K–12 schools.* Utah State University.

Andjic, B., Grujičić, R., & Markuš, M. M. (2015). Robotics and its effects on the educational system of Montenegro. *World Journal of Education, 5*(4), 52.

Azarfam, A. Y., & Jabbari, Y. (2012). Dealing with teachers' technophobia in classroom. *Advances in Asian Social Science, 2*(2), 452–455.

Bauerle, A., & Gallagher, M. (2003). Toying with technology: Bridging the gap between education and engineering. In C. Crawford, N. Davis, J. Price, R. Weber, & D. Willis (Eds.), *Proceedings of Society for Information Technology and Teacher Education International Conference* (pp. 3538–3541). AACE.

Benitti, F. B. V. (2012). Exploring the educational potential of robotics in schools: A systematic review. *Computers & Education, 58*(3), 978–988.

Bers, M. U., Ponte, I., Juelich, C., Viera, A., & Schenker, J. (2002). Teachers as designers: Integrating robotics in early childhood education. *Information Technology in Childhood Education Annual, 2002*(1), 123–145.

Bers, M. U., & Portsmore, M. (2005). Teaching partnerships: Early childhood and engineering students teaching math and science through robotics. *Journal of Science Education and Technology, 14*(1), 59–73.

Bers, M., Seddighin, S., & Sullivan, A. (2013). Ready for robotics: Bringing together the T and E of STEM in early childhood teacher education. *Journal of Technology and Teacher Education, 21*(3), 355–377.

Buabeng-Andoh, C. (2012). Factors influencing teachers' adoption and integration of information and communication technology into teaching: A review of the literature. *International Journal of Education and Development using Information and Communication Technology, 8*(1), 136.

Carano, E. L., Liu, S. Y., & Hedrick, J. K. (2014, October). Applying the Gale-Shapley Stable Matching Algorithm to peer human-robot task allocation. In *ASME 2014 Dynamic Systems and Control Conference*. American Society of Mechanical Engineers. https://asmedigitalcollection.asme.org/DSCC/proceedings-abstract/DSCC2014/46209/V003T38A001/229705

Chalmers, C. (2013). Learning with FIRST LEGO League. In *Proceedings of Society for Information Technology and Teacher Education (SITE) Conference* (pp. 5118–5124). AACE.

Chalmers, C. (2017). Preparing teachers to teach STEM through robotics. *International Journal of Innovation in Science and Mathematics Education, 25*(4), 17–31.

Chalmers, C., Chandra, V., Hudson, S. & Hudson, P. (2012). *Preservice teachers teaching technology with robotics*. Paper presented to Australian Teacher Education Association (ATEA) Conference, Adelaide (Glenelg), SA, 1–4 July,

Chambers, J., & Carbonaro, M. (2003). Designing, developing and implementing a course on LEGO robotics for technology teacher education. *Journal of Technology and Teacher Education, 11*(2), 209–241.

Chen, G. D., & Chang, C. W. (2008, November). Using humanoid robots as instructional media in elementary language education. In *Digital games and intelligent toys based education, Second IEEE International Conference* (pp. 201–202). IEEE.

Cox, M. J., Preston, C., & Cox, K. (1999). *What factors support or prevent teachers from using ICT in their classrooms?* Paper presented at the BERA 1999 Conference. Brighton, UK, Sept 2–9.

Craig, D. C. (2014). Robotics programs: Inspiring young women in STEM. In J. Koch, B. Polnick, & B, Irby (Eds.), *Girls and women in STEM* (pp. 153–174). Information Age Publishing, Inc.

Creswell, J. W. (2014). *Research design: Qualitative, quantitative and mixed methods approaches* (4th ed.). Sage.

Davis, F. D. (1989). Perceived usefulness, perceived ease of use, and user acceptance of information technology. *MIS Quarterly, 13*(3), 319–339.

21st Digital Class. (2015). *Teacher questionnaire on the use of information and communication technology* (ICT). Retrieved January 15, 2019 from http://www.21digitalclass.com/uploads/4/7/2/9/47298253/teachers__questionnaire_on_the_use_of_ict.pdf.

Drent, M., & Meelissen, M. (2008). Which factors obstruct or stimulate teacher educators to use ICT innovatively? *Computers & Education, 51*(1), 187–199.

Eguchi, A. (2007). Educational robotics for elementary school classroom. In R. Carlsen, K. McFerrin, J. Price, R. Weber & D. Willis (Eds.), *Proceedings of SITE 2007*. Society for Information Technology & Teacher Education International Conference (pp. 2542–2549). Association for the Advancement of Computing in Education (AACE).

Eguchi, A. (2010, March). What is educational robotics? Theories behind it and practical implementation. In D. Gibson & B. Dodge (Eds.), *Proceedings of SITE 2010--Society for Information Technology & Teacher Education International Conference* (pp. 4006– 4014). San Diego, CA, USA: Association for the Advancement of Computing in Education (AACE).

Eickelmann, B. (2011). Supportive and hindering factors to a sustainable implementation of ICT in schools/Förderliche und hemmende Bedingungen der nachhaltigen Implementierung von IKT in Schulen. *Journal for Educational Research Online, 3*(1), 75.

Ertmer, P. A., & Ottenbreit-Leftwich, A. T. (2010). Teacher technology change: How knowledge, confidence, beliefs, and culture intersect. *Journal of Research on Technology in Education, 42*(3), 255–284.

Ertmer, P. A., & Ottenbreit-Leftwich, A. (2013). Removing obstacles to the pedagogical changes required by Jonassen's vision of authentic technology-enabled learning. *Computers & Education, 64*, 175–182.

Eteokleous, N. (2008). Evaluating computer technology integration in a centralized educational system. *Computers and Education Journal, 51*(2), 669–686.

Eteokleous, N., Demetriou, A. Y., & Stylianou, A. (2013). The pedagogical framework for integrating robotics as an interdisciplinary learning—Cognitive tool. In J. Roselli & E. Gulick (Eds.), *Information and communications technology: New research* (pp. 141–158). Nova Science Publishers, Inc.

Eteokleous, N., & Ktoridou, D. (2014). Educational robotics as learning tools within the teaching and learning practice. In *Global engineering education conference (EDUCON), 2014 IEEE* (pp. 1055–1058). IEEE.

Fullan, M. (2008). *The six secrets of change.* Jossey-Bass.

Gerick, J., & Eickelmann, B. (2014). Einsatz digitaler Medien im Mathematikunterricht und Schülerleistungen. Ein internationaler Vergleich von Bedingungsfaktoren auf Schulebene auf der Grundlage von PISA 2012 [Use of digital media in math classes and student performance. An international comparison of conditional factors. School level based on PISA 2012]. *Tertium Comparationis, 20*(2), 152.

Heinssen, R. K., Glass, C. R., & Knight, L. A. (1987). Assessing computer anxiety: Development and validation of the computer anxiety rating scale. *Computers in Human Behavior, 3*, 49–59.

Hermans, R., Tondeur, J., van Braak, J., & Valcke, M. (2008). The impact of primary school teachers' educational beliefs on the classroom use of computers. *Computers & Education, 51*(4), 1499–1509.

Hew, K. F., & Brush, T. (2007). Integrating technology into K–12 teaching and learning: Current knowledge gaps and recommendations for future research. *Educational Technology Research and Development, 55*(3), 223–252.

Holden, R., & Karsh, B-T. (2010). The Technology Acceptance Model: Its past and its future in health care, *Journal of Biomedical Informatics, 43*(1), 159–172.

Jonassen, D. H. (1999). *Computer as mindtools in schools: Engaging critical thinking,* (2nd ed.). Prentice Hall.

Kim, C., Kim, D., Yuan, J., Hill, R. B., Doshi, P., & Thai, C. N. (2015). Robotics to promote elementary education preservice teachers' STEM engagement, learning, and teaching. *Computers & Education, 91*, 14–31.

Khanlari, A. (2013). Effects of robotics on 21st century skills. *European Scientific Journal, ESJ, 9*(27), 27–36.

Kucuk, S., & Sisman, B. (2018).Preservice teachers' experiences in learning robotics design and programming. *Informatics in Education, 17* (2), 301–320.

Kvale, S. (1996). *Interviews: An introduction to qualitative research interviewing.* Sage.

Looi, C. K., Lim, W. Y., & Chen, W. (2008). Communities of practice for continuing professional development in the twenty-first century. In *International handbook of information technology in primary and secondary education* (pp. 489–505). Springer.

Ma W. W., Andersson, R., & Streith, K. (2005). Examining user acceptance of computer technology: An empirical study of student teachers. *Journal of Computer Assisted Learning, 21,* 387–395.

Ma, Y., & Williams, D. C. (2013). The potential of a first LEGO league robotics program in teaching 21 st century skills: An exploratory study. *Journal of Educational Technology Development and Exchange, 6*(2), Article 2.

Malec, J. (2001). *Some thoughts on robotics for education.* Paper presented at the 2001 AAAI Spring Symposium on Robotics and Education. AAAI Press.

Mataric, M. J. (2004). *Robotics education for all ages.* Paper presented at the American Association for Artificial Intelligence Spring Symposium on Accessible, Hands-on AI and Robotics Education. AAAI Press.

Maykut, P. , & Morehouse, R. (1994). *Beginning qualitative research: A philosophic and practical guide.* Falmer Press/Taylor & Francis, Inc.

McFarland, D., & Hamilton, D. (2006). Adding contextual specificity to the technology acceptance model. *Computers in Human Behavior, 22*(3), 427–447.

Miglino, O., Lund, H. H., & Cardaci, M. (1999). Robotics as an educational tool. *Journal of Interactive Learning Research, 10*(1), 25–47.

Mikropoulos, T. A., & Bellou, I. (2013). Educational robotics as mindtools. *Themes in Science and Technology Education, 6*(1), 5–14.

Miller, D. P., Nourbakhsh, I. R., & Siegwart, R. (2008). Robots for education. In *Springer handbook of robotics* (pp. 1283–1301). Springer.

Mitra, A. (1998). Categories of computer use and their relationships with attitudes toward computers. *Journal of Research on Computing in Education, 30,* 281–296.

Mumtaz, S. (2000). Factors affecting teachers' use of information and communications technology: A review of the literature. *Journal of Information Technology for Teacher Education, 9*(3), 319–342.

Nickell, G. S., & Pinto, J. N. (1986). The computer attitude scale. *Computers in Human Behavior, 2*(4), 301–306.

Ortiz, A., Bos, B., & Smith, S. (2015). The power of educational robotics as an integrated STEM learning experience in teacher preparation programs. *Journal of College Science Teaching, 44*(5), 42–47. http://www.jstor.org/stable/43631847.

Papert, S. (1980). Constructionism vs. instructionism. In *Proceedings from Japanese Educators Conference.* http://www. papert. org/articles/const_inst

Papert, S. (1993). *Mindstorms: Children, computers, and powerful ideas* (2nd ed.). Basic-Books.

Petre, M., & Price, B. (2004). Using robotics to motivate "back door" learning. *Education and Information Technologies, 9*(2), 147–158.

Player-Koro, C. (2012). Factors influencing teachers' use of ICT in education. *Education Inquiry, 3*(1), 93–108.

Prestridge, S. (2012). The beliefs behind the teacher that influences their ICT practices. *Computers & Education, 58*(1), 449–458.

Resnick, M. (2003). Playful learning and creative societies. *Education Update, 8*(6). http://web.media.mit.edu/wmres/papers/education-update.pdf.

Rogers, C. B. (2012). Engineering in kindergarten: How schools are changing. *Journal of STEM Education: Innovations and Research, 13*(4), 4–9.

Roussos, P. (2007). The Greek computer attitudes scale: construction and assessment of psychometric properties, *Computers in Human Behavior, 23,* 578–590.

Rozell, E. J., & Gardner, W. L. (2000). Cognitive, motivation, and affective processes associated with computer-related performance: a path analysis. *Computers in Human Behavior, 16*, 199–222.

Sang, G., Valcke, M., van Braak, J., & Tondeur, J. (2009). Investigating teachers' educational beliefs in Chinese primary schools: Socioeconomic and geographical perspectives. *Asia-Pacific Journal of Teacher Education, 37*(4), 363–377.

Shiomi, M., Kanda, T., Howley, I., Hayashi, K., & Hagita, N. (2015). Can a social robot stimulate science curiosity in classrooms? *International Journal of Social Robotics, 7*(5), 641–652.

Sisman, B., & Kucuk, S. (2019). An educational robotics course: Examination of educational potentials and preservice teachers" experiences. *International Journal of Research in Education and Science (IJRES), 5*(2), 510–531

Spektor-Levy, O., & Granot-Gilat, Y. (2012). The impact of learning with laptops in 1:1 classes on the development of learning skills and information literacy among middle school students. *Interdisciplinary Journal of E-Learning and Learning Objects, 8*(1), 83–96.

Talaiver, M., & Bowen, R. (2010). Developing 21st-century skills: Game design and robotics exploration. In D. Gibson & B. Dodge (Eds.), *Proceedings of Society for Information Technology & Teacher Education. International Conference 2010* (pp. 2089–2090). AACE.

Teachers Inspiring Life Long Learning. (n.d.). *Teacher questionnaire*. Retrieved January 15, 2019, from http://www.till.org.uk/wp-content/uploads/2019/03/TEACHER-AND-ICT.pdf.

Venkatesh, V., & Davis, F. D. (2000). A theoretical extension of the technology acceptance model: Four longitudinal field studies. *Management Science, 46*(2), 186–204. doi:10.1287/mnsc.46.2.186.11926.

Vollstedt, A-.M. (2005). *Using robotics to increase student knowledge and interest in science, technology, engineering and math* (Master's thesis). Retrieved from: ProQuest Dissertation and Theses database.

Wadmany, R., & Levin, T. (2004). The use of Information technologies in the classrooms: Patterns of change and development in educational beliefs and in educational practices among teachers and their students. In *Society for Information Technology & Teacher Education International Conference* (pp. 4295–4299). AACE.

Ward, R., Miller, J. L., Sienkiewicz, R., & Antonucci, P. (2012). ITEAMS: Increasing the self-identification for girls and underserved youth in pursuing STEM careers. *Journal of Systemics, Cybernetics & Informatics, 10*(1), 95–99.

Williams, D., Ma, Y., & Prejean, L. (2010). A preliminary study exploring the use of fictional narrative in robotics activities. *Journal of Computers in Mathematics and Science Teaching, 29*(1), 51–71.

Williams, D. C., Ma, Y., Prejean, L., Ford, M. J., & Lai, G. (2007). Acquisition of physics content knowledge and scientific inquiry skills in a robotics summer camp. *Journal of Research on Technology in Education, 40*(2), 201–216.

Whitehead, S.H. (2010). *Relationship of robotic implementation on changes in middle school students' beliefs and interest toward science, technology, engineering and mathematics* (Doctoral Dissertation). Retrieved from: ProQuest Dissertation and Theses database. Indiana University of Pennsylvania.

CHAPTER 4

ELICITING PEDAGOGICAL CONTENT KNOWLEDGE FOR COMPUTER SCIENCE TEACHING

Aleata Hubbard and Yvonne Kao

A growing number of pre-service programs are emerging to support teachers in developing the competencies and knowledge needed for effective computer science instruction. A requisite focal area for any teacher training program is the connection of content knowledge with pedagogy. This interwoven knowledge base, which Shulman termed pedagogical content knowledge, is needed to move towards teaching expertise. However, pedagogical content knowledge is a known difficulty for pre-service teachers and not well covered in many computer science teacher preparation programs. In this chapter, we present several tools to elicit this specialized form of knowledge, discuss examples of educators' responses to the items, and share our reflections on the content and structure of their responses as well as the features specific to the computer science discipline. We conclude with recommendations to guide the use of pedagogical content knowledge measures in teacher preparation programs and suggested avenues for further research.

Keywords: Pedagogical Content Knowledge, Teacher Preparation

Preparing Pre-Service Teachers to Teach Computer Science: Models, Practices, and Policies,
pages 69–88.

INTRODUCTION

Many countries are pursuing ambitious initiatives to expand computer science education at the primary and secondary levels (Hubwieser et al., 2015). Like any other educational reform, the success of these initiatives will depend on teachers bringing computer science into their classrooms. However, unlike many other K–12 disciplines, computer science is a relatively young field, first appearing in schools in the 1950s (e.g., Buchman, 1956). As such, many aspiring teachers have not experienced computer science during their own education. And teachers that have learned computer science are confronted with an evolving discipline, new curricula, and new programming environments they need to learn.

A growing number of pre-service programs are emerging to support teachers in developing the competencies and knowledge needed for effective computer science instruction. A requisite focal area for any teacher training program is the connection of content knowledge with pedagogy, a known difficulty for pre-service teachers (Ball, 2000). This interwoven knowledge base, which Shulman (1986) termed pedagogical content knowledge, is not well covered in many computer science teacher preparation programs (Armoni, 2011). However, since pedagogical content knowledge is needed to move towards teaching expertise (Berliner, 2004), we argue that computer science teacher preparation must attend to this specialized form of knowledge.

If pedagogical content knowledge becomes a foundational component of pre-service education, how might we learn what aspects of this knowledge base teachers develop during their training? And how might we identify areas of growth for individual educators? In this conceptual chapter, we briefly introduce pedagogical content knowledge and how it can be used as a framework for supporting pre-service teacher preparation. Drawing on our work with in-service educators new to teaching computer science, we present examples of instruments designed to elicit pedagogical content knowledge that can be incorporated into pre-service computer science programs. We then conclude with suggestions for both the research community and the practitioner community to expand our understanding and use of pedagogical content knowledge in the preparation of future computer science teachers.

BACKGROUND ON PEDAGOGICAL CONTENT KNOWLEDGE

Shulman (1986, 1987) developed the construct of pedagogical content knowledge (PCK) to describe the knowledge of how to teach particular subject matter. PCK emerged during a time of reform in the teaching profession and supported scholars in articulating, theorizing, and investigating one component of the teaching knowledge base. Namely, PCK constituted "the blending of content and pedagogy into an understanding of how particular topics, problems, or issues are organized, represented, and adapted to the diverse interests and abilities of learners, and presented for instruction" (Shulman, 1987, p. 8). For example, recognizing that an egg carton can serve as a productive visual metaphor for two-dimensional arrays demonstrates PCK. As use of PCK spread in the academic community, scholars expanded its original definition to include additional components such as knowledge of assessment, curriculum, media, educational ends, and particular types of content knowledge (Depaepe et al., 2013). Although the varied definitions of PCK can be difficult to distinguish (Hashweh, 2005; Matthews, 2013), Shulman (2015) recently encouraged multiple perspectives of the construct to account for the varying sociocultural contexts of teaching and professional learning. While PCK has evolved into an umbrella term often encompassing multiple aspects of teaching knowledge specific to content, it remains a useful guide for investigating the development of teaching expertise.

Decades of PCK scholarship in other disciplinary communities has informed our understanding of this type of teaching knowledge, particularly its relationship to subject matter knowledge (e.g., Depaepe et al., 2013). Studies such as the multinational Teacher Education and Development Study: Learning to Teach Mathematics (TEDS-M) demonstrated a positive correlation between content knowledge and PCK (Blömeke & Delaney, 2012). Strong content knowledge allows teachers to better notice student thinking and leads to changes in practice that better support student learning (Goldsmith et al., 2014). Given the link between these two knowledge bases, the PCK for computer science will be distinct from the PCK of other disciplines.

The computer science education community is beginning to build its own understanding of PCK that includes new conceptualizations of the construct, insights related to unique aspects of teaching the discipline, and innovative methods of measurement (Hubbard, 2018). For example, Woollard (2005) created a framework to categorize metaphors used in computer science teaching along two dimensions: (a) novel or traditional, and (b) theoretical or kinesthetic. The use of Russian dolls to explain recursion is classified as a traditional, kinesthetic metaphor. As another example, Liberman et al. (2012) identified regressed expertise as a phase computer science teachers experience when they change programming paradigms (e.g., going from a procedural language like C to an object-oriented language like Java). They observed that teachers with strong PCK in procedural programming used less effective teaching strategies when faced with unexpected instructional situations in their new courses, but that these ineffective tactics were less frequent during computer lab sessions than in classroom lectures.

Scholars have explored various methods to examine computer science PCK. Some of these efforts draw on work from other education research communities. For example, several researchers have adapted Loughran et al.'s (2004) group interview guide called Content Representations (CoRe) to document the knowledge of experienced computer science educators and to assess the development of PCK in pre-service teachers (Buchholz et al., 2013; Saeli et al., 2010). However, most researchers tend to create their own instruments and methods to measure computer science PCK. The KUI project used both content analysis of teacher education curricula and interviews where teachers reacted to hypothetical teaching scenarios to refine and test their two-dimensional model of computer science

PCK (Hubwieser et al., 2013; Margaritis et al., 2015). Similarly, Yadav and colleagues (Yadav et al., 2016; Yadav & Berges, 2019) used teaching vignettes and open-ended questionnaire items to understand how teachers might use their PCK to respond to student thinking.

While the construct of PCK has proved fruitful for scholarship, its utility for informing teaching practice and preparation has been questioned (Settlage, 2013), leading some researchers to focus on ways of eliciting and portraying PCK that can be easily shared with teachers. This shift in focus has identified several benefits for using PCK as a framework in pre-service teacher preparation including encouraging reflection on practice, preparing pre-service teachers to obtain PCK in the future, and helping pre-service teachers examine the difference between learners knowing an answer and understanding the process (Mecoli, 2013). In this chapter, we present different methods we have used to elicit PCK for computer science and discuss their affordances and challenges in supporting pre-service teacher education.

EXEMPLARS

In the early 2010s, we began our foray into computer science education through an NSF-funded research project called *Developing Computer Science Pedagogical Content Knowledge through On-the-Job Learning*. The goals of our study were: (a) identify the components of an on-the-job training model that effectively prepared in-service high school educators to teach computer science, and (b) develop a theoretical framework and a suite of assessment items to measure PCK for computer science. For five years, we worked with teachers to address these goals within introductory courses focused on the block-based language Snap! and AP Computer Science A courses focused on Java. Since that time, we have also worked with school districts and informal learning organizations to grow and develop their secondary computer science teaching forces. In exploring PCK across these projects, our focus has shifted from assessing PCK to eliciting PCK. Assessments, which are sometimes viewed as a form of testing needed for accountability, felt orthogonal to the benefits we strove to provide with our PCK instruments. To move closer to our goal, we began developing tools that would offer insight into PCK while also providing teachers with activities centered around authentic artifacts of practice (Ball & Cohen, 1999). The question driving our work now is: how can we design activities that encourage teachers to share and reflect upon teaching computer science with a focus on specific content?

Eliciting PCK requires attending to the development and nature of teacher knowledge. As teachers gain more experience planning, delivering, and reflecting on their lessons, their understanding of how to support student learning evolves and is incorporated into their PCK. Also, as PCK builds on specific experiences, it is not uncommon to hear teachers describe a story about a teaching episode or use figurative language to explain their ideas. Lastly, PCK presents itself in different forms, each of which is better elicited with different methods (Shavelson et al.,

2005). For example, identifying a teacher's knowledge of common misconceptions might be easily measured with close-ended items on a survey, but this method might fall short of capturing evidence of how an educator responds to those misconceptions while teaching. Park and Oliver (2008) identified two forms of teaching knowledge in which PCK plays an important role: knowledge-in-action which is used during the enactment of teaching and knowledge-on-action which is used to prepare for teaching lessons. On the following pages, we provide examples of two activities we have used with teachers to elicit knowledge-on-action related to their computer science teaching.

Eliciting PCK through CoRe

Background on CoRe

CoRe is an interview guide developed by Loughran et al. (2004) to capture and document PCK for science. In this collaborative activity, a group of teachers first identifies a set of "big ideas" they want students to learn about their content area and then they discuss seven open-ended prompts related to teaching each idea (see Table 4.1). The output of these discussions is then exemplified through PaP-eR (i.e. pedagogical and professional-experience repertoires), or a narrative description of how a teacher enacted the related PCK in practice. In a longitudinal study with six primary and secondary science teachers, Bertram and Loughran (2012) found the CoRe promoted reflection on teaching practice, increased awareness of student conceptions and strategies for responding to learners' ideas, helped teachers approach the teaching of unfamiliar content, and was beneficial to both new and experienced educators. While originally developed for experienced teachers, using CoRe to introduce pre-service teachers to the concept of PCK also encourages a deeper understanding of the connections between teaching and learning of subject matter (Loughran et al., 2008).

TABLE 4.1. CoRe Prompts (Loughran et al., 2004)

Prompt
1. What you intend the students to learn about this idea
2. Why it is important for students to know this
3. What else you know about this idea (that you do not intend students to know yet)
4. Difficulties/limitations connected with teaching this idea
5. Knowledge about students' thinking which influences your teaching of this idea
6. Other factors that influence your teaching of this idea
7. Teaching procedures (and particular reasons for using these to engage with this idea)
8. Specific ways of ascertaining students' understanding or confusion around this idea (include likely range of responses)

CoRe has been incorporated into computer science teacher preparation and training. Buchholz et al. (2013) used CoRe with fourteen computer science education undergraduate students to both gauge their PCK development before and after a teaching experience and to encourage their reflection on planning and teaching. Using this data, they proposed a preliminary competency model of pre-service teachers' PCK development. The model hypothesizes that pre-service teachers progress (a) from identifying particular teaching topics to understanding how those topics connect to the larger world and (b) from a more teacher-centric view to a more learner-centric view when considering knowledge about student thinking. As another example, Saeli et al. (2010) held workshops with thirty experienced computer science educators in an effort to document PCK related to programming that can be shared with other teachers. Teachers worked in groups of five for two hours discussing ideas they identified as core to programming. Discussions were summarized for the topics of loops, data structures, arrays, decomposition, parameters, and algorithms.

Exemplars of the Modified CoRe Questionnaire

As part of our NSF-funded study, we used the CoRe to help us understand how PCK developed as teachers gained more experience in computer science teaching. All teachers, while experienced mathematics educators, were within their first three years of teaching computer science. We spent one year working closely with these teachers as they taught introductory level computer science courses, visiting them in their classrooms monthly. Teachers completed a questionnaire version of the CoRe the day before our observations. Attending to the episodic nature of PCK, we further modified the CoRe by shifting the focus from a big idea of the discipline to the learning objective for the observed lesson. Also, given the various goals of lessons (e.g., learn new content, complete an assignment, research a topic), we replaced the eighth CoRe prompt with "how will you know if this lesson is a success."

In the following paragraphs, we provide examples of responses to the CoRe questionnaire and to interviews where teachers expanded on their written responses. The exemplars were selected to show the range of responses we received in terms of their focus (e.g., general teaching knowledge versus PCK specific to computer science) and their level of detail. We highlight these examples not to critique responses, but rather to emphasize the interconnectedness of all knowledge bases teachers draw upon in their craft. Teaching is a complex process and it may be natural for educators to consider PCK prompts in relation to other factors such as classroom logistics and prior experiences from other disciplines.

An example of a modified CoRe questionnaire collected in the middle of the school year from a teacher who felt completely prepared to teach her students about lists is shown in Table 4.2. While these comments may be considered ideal in some respects given the teacher's focus on the content topic for each prompt, they are not representative of the responses we received across the school year.

Our decision to focus the CoRe on individual lessons sometimes invited responses related more to the realities of daily teaching and less to ideas about PCK. For example, when asked what other factors will influence their teaching of a topic, some teachers wrote comments akin to "crazy schedule of these 2 weeks is getting in the way" or "the fact that some days have started without Internet access explains why I added the topic of binary numbers to the curriculum." We also noticed responses sometimes described general pedagogical knowledge, especially as it related to teaching strategies used in the classroom. Consider the following responses provided by the same teacher to the seventh CoRe prompt:

> I plan to review the previous day's material with a PowerPoint presentation. I will ask individual students questions to assess their understanding. They will then work on a lab, at times asking peers and instructors for help. (Visit 2)

> Students learn by grappling with the programming language themselves. I intend to let them develop a working program. Providing them with a skeleton code allows students to know where to start and can eliminate much of the frustration of starting from scratch. (Visit 6)

TABLE 4.2.   Response to Modified CoRe Prompts About Lists

Prompt	Response
What is the learning objective of this lesson?	Students will learn attributes of a list, how to manipulate it, and how to iterate.
Why is it important for students to know this?	Lists are used frequently in computer programming, like in sorting.
What else do you know about this idea that you do not intend students to know yet?	I know there is something called "linked lists" which we are not doing in SNAP. Also, there is a difference between arrays and lists.
What are the difficulties or limitations connected with teaching this topic?	Snap starts with item 1 while in computer programming, people start with 0. There are two "length of" blocks in SNAP which students get mixed up. They also get confused with "item any" when they are trying to see if a list contains something. Also, SNAP's blank list contains a blank item #1.
What do you know about students' thinking that will influence your teaching of this topic?	The items noted above.
What other factors will influence your teaching of this topic?	We teach whatever list blocks are available in SNAP.
What teaching procedures will you use to engage with this topic and why?	We had some students stand in a row and people act as variables to help engage students kinesthetically.
How will you know if this lesson is a success?	Students will create the Hangman project

The first response demonstrates general pedagogical knowledge that could be applied in any lesson and even in other subject areas. In contrast, the second response highlights the benefit of providing learners with starter code, a strategy unique to working with programming languages. This tendency to focus on general pedagogical knowledge was not simply a reflection of the teacher's level of experience or confidence in the subject matter; we also received these comments from the most experienced teachers in our group.

Similar to Bertram's (2010) observation from using the CoRe with science teachers, we noticed variation in the level of detail teachers provided in their responses. Some teachers wrote ambiguous comments such as "expand their thinking" or "nothing." Others provided terse responses that did not reflect the richness of the teaching we observed during our visits. We found that probing these responses through interviews provoked more detailed ideas and recollections in most teachers. In the middle of the school year, we visited a teacher during a lesson focused on building a fraction calculator in Java. In describing the difficulties and limitations connected with teaching the lesson on her CoRe questionnaire, she wrote, "Students aren't used to working with a larger program or with phases. Sometimes they have a lot of trouble following the instructions." After the lesson, we asked her for additional thoughts about these difficulties and she said:

> So, the first two checkpoints could be done right in this one method that they gave you...But now all of a sudden they have to get data that they got in the first checkpoint and use that along with data that they got in the second checkpoint and then go do the calculations, and now they need program design, which they haven't had to do really. So, we've done pseudocoding and even a short exercise it is hard for them to think in pseudocode. What they do is they code it and then they write the pseudocode. Or they write the pseudocode very close to code.

Simply reading her questionnaire response might suggest that she is aware students have some difficulty writing large programs, but that she does not yet fully understand why. However, the interview provided an opportunity to describe her ideas in more detail and to reveal her understanding of students' conceptions of pseudocode. For all but one of our teachers, talking through ideas resulted in more detailed PCK responses than questionnaires alone. So, we encourage such dialogue when using the modified CoRe questionnaire. However, there may be situations when it is not feasible to speak to every teacher in your program. In the next section, we describe how we approached eliciting PCK at scale.

Eliciting PCK through Online Questionnaires

To gather data from a larger group of teachers, we developed an online PCK questionnaire. This questionnaire contained nine items covering three introductory computer science topics: algorithms, variables and assignment, and control structures. Each question was situated within a common teaching scenario. The design and structure of the questionnaire was informed by the Mathematical Work of Teaching Framework (Selling et al., 2016) as well as the CoRe (Loughran et al., 2004) (see Kao et al., 2018 for a detailed discussion of this instrument). High school CS teachers and industry professionals volunteering in the teachers' CS classes completed the questionnaire at the beginning and end of the school year. The discussion and exemplars presented below are drawn from three of the questions: two questions ask teachers to identify learning goals for introductory CS topics and one question asks teachers to evaluate a piece of student work. Participants' responses were categorized using an open coding process. Many responses reflected multiple aspects of PCK, however, we present exemplars that clearly illustrate the types of teaching knowledge prevalent in the data set.

Identifying Learning Goals

We first discuss exemplars from two questions that asked teachers to identify learning goals for introductory CS topics. The prompts relate to the topics of variables and control structures:

> *Variables:* You are teaching an introductory computer science course. It is still early in the semester, and students have mainly been programming short code segments to perform simple tasks (e.g., "Hello, World"). You are about to teach a lesson to introduce your students to the idea of variables and assignment. What is most important for your students to learn about variables and assignment in this lesson?

> *Control Structures:* You are teaching an introductory computer science course. Your students have already learned about Booleans, logical operators, and how to evaluate Boolean expressions. The next unit covers control structures: conditional statements, loops, and nested loops. What is most important for your students to understand about control structures in this unit?

Teachers' responses to both questions revealed three major themes: (a) big ideas about the discipline of computer science, (b) specific knowledge and skills, and (c) pedagogical approaches. Tables 4.3, 4.4, and 4.5 show examples of responses that fit each theme for each question.

The responses in Table 4.3 (Examples 1–4) link understanding of variables and control structures to bigger ideas in programming. All these examples describe how variables and control structures increase the power and usefulness of computer programs by allowing for abstraction and adaptability.

In contrast to these "big ideas" responses, the responses in Table 4.4 (Examples 5–12) identify specific knowledge and skills for students to learn. The scope of the knowledge and skills in these responses is much narrower than the knowledge described in Examples 1–4. Example 5 provides a long list of declarative facts about variables that students should learn, some of which are echoed in Example 6. Example 7 and the latter part of Example 9 describe contrasts that students should understand. Example 8 and the first part of Example 9 provide similar facts about control structures. Examples 10, 11, and 12 describe skills students should acquire so they can effectively program with control structures.

TABLE 4.3. Example Responses that Reflect Big Ideas of the Discipline

Variables	Control Structures
Example 1. Variables are an important building block in computer code. Being able to store and recall values in a program, is crucial in making programs work. One of the "super powers" of a computer (compared to humans) is the ability to store and recall tremendous amounts of information in perfect detail and accuracy. Students should take advantage of this with their programs. [Introductory CS volunteer, pre-test]	**Example 3.** Control structures are what's needed to make computer programs truly complex and useful. Without them, programs are just simple instructions that do the same thing over and over again, regardless of the situation. But with control structures (especially conditional statements and the repeat-until loops), you can make programs that adapt to all sorts of different situations. [Introductory CS volunteer, pre-test]
Example 2. Variables are adaptable and make lengthy programs adapt to minor changes without a complete overhaul of code. [Introductory CS teacher, post-test]	**Example 4.** Control structures are statements that are only executed when the boolean expression controlling their execution is true. You can use control structures to create programs which behave in different ways depending on the the [sic] conditions present when the program is executed. For example, you can use them to create programs that respond to user input, or perform calculations differently depending on the types of values they encounter. [AP CS teacher, post-test]

The two categories of responses shown in Tables 4.3 and 4.4 are consistent with Buchholz et al.'s (2013) model of preservice teachers' PCK development. Some of the responses demonstrated greater focus on identifying specific topics for a lesson while others focused on drawing connections to the larger world of computer science.

A third category, pedagogically-oriented responses, are shown in Table 4.5 (Examples 13–17). These responses sometimes identified a specific idea, fact, or skill as a goal for the lesson/unit, but the focus of the response was in describing a pedagogical strategy for helping students learn the desired content. Respondents described examples and analogies to illustrate the concept as well activities and exercises for students.

Analyzing Student Work

In the third question, teachers were given a code-writing prompt and analyzed an example of student work in response to that prompt (see Figure 4.1). Two major categories emerged from these responses: repetition-focused responses and abstraction-focused responses (Table 4.6).

In repetition-focused responses, the respondent identifies code repetition or inefficiency as the major issue. The respondent recognizes that Alice understands "IF" statements but not loops. The feedback is to steer Alice towards thinking about loops. Some respondents provided direct instruction to Alice to use loops,

TABLE 4.4.   Example Responses that Reflect Specific Knowledge and Skills

Variables	Control Structures
Example 5. 1. Variable is like a storage box with a meaningful label so you can remember what kind of things you will store in it and be able to find it later. 2. Variable can store one value of its kind at a time. If you want to put a different thing of the same kind into it, the new one will displace the one that's already in the box. 3. Assignment is similar to the action of putting the thing into the box. 4. Since we are in the intro level, we will just limit to assignment by value. So, when A := B, in this assignment, a copy of the value of B is put into A, but B will still retain it's [sic] value. 5. The assignment statement is the work horse of programming. [Introductory CS volunteer, pre-test]	**Example 8.** They must contain a control variable, test or condition, and a change to the control variable. [AP CS teacher, pre-test]
Example 6. Declaration and assignment are two different things. You cannot assign before you declare. Also, variables have a type and it is important to understand the differences between the types. [AP CS teacher, pre-test]	**Example 9.** Regarding loops, they need to understand that for loops are for a pre-defined number of iterations and while loops are for an indefinite number of iterations. Conditional statements such as if/else if/else statements are different than if/if/if statements and nested if statements. I think they should know the differences. [AP CS teacher, post-test]
Example 7. The differences between variables in math and variables in a computer program. [AP CS volunteer, pre-test]	**Example 10.** Students need to physically trace where the computer is reading and processing as it goes through the loop, almost similar to following a debugger through a program. In control structures, I've learned that students can get them to work but may not always understand what the computer is processing at different moments. [Introductory CS teacher, pre-test]
	Example 11. I think it is import [sic] for students to be able to identify a loop that produces an error or an infinite loop. [Introductory CS teacher, pre-test]
	Example 12. How to properly use Boolean operators. Most students will have a grasp of >, =, <=, and == based on their math counterparts. Boolean logic (which is behind all of the control logic operators) is more abstract and probably unfamiliar. [AP CS volunteer, post-test]

as in Example 18, while other respondents were more student-centered, as in Example 19. A shift from a more teacher-centered to a more student-centered view of teaching would be consistent with Buchholz et. al.'s (2013) model of pre-service teachers' PCK development.

In abstraction-focused responses, the respondent moves beyond issues of code repetition or inefficiency and discusses how Alice's code lacks generality. In Example 20, the respondent discusses developing a solution that can handle an arbitrary number of test items. In Example 21, the respondent discusses "programming idioms," or schema for solving programming problems. It is worth mentioning that the respondents in Examples 20 and 21 have answered a slightly different question than the given prompt. The question explicitly asks what Alice does and does not understand about *control structures*, not programming in gener-

TABLE 4.5. Example Responses that Reflect Pedagogical Approaches

Variables	Control Structures
Example 13. Help students make connections to prior knowledge of variables (math, science class). Give students examples of how variables are used broadly as numbers, lists, strings, and more. Show students one clear example of how a variable can be powerful: Ex: Draw a spiral. 1. Ask students for verbal instructions for how to draw with marker 2. Approximate smooth spiral with straight segments of increasing length on whiteboard with marker 3. Show an example of how we could use a 'length' variable in a loop, with increasing length 4. Create code to draw spiral 5. Ask students to take sample code and tweak at least 1 setting: angle, colors, line-width, etc. and make their own spiral. Conclude class with asking students to explain how variables can be used in CS. [Introductory CS teacher, pre-test]	**Example 16.** Students don't have much trouble generating if-then statements, but they don't often think of ways to use other varieties of conditional statements, loops, and nested loops. I see students overuse forever loops and not sure when to use 'if-else' blocks, etc. I think it would be important to give students clear examples of when various conditional statements, loops, and nested loops would be appropriate to use for a variety of tasks or programming challenges. Question to explore with students: What control structures exist and when might we use or avoid them? [Introductory CS teacher, pre-test]
Example 14. I think it's important to make sure students learn what exactly a variable is and how to assign values to relevant variables. First, I would explain to students the different types of variables (integer, String, boolean, etc). I would then go into showing why variables are useful by using a real-life example. Perhaps I would go through an example that uses one of the students and illustrates variable conventions. I would also explain how to go about assigning a value to a variable and how once a variable is assigned, it can be re-assigned if necessary. [Introductory CS volunteer, pre-test]	**Example 17.** It is most important to understand how conditional statements, loops, and nested loops translate into English. When we think about a process, we frequently express instructions using words/phrases like "if," "when," "as long as," "while," "until," etc. These kinds of statements are directly translatable into control structures. Once students understand that translation, they are typically more comfortable using them in code. [Introductory CS volunteer, pre-test]
Example 15. We make the comparison to Algebra and equations. We show that like equations we can vary the input to a function to change its outcome but still follow the same rules. [AP CS volunteer, post-test]	

al. The contrast between the repetition-focused and abstraction-focused responses once again seem to be broadly consistent with Buchholz et al.'s (2013) model of pre-service teachers' PCK development.

Summary of Exemplars

We presented examples from the modified CoRe and the online questionnaire to demonstrate broad categories of responses one might uncover when using dif-

Your unit on control structures is almost over. Students have been practicing with conditionals and loops for several weeks. As a final exercise, you assign your students the following code-writing prompt:

> *Write a code segment that will grade a 5-question multiple-choice quiz. Assume that* ***responses*** *is a list that contains a student's responses to each question and* ***answers*** *is another list that contains the correct answers. Award one point for every question answered correctly and <report/print> a letter grade as follows:*
>
> *A if the total score is 5*
> *B if the total score is 4*
> *C if the total score is 3*
> *D if the total score is 2*
> *F if the total score is 1 or 0*

A student in your class, Alice, turned in the following code:

```
int score = 0;

if (responses[0] == answers[0])
    score++;

if (responses[1] == answers[1])
    score++;

if (responses[2] == answers[2])
    score++;

if (responses[3] == answers[3])
    score++;

if (responses[4] == answers[4])
    score++;

if (score == 5)
    System.out.println("A");

if (score == 4)
    System.out.println("B");

if (score == 3)
    System.out.println("C");

if (score == 2)
    System.out.println("D");

if (score == 1 | score == 0)
    System.out.println("F");
```

What does Alice understand well about control structures? What doesn't Alice understand well about control structures?

What kind of feedback would you provide Alice to improve her understanding of control structures?

FIGURE 4.1.   PCK Questionnaire Item on Analyzing Student Work. Note. Teachers of the block-based introductory course saw the code on the left. AP CS A teachers saw the Java code on the right.

ferent methods to elicit PCK. The responses to our instruments represented all areas of PCK as conceptualized by Shulman (1986): general pedagogical knowledge, content knowledge, and pedagogical content knowledge. The pedagogically-oriented responses aligned with existing models of computer science teachers' PCK development (Buchholz et al., 2013). In addition, the content-oriented responses reflect models of computer science content knowledge development, suggesting a range of computer science content expertise among teachers in our sample. Studies of expert-novice differences in programming knowledge have found that novices' programming difficulties are rooted in poor planning and design and a lack of knowledge of higher-level programming strategies (see de Raadt, 2007; Robins et al., 2003 for literature reviews). For example, novice programmers may be unaware of "programming idioms" as described and taught by the respondent

TABLE 4.6. Repetition-focused versus Abstraction-focused Responses

Repetition-Focused	Abstraction-Focused
Example 18. Alice understands the correct order and conditional statements. Alice does not understand how loops can do the same thing but more efficiently. I would advise Alice to use a loop to minimize her coding. [Introductory CS teacher, post-test]	**Example 20.** Understands: use of Boolean expressions to properly determine correct answers. use of Boolean expressions to properly identify letter grade. Does not understand: Use of loops to repeat common logic. Use of loops to "future proof" the code. The use of If/Else to capture remaining cases. I would ask her to identify nearly identical pieces of code. Once identified I would ask here [sic] if she could, using the techniques we have learned in class, represent that code only once in her program. I would follow up asking her now, what would need to change in your program to handle grading a quiz with 6 questions? How about 60 questions? How about 600 questions? [Introductory CS volunteer, post-test]
Example 19. Alice understands if statements well! However, she doesn't seem to recognize that the repetitive code checking answers could go into a for loop. I would push her to think about what's repetitive about each part, and whether it can be put into a different control structure to reduce the amount of code she has to write. [AP CS A volunteer, pre-test]	**Example 21.** How to test for conditions but not how to recognize repeating structures. Did not see this as two list traversals. In our class we spend a lot of time on programming idioms like list traversals. These are programming structures that are used often and are made up of a number of commands. Here I would ask what do we usually do with lists? (all list traversals have 4 parts: an index to keep track of where you are, a starting point, and an ending condition, and a step increment.) Other idioms include multiple IF's to make a Case of structure, how to make a matrix out of nested lists, use modulo w/index origin. [Introductory CS volunteer, post-test]

in Example 21. These findings are consistent with studies of expert-novice differences in other academic content areas, such as mathematics (e.g., Koedinger & Anderson, 1990; Schoenfeld, 1992) and physics (e.g., Chi et al., 1981), and have implications both for CS teacher preparation and CS curriculum design, which will be discussed further below.

We want to emphasize that it is not our intention to evaluate our participants' PCK based on their responses to the CoRe or to our questionnaire. For example, it is not necessarily the case that a teacher who focused more on general pedagogy in the CoRe is less experienced than a teacher who focused more on specific aspects of CS teaching. Nor does a teacher who responded to the questionnaire with big ideas necessarily possess stronger PCK than one who focused on specific knowledge and skills. Although such a shift in teacher perspective could be consistent with growth in PCK, as proposed by Buchholz et al. (2013), our instruments would need to undergo additional validation testing before they could be used to draw such conclusions. However, we believe that as teachers gain expertise in the subject area and their craft, they will develop knowledge in all the categories shown above and the ability to flexibly apply that knowledge effectively when teaching.

We conclude this section with practical suggestions for eliciting PCK in practice. When using PCK instruments, we have found that it is important to ask about particular CS content, which could be a big idea in CS or a specific learning objective. We have also found the framing of PCK questions is important. In the case of the CoRe, it is important to convey what the questions are trying to elicit, as the language of the CoRe may not align with teachers' normal ways of thinking about teaching. For questions such as those on our online questionnaire, it is important to situate them in specific teaching contexts (e.g., describing what students in the scenario already know). Otherwise teachers may be overwhelmed by the range of possibilities and unable to answer concisely.

NEXT STEPS

Teaching is a complex craft that requires a wide repertoire of knowledge and skills. Although pedagogical content knowledge is just one of the core competencies pre-service teachers will need to develop as they begin their careers, we believe it serves as a useful framing for teacher preparation because it keeps the focus on subject matter. Within computer science, attending to PCK is particularly important given many pre-service teachers have limited prior experiences with the discipline. An explicit focus on PCK brings additional opportunities for pre-service teachers to develop knowledge of computer science within the context of teaching. In the remainder of this section, we offer concrete examples of how PCK can be incorporated into pre-service programs and offer ideas for future research to further support the design of tools to elicit PCK from pre-service candidates.

Incorporating PCK into Pre-service Programs

A core feature of the highest-quality teacher preparation programs is coherence between courses. A typical pre-service teacher preparation sequence might include a series of courses to learn subject-matter content, a separate course on teaching methods, and another course on general learning theory. These courses may or may not directly reference content from other courses. A graduate from such a program may still lack a clear understanding of what learning theory informs specific curriculum design or underlies specific pedagogical techniques and which pedagogical techniques are best suited for different concept areas.

In contrast, imagine a course sequence in which the computer science content is addressed alongside pedagogy (Darling-Hammond, 2006). In each course, pre-service teachers would learn computer science content, techniques for teaching that content, and learning theories as applied to the teaching and learning of that specific content. The computer science content for each course would get progressively more advanced and integrated, culminating with direct teaching of expert-like representations and organization of computer science knowledge and expert-like problem-solving schema. For example, pre-service teachers may learn about looping in an early course, including ways of presenting looping to students, practice exercises for looping, and common student conceptions regarding looping. In a later course, pre-service teachers could learn about looping as it is used in array traversals, applications of array traversals in programming problem-solving, and common student conceptions regarding array traversals. In this way, pre-service teachers would receive direct instruction on expert representations and schema for computer science content, a technique that is likely to improve their own learning of the content (de Raadt et al., 2009). Pre-service teachers would also develop greater knowledge of how different computing concepts connect, how students think and learn about different concepts, and how to represent abstract concepts for students—all characteristics of expert teachers (Hogan et al., 2003). A pre-service preparation program designed in this way would allow teachers the opportunity to develop a pedagogically integrated view of foundational computer science concepts and all the facets of PCK we described above.

Another core feature of high-quality teacher preparation is course work closely integrated with clinical practice. The clinical practice should be extensive and supervised by an experienced teacher who can model expert practice (Darling-Hammond, 2006). Eliciting PCK from pre-service teachers can help clinical supervisors monitor their preparation. The CoRe and items like those found on our online PCK questionnaire can be given following course work and at different time points during clinical practice to determine how PCK is evolving. This information can be used formatively to mentor an individual teaching candidate as well as evaluating the program as a whole. Participating in PCK activities can also provide pre-service teachers with a structure to organize the theory they learn in their training and their experiences working directly with learners in classrooms.

We recognize that providing pre-service teachers with the type of clinical experience recommended by Darling-Hammond (2006) can be logistically difficult, as few master CS teachers who can supervise clinical practice exist in K–12 schools. Eliciting PCK could also fit into a clinical experience centered around tutoring individual introductory CS students at the university level, like in the Disciplinary Focus Tutoring (DFT) model described by Ragonis and Hazzan (2009). In this model, pre-service teachers are paired with a tutee enrolled in an introductory CS course for a series of five tutoring sessions. All tutors are supervised by an experienced teacher who coordinates the tutoring sessions and provides coaching throughout the process. Activities that elicit the tutor's PCK can be interspersed between tutoring sessions and used to inform the coaching.

Avenues for Further Research

Our experience is that it is possible to elicit some aspects of PCK from teachers through questionnaires or interviews. The exemplars provided above illustrate the wide range of knowledge CS teachers bring to bear when thinking about and discussing CS instruction. Some exemplars addressed general ideas in teaching and pedagogy and most touched on some aspect of CS content knowledge. However, getting a complete picture of any individual candidate's PCK requires time and a convergence of methods. For those interested in developing more robust measures of CS teacher PCK, there are two clear avenues for further research.

The first avenue is to conduct research into the methodology used to elicit PCK. What types of prompts yield the most valid and reliable responses? Does the CS content affect how easy it is to obtain a valid and reliable measure of PCK? When should PCK be assessed and how do different assessment contexts affect teachers' responses? Should teachers be asked about PCK just after a lesson related to the same topic is taught, so it is fresh in their minds? How much change in PCK is expected during a teacher preparation program? How much change is expected after a year or more of teaching? The second avenue is to conduct research on learning progressions in CS PCK, validating and building on the preliminary model proposed by Buchholz et al. (2013). How can we determine the depth of teachers' CS PCK? What does the PCK of an expert teacher look like? And how does it compare to the PCK of a novice teacher? Does the trajectory of PCK development depend on the teacher's educational background?

CONCLUSION

Computer science teacher preparation in the United States has made considerable progress in the last decade. Until now, many of these efforts have focused on CS content as many future CS teachers have had minimal exposure to the discipline. However, CS teachers also need knowledge of pedagogy—not just general techniques, but the intersection between CS content, specific techniques for teaching that content, and student learning. In this chapter, we presented exemplars from in-service teachers that show the range of pedagogical content knowledge they employ when teaching CS and discussed several ways of eliciting this knowledge. Moving forward, we hope more pre-service programs incorporate PCK into their training so that future teachers develop the necessary foundation for effective CS teaching.

REFERENCES

Armoni, M. (2011). Looking at secondary teacher preparation through the lens of computer science. *Trans. Comput. Educ.*, *11*(4), 23:1–23:38. https://doi.org/10.1145/2048931.2048934

Ball, D. L. (2000). Bridging practices: Intertwining content and pedagogy in teaching and learning to teach. *Journal of Teacher Education, 51*(3), 241–247. https://doi.org/10.1177/0022487100051003013

Ball, D. L., & Cohen, D. (1999). Developing practice, developing practitioners: Toward a practice-based theory of professional education. *Teaching as the learning profession.* Jossey-Bass.

Berliner, D. C. (2004). Describing the behavior and documenting the accomplishments of expert teachers. *Bulletin of Science, Technology & Society, 24*(3), 200–212. https://doi.org/10.1177/0270467604265535

Bertram, A., & Loughran, J. (2012). Science teachers' views on CoRes and PaP-eRs as a framework for articulating and developing pedagogical content knowledge. *Research in Science Education, 42*(6), 1027–1047. https://doi.org/10.1007/s11165-011-9227-4

Bertram, A. R. (2010). *Enhancing science teachers' knowledge of practice by explicitly developing pedagogical content knowledge* [PhD Thesis]. Monash University. https://bridges.monash.edu/articles/thesis/Enhancing_science_teachers_knowledge_of_practice_by_explicitly_developing_pedagogical_content_knowledge/4546342

Blömeke, S., & Delaney, S. (2012). Assessment of teacher knowledge across countries: A review of the state of research. *ZDM Mathematics Education, 44*(3), 223–247.

Buchholz, M., Saeli, M., & Schulte, C. (2013). PCK and reflection in computer science teacher education. *Proceedings of the 8th Workshop in Primary and Secondary Computing Education* (pp, 8–16). https://doi.org/10.1145/2532748.2532752

Buchman, A. L. (1956). Computer programming and coding at the high school level. *Proceedings of the 1956 11th ACM National Meeting* (pp. 118–121). https://doi.org/10.1145/800258.808964

Chi, M. T. H., Feltovich, P. J., & Glaser, R. (1981). Categorization and representation of physics problems by experts and novices. *Cognitive Science, 5,* 121–152.

Darling-Hammond, L. (2006). Constructing 21st-century teacher education. *Journal of Teacher Education, 57*(3), 300–314. https://doi.org/10.1177/0022487105285962

Depaepe, F., Verschaffel, L., & Kelchtermans, G. (2013). Pedagogical content knowledge: A systematic review of the way in which the concept has pervaded mathematics educational research. *Teaching and Teacher Education, 34,* 12–25. https://doi.org/10.1016/j.tate.2013.03.001

de Raadt, M. (2007). A review of Australasian investigations into problem solving and the novice programmer. *Computer Science Education, 17,* 201–213.

de Raadt, M., Watson, R., & Toleman, M. (2009). Teaching and assessing programming strategies explicitly. *Proceedings of the 11th Australasian Computing Education Conference (ACE 2009), 95,* 45–54.

Goldsmith, L., Doerr, H., & Lewis, C. (2014). Mathematics teachers' learning: A conceptual framework and synthesis of research. *Journal of Mathematics Teacher Education, 17*(1), 5–36.

Hashweh, M. (2005). Teacher pedagogical constructions: A reconfiguration of pedagogical content knowledge. *Teachers and Teaching, 11*(3), 273–292.

Hogan, T., Rabinowitz, M., & Craven III, J. A. (2003). Representation in teaching: Inferences from research of expert and novice teachers. *Educational Psychologist, 38*(4), 235–247.

Hubbard, A. (2018). Pedagogical content knowledge in computing education: A review of the research literature. *Computer Science Education, 28*(2), 117–135. https://doi.org/10.1080/08993408.2018.1509580

Hubwieser, P., Berges, M., Magenheim, J., Schaper, N., Bröker, K., Margaritis, M., Schubert, S., & Ohrndorf, L. (2013). Pedagogical content knowledge for computer science in German teacher education curricula. *Proceedings of the 8th Workshop in Primary and Secondary Computing Education* (pp. 95–103). https://doi.org/10.1145/2532748.2532753

Hubwieser, P., Giannakos, M. N., Berges, M., Brinda, T., Diethelm, I., Magenheim, J., Pal, Y., Jackova, J., & Jasute, E. (2015). A global snapshot of computer science education in K–12 schools. *Proceedings of the 2015 ITiCSE on Working Group Reports* (pp, 65–83). https://doi.org/10.1145/2858796.2858799

Kao, Y., D'Silva, K., Hubbard, A., Green, J., & Cully, K. (2018). Applying the mathematical work of teaching framework to develop a computer science pedagogical content knowledge assessment. *Proceedings of the 49th ACM Technical Symposium on Computer Science Education* (pp. 888–893). https://doi.org/10.1145/3159450.3159521

Koedinger, K. R., & Anderson, J. R. (1990). Abstract planning and perceptual chunks: Elements of expertise in geometry. *Cognitive Science, 14*(4), 511–550.

Liberman, N., Kolikant, Y. B.-D., & Beeri, C. (2012). "Regressed Experts" as a new state in teachers' professional development: Lessons from computer science teachers' adjustments to substantial changes in the curriculum. *Computer Science Education, 22*(3), 257–283.

Loughran, J., Mulhall, P., & Berry, A. (2004). In search of pedagogical content knowledge in science: Developing ways of articulating and documenting professional practice. *Journal of Research in Science Teaching, 41*(4), 370–391. https://doi.org/10.1002/tea.20007

Loughran, J., Mulhall, P., & Berry, A. (2008). Exploring pedagogical content knowledge in science teacher education. *International Journal of Science Education, 30*(10), 1301–1320. https://doi.org/10.1080/09500690802187009

Margaritis, M., Magenheim, J., Hubwieser, P., Berges, M., Ohrndorf, L., & Schubert, S. (2015). Development of a competency model for computer science teachers at secondary school level. *2015 IEEE Global Engineering Education Conference (EDUCON)* (pp. 211–220). https://doi.org/10.1109/EDUCON.2015.7095973

Matthews, M. E. (2013). The influence of the pedagogical content knowledge framework on research in mathematics education: A review across grade bands. *Journal of Education, 193*(3), 29–37.

Mecoli, S. (2013). The influence of the pedagogical content knowledge theoretical framework on research on preservice teacher education. *Journal of Education, 193*(3), 21–27.

Park, S., & Oliver, J. S. (2008). Revisiting the conceptualisation of pedagogical content knowledge (PCK): PCK as a conceptual tool to understand teachers as professionals. *Research in Science Education, 38*(3), 261–284.

Ragonis, N., & Hazzan, O. (2009). Integrating a tutoring model into the training of prospective computer science teachers. *Journal of Computers in Mathematics and Science Teaching, 28*(3), 309–339.

Robins, A., Rountree, J., & Rountree, N. (2003). Learning and teaching programming: A review and discussion. *Computer Science Education, 13*, 137–172.

Saeli, M., Perrenet, J., Jochems, W., & Zwaneveld, B. (2010). *Portraying the pedagogical content knowledge of programming—The technical report.* https://www.tue.nl/fileadmin/content/universiteit/Over_de_universiteit/Eindhoven School_of_Education/Onderzoek/Projecten_promovendi/Mara_Saeli_SPJZ_Technical_Report.pdf

Schoenfeld, A. H. (1992). Learning to think mathematically: Problem solving, metacognition, and sense making in mathematics. *Handbook of Research on Mathematics Teaching and Learning* (pp. 334–370). Macmillan.

Selling, S. K., Garcia, N., & Ball, D. L. (2016). What does it take to develop assessments of mathematical knowledge for teaching?: Unpacking the mathematical work of teaching. *The Mathematics Enthusiast, 13*(1/2), 35.

Settlage, J. (2013). On acknowledging PCK's shortcomings. *Journal of Science Teacher Education, 24*(1), 1–12. https://doi.org/10.1007/s10972-012-9332-x

Shavelson, R. J., Ruiz-Primo, M. A., & Wiley, E. W. (2005). Windows into the mind. *Higher Education, 49*(4), 413–430. https://doi.org/10.1007/s10734-004-9448-9

Shulman, L. (1986). Those who understand: Knowledge growth in teaching. *Educational Researcher, 15*, 4–14.

Shulman, L. (1987). Knowledge and teaching: Foundations of the new reform. *Harvard Educational Review, 57*(1), 1–23. https://doi.org/10.17763/haer.57.1.j463w79r56455411

Shulman, L. (2015). PCK: Its genesis and exodus. In A. Berry, P. Friedrichsen, & J. Loughran (Eds.), *Re-examining pedagogical content knowledge in science education* (pp. 3–13). Routledge.

Woollard, J. (2005). The implications of the pedagogic metaphor for teacher education in computing. *Technology, Pedagogy and Education, 14*(2), 189–204.

Yadav, A., & Berges, M. (2019). Computer science pedagogical content knowledge: Characterizing teacher performance. *ACM Transactions on Computing Education, 19*(3), 29:1–29:24. https://doi.org/10.1145/3303770

Yadav, A., Berges, M., Sands, P., & Good, J. (2016). Measuring computer science pedagogical content knowledge: An exploratory analysis of teaching vignettes to measure teacher knowledge. *Proceedings of the 11th Workshop in Primary and Secondary Computing Education* (pp. 92–95). https://doi.org/10.1145/2978249.2978264

PART II

COURSE DESIGN MODELS FOR PREPARING PRE-
SERVICE TEACHERS TO TEACH COMPUTER SCIENCE

CHAPTER 5

CREATING CHANGE AGENTS

A Teacher Preparation Model That Prepares All Teachers to Facilitate Computer Science Concepts

Chery Lucarelli, Jill Long, Jennifer Rosato,
Christa Treichel, and Heather Benedict

This book chapter shares a conceptual model, TeachCS@CSS, that provides a framework for the implementation of a pilot teacher preparation model that integrates computational thinking (CT) and computer science (CS) throughout the undergraduate and graduate teacher preparation programs at The College of St. Scholastica (CSS). A critical component of this model is the unique and collaborative partnership between faculty from Education and Computer Information Systems (CIS) departments at The College of St. Scholastica. The primary aim of the TeachCS@CSS model is to create an interdisciplinary, sustainable curriculum strand that infuses computational thinking and computer science (CT/CS) so that *all* K–12 pre-service teachers have the knowledge and skills to teach CS through interdisciplinary or stand-alone approaches. Foundational to this work is a focus on equity with the hope that teacher candidates will become change agents able to champion "CS for All" in their schools. Additional aspects of the model are shared

Preparing Pre-Service Teachers to Teach Computer Science: Models, Practices and Policies, pages 91–112.

including the process to provide professional development to Education faculty as well as a developmental coaching model that supports curriculum development. The model includes a blended CT mini-course, scaffolded lessons in required education and content methods courses, and a field experience placement. Equally important is the work with key K12 school partners that support our teacher candidates. Program outcomes address knowledge in the areas of CT/CS content, curriculum, and pedagogy. An intentional lens of equity was used throughout the project with a focus on effective teacher dispositions to support equitable learning for *all* students.

Keywords: Teacher Education, Computational Thinking, Computer Science, Curriculum Model

INTRODUCTION—A CALL TO ACTION

The United States has a computer science (CS) educational gap at every level, pre-school through college. In order to achieve K–12 CS education at scale, we need to consider how to prepare future teachers as part of the nation's teacher preparation programs. Imagine, as Krauss and Prottsman suggest (2016), that very few people had ever learned mathematics but that parents, industry, and government believed that all children should learn mathematics. To solve this problem, teacher education faculty could be asked to prepare teacher candidates on how to teach mathematics, but they themselves had never taken a mathematics class. This is the problem we now face in CS. Without changing teacher preparation programs to incorporate CS concepts as part of the curriculum, it will be unlikely that the United States will be able to create a sustainable K–12 educational system that provides equitable access to CS for all students.

A critical component of changing the teacher preparation landscape will require overcoming the highly regulatory governance structures that shape and drive teacher preparation programs (Metzler, 2009). The U.S. does not have a national system for teacher preparation, consequently, teacher preparation programs vary greatly from one state to another and even those within one state may be very different from each other. The nation's teacher preparation programs are almost always aligned with state adopted standards, which are typically based on standards issued by national organizations.

For example, at the national level, the Interstate New Teacher Assessment and Support Consortium (InTASC) provides a set of teacher preparation standards that many states use for teacher licensure (Council of Chief State School Officers, 2016). Minnesota uses the InTASC standards to inform its Minnesota Standards of Effective Practice (SEPs). As Erickson and Wentworth (2010) noted, "Like standards for accreditation, these licensure requirements frame the design and implementation of teacher preparation programs" (p. 5). Within this context, infusing CS into the teacher preparation curriculum is difficult as there is no mention of computer science in national or state teacher preparation standards. A 2013 Computer Science Teachers Association (CSTA) report, *Bugs in the System,* found that as a result of different state requirements, the CS teacher preparation system in the U.S. is flawed (CSTA, 2013).

Infusing CS into teacher preparation programs requires multi-level systemic changes with intentional design and implementation, including plans for developing the computing knowledge of Education faculty. The *Priming the Computer Science Teacher Pump* report (DeLyser et al., 2018) offered recommendations for pre-service teacher programs to integrate CS into their education programs. These recommendations included: attending to required CS content, CS teaching methods, and alignment with state and national CS standards. The report states that Education faculty should be prepared to integrate CS into foundation courses, content methods courses, and field experiences. In order to integrate CS into the respective courses, Education faculty must have the CS subject matter and pedagogical content knowledge along with knowledge of the curriculum (Shulman, 1986). In addition, the *Priming the Pump* report suggested that developing this CS-specific knowledge requires collaboration between CS and Education faculty given that Education faculty have pedagogical expertise while CS faculty have CS content knowledge.

More recently, the *CS for All* movement (National Science Foundation, n.d.), was established to further support the call for action and address CS education for all K–12 learners in every school setting. The College of St. Scholastica's School of Education (SOE) responded to this call to action by creating the TeachCS@ CSS project. The TeachCS@CSS project is grounded in the following tenets that support CS for All: (1) CS is a new literacy that all K–12 students have the right to learn; (2) CS professional developments (PD) needs to include teacher preparation programs so that pre-service teachers are prepared before they leave their programs and begin teaching; and (3) If CS for All *teachers* is necessary, then CS for All *Education faculty* needs to be addressed as they are the critical stakeholders in designing teacher preparation programs.

The ambitious goal of TeachCS@CSS is to prepare *all K–12 teacher candidates*, regardless of licensure area, to have a basic foundation in CS concepts and to understand the critical equity issues that exist in this content area. To be clear, the TeachCS@CSS focus on CS and computational thinking (CT) literacy does not suggest that teacher candidates should have the same knowledge and skills as computer scientists or CS teachers. Rather, TeachCS@CSS posits that the same attention and importance should be given to CS that is given to other subject areas such as mathematics, science, and reading across all grade levels and subjects.

In this chapter, we describe the context for and background of the TeachCS@ CSS project, the rationale and design of the project, how the phases were implemented, lessons learned from the project, and next steps for future directions in understanding how to integrate CT/CS in teacher preparation programs.

BACKGROUND

The College of St. Scholastica (CSS), with funding from a Google grant, created TeachCS@CSS, a model for integrated CT/CS curriculum across teacher preparation programs (see Figure 5.1). With TeachCS@CSS, the School of Education (SOE) has committed to addressing CS across all teacher education programs, regardless of licensure area, so that students see CS as a critical literacy and can integrate CT into their teaching practice. CSS is a small liberal arts college located in the upper Midwest in Duluth, MN, with extended campus locations in the Twin Cities and St. Cloud metro areas and provides several paths for teacher licensure for elementary and secondary teachers. The teaching licensure pathways include a traditional undergraduate program, a degree completion program, and a graduate licensure program. TeachCS@CSS is offered in all three programs and is the only model in the country that has attempted to fully integrate CT throughout its curriculum for all licensure candidates.

The design and implementation of the TeachCS@CSS model included three phases: (1) PD for all Education faculty; (2) disciplinary connections to support the teacher preparation curriculum; and (3) field experiences with K–12 school partners. Throughout these phases is a focus on equity and broadening participation for all stakeholders. Within each of the three phases, intentional steps were developed and implemented in order to effectively embed CS content into the teacher preparation program.

The TeachCS@CSS project utilized a collaborative partnership with CT/CS content experts, Education faculty, and K12 partners. Combining the expertise and pedagogical knowledge of the Education faculty with the expertise of CS

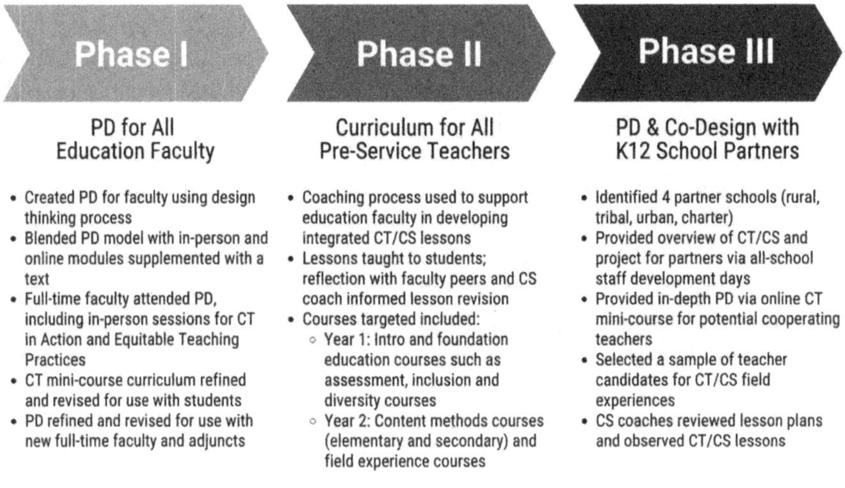

FIGURE 5.1. TeachCS@CSS Model

content experts provided a space to support innovation in a safe environment where each stakeholder group brought something important for consideration. The TeachCS@CSS project was led by a team that included two Education faculty members, Long and Lucarelli, representing both undergraduate and graduate teacher preparation programs, respectively. CS expertise was provided by Rosato, a Computer Information Systems faculty member, and Benedict, a consultant with experience in coaching and CT curriculum development, both of whom served as CT/CS content coaches as well. Treichel, an external consultant, was the evaluator for the project.

DESIGN OF TEACHCS@CSS

During the design phase of the project, which informed the creation of the project's three phases described in Figure 5.1, the TeachCS@CSS team began to understand the need for a common definition and understanding of CT and CS and realized that in order to apply CS concepts, a common conceptual idea, as well as common language, was needed. After much discussion, reading, and consulting with the CS faculty, the project team made the decision to use the CS concept of CT. Wing (2006) argued for CT as a "fundamental skill for everyone, not just for computer scientists. To reading, writing, and arithmetic, we should add computational thinking to every child's analytical ability" (p. 33). Wing encouraged computational exposure to pre-college audiences, especially to teachers and students. The TeachCS@CSS project advocates for the idea that CT is a new literacy that all members of society should be able to learn. Krauss and Prottsman's book, *Computational Thinking and Coding for Every Student: The Teacher's Getting-Started Guide,* was adopted as the primary book for the PD phase, as it provided an accessible entry point for educators with little to no experience in CS. In addition, it defined foundations of CT, including: Decomposition, Pattern Recognition, Pattern Matching, Abstraction, Algorithms, and Automation. These definitions and terms were central to the design of TeachCS@CSS.

The TeachCS@CSS project team, described above, considered each stakeholder group (e.g., students, field clinical supervisors, faculty—including adjuncts, and school partners) and the strengths and challenges that each group brought to learning CT/CS. To manage the complexities and progressions of the project, the TeachCS@CSS team utilized a design thinking process to address the components and implementation of the model through the three phases of the project (see Figure 5.1) described later in this chapter. The design thinking process, proposed by Stanford, includes five stages that support creative problem solving for complex issues. The first stage, empathy, provides a critical foundation of the process and focuses on the human aspect of the problem and was especially helpful as the team addressed the issues in integrating CS into the teacher preparation program. The other four stages include define, ideate, prototype, and test. Each of these stages were part of the design process to support the project.

Faculty Professional Development

The first consideration for the TeachCS@CSS project was to focus on the needs of the Education faculty members as indicated in Phase 1 of the project. Education faculty are critical stakeholders who design and implement curriculum for teacher preparation programs and are influenced, like all college faculty, by their past educational and work experiences and research. Education faculty are almost always former K–12 teachers who have had little to no academic preparation or experience in CS. Therefore, with the mandate of state licensure standards that do not name CS and the general lack of computer science experience, Education faculty are unlikely to have the depth of understanding necessary to create curriculum for future teachers that addresses CS without additional support and PD. Hence, it was critical that the project included an early focus on PD for Education faculty.

The project team had prior experience in providing CS PD to other groups of teachers, which informed the importance of creating a safe and accessible experience for faculty who, for the most part, were not familiar with teaching CS concepts. In addition, we drew upon the guiding principles for effective teacher PD (e.g., Darling-Hammond et al., 2017).

Darling-Hammond et al. (2017) noted that effective teacher PD includes seven key elements: (1) focused on content, (2) active learning, (3) collaboration, (4) models of effective practice, (5) coaching and mentoring, (6) reflection, and (7) long term and sustained. Specifically, Darling-Hammond et al. noted that PD should last at least 50 hours spread from 6 to 12 months.

Active learning as an effective PD technique is also reinforced by a large-scale study on effective teacher PD in mathematics. Garet et al., (2001) found that effective teacher PD includes active learning and collective learning experiences. Additionally, Darling-Hammond, et al. (2017) stated, "The opportunity for teachers to engage in the same learning activities that are designed for their students is often utilized as a form of active learning" (p. 8). The authors noted that effective active learning during teacher PD may also include hands-on experience as well as the planning of instruction and lesson observations.

To ensure that the team implemented effective PD guiding principles, the TeachCS@CSS project started by developing a time frame for the Education faculty in order to meet the recommended guidelines of a minimum of six months with PD activities extending over 50 hours. In addition, the model incorporated PD experiences that Education faculty participated in which became the foundation of the introductory modules for preservice teachers. In essence, the PD modeled the pre-service teacher curriculum as much as possible. These TeachCS@CSS PD components align with the recommendations for effective PD as well as the needs of the Education faculty who were novices to CT/CS content and pedagogy, similar to the knowledge level of the pre-service teachers.

A blended PD model was created that incorporated online modules and face-to-face sessions to provide flexibility for faculty schedules. The face-to-face sessions incorporated active and collaborative learning methods, such as a "computational thinking in action" workshop session where faculty participated in hands-on centers focused on different CT activities. These centers encouraged hands-on exploration with other faculty in a low-stakes manner and emphasized exploration and inquiry. To address the mentoring and coaching PD recommendation, the TeachCS@CSS project utilized a coaching model, described in Chapter 9 later in this book, providing support to faculty as they designed and taught lessons that infused CS concepts in their foundation and methods courses.

In addition, Education faculty co-constructed lesson plans for the pre-service teacher curriculum with CT/CS coaches (content experts), another form of active learning and a recommended PD strategy as noted earlier. As part of this component, the Education faculty members were provided with a classroom visit by a CT/CS content expert who was referred to as the "CS coach" to provide ongoing support and mentoring (see Chapter 9).

Effective PD should also "emphasize content and pedagogy aligned with national, state and local standards, frameworks" (Garet et al., 2001, p. 928). To address this recommendation and to provide a rationale for integrating CT/CS into the teacher preparation curriculum to the Education faculty, the project utilized the School of Education's (SOE) conceptual framework (see Figure 2) which consists of the following major components: equity, content knowledge, educational technology, pedagogy, dispositions, and collaborative partnerships. Additionally, the project team aligned the project with national and state standards.

Alignment to Standards and Frameworks

The SOE conceptual framework (see Figure 5.2) was developed by the Education faculty, and is grounded in evidence-based practice, and provides a set of guiding principles for the teacher preparation program. The TeachCS@CSS project provided opportunities to have faculty engage in reflection and discussion during a PD face-to-face session on how the components of the SOE conceptual framework align with the ideals of the CS for All movement, particularly in the areas of equity, technology, and innovation. By connecting the TeachCS@ CSS project to the conceptual framework, a rationale for infusing CT into the teacher preparation curriculum was established. For example, the project team brought awareness to the inequities that exist in access to CS in K–12 schools. The team was also able to demonstrate how CS can be an innovative opportunity to strengthen the teacher preparation program in educational technology.

In addition, to the School of Education's Conceptual Framework, the TeachCS@ CSS project was informed by the International Society in Technology Education (ISTE, 2016) Standards. The School of Education utilized the ISTE standards for educators and students as part of the program's instructional planning process for over 10 years. Therefore, this served as an opportunity to connect the project to the faculty's prior knowledge with standards and curriculum alignment. The new version of the *ISTE Standards for Students* (STE, 2016), includes CT as a standard with several related benchmarks. Bringing awareness to the ISTE CT standard

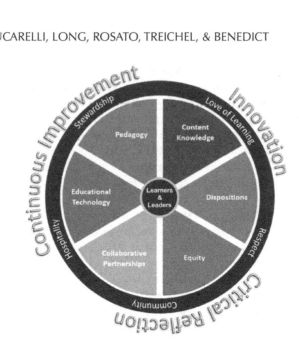

FIGURE 5.2.   The School of Education's Conceptual Framework (revised 2018)

was helpful to support the rationale of the project as ISTE is a highly regarded national organization and the SOE faculty are familiar with the ISTE standards. In the absence of state K–12 CS standards, the project introduced the national Computer Science Teacher Association Standards (CSTA, 2017) to the faculty as part of the curriculum design process. The use of standards for instructional planning is a required and best practice for Education faculty as they prepare their instruction and support teacher candidates. Thus, the use of ISTE and CSTA standards was helpful in connecting the TeachCS@CSS project to current practice.

Teacher Candidate CS Knowledge Gap

Like the Education faculty, most teacher candidates in the U.S have had little to no academic preparation or experience in CS and this is true for the teacher candidates at CSS. Some teacher candidates may have had a CS course in high school or college but this is rare. Without CS preparation at the pre-service level, teacher candidates will most likely enter the teaching profession unable to support K–12 students in learning CS. This scenario, where new teachers enter the teaching profession without CS knowledge, has the potential to perpetuate the CS education gap for K–12 students. Teachers are unlikely to teach a subject they are unfamiliar with or in which they do not feel confident. Therefore, it is critical that all teacher candidates have a basic understanding of Cs concepts so that they have the confidence needed to teach it in their future classrooms.

Finally, teacher candidates should have experience in creating and teaching CT/ CS lessons in the classroom as they do for all other content areas. A critical component of preparing teacher candidates is providing an opportunity to apply theory to practice in field experiences. In order for this to be possible, potential school partners and cooperating teachers at each school needed to be identified. These partners often do not have the CT/CS background either and need an understanding of the motivation for CS for All as well as have some experiences with CT/CS content.

The TeachCS@CSS project team attempted to address the teacher candidate CS knowledge gap by integrating CS integrated curriculum throughout the teacher preparation program. Additionally, the team understood the need to support teacher candidates in teaching CS integrated lessons in their required field experiences. Therefore, the project planned and worked with critical stakeholders in partner schools to implement these unique requirements for the field experiences. The process for implementation of the three project phases is explained below.

IMPLEMENTATION

The following section describes how the three phases of the TeachCS@CSS model (see Figure 1) were implemented at the CSS and with school partners. Included are details of the implementation, feedback from faculty and student reflections, surveys, and lessons learned from each phase of the project. The TeachCS@CSS project utilized a variety of methods to capture stakeholder feedback on each phase in order to inform the team and improve the project. The project hired and consulted with a project evaluator who provided evaluation consultation as well as created and provided surveys to each stakeholder group. In some cases, the evaluator provided focus group sessions with stakeholders. Faculty also provided opportunities for teacher candidates to provide anonymous feedback on their experiences in courses. In other cases, the project team provided opportunities for stakeholder groups to share their experiences in meetings through discussions and written reflections. The project team itself was able to identify strengths and challenges during team meetings by sharing observations and reflections.

Phase I—PD for Education Faculty

Phase I was designed focused on providing PD to Education faculty, critical stakeholders who design and implement curriculum in the SOE. The goal of the PD was to support faculty in acquiring basic CS content knowledge with a focus on CT. Simply put, Education faculty cannot plan curriculum or teach what they do not know. The PD utilized a blended format, which included an online course accompanied by face-to-face sessions. The online course includes four modules, with each module requiring approximately five hours to complete. Face-to-face sessions, such as CT in Action, were strategically planned as part of regular SOE meetings or retreats so that faculty progressed together throughout the course. The online modules provided the CT/CS content foundational knowledge needed

for integrating CS lessons within their respective foundations and methods courses taught in the teacher preparation program across all licensure levels. Current
faculty were invited to participate and were provided with a stipend. A majority
(85%, n=18) of the faculty participated. All new faculty, including adjuncts, are
now required to participate in the online PD modules as part of the on board-
ing process in the SOE. The team also saw the benefits of prototyping the four
modules that were designed in the PD online course, centered on the concepts of
CT. The modules were improved, revised, and eventually utilized in the teacher
preparation curriculum.

There are key components in each module that provide support, structure, and
consistency for participants. A course moderator supported faculty through the
online PD and facilitated the modules by answering questions via discussions and
email. Faculty could move through the modules at their own pace which allowed
for individual comfort levels and time commitments. This was an intentional design consideration as for most faculty, this was their first exposure to CT/CS content. The online format also created the space for the TeachCS@CSS team to be
mindful and responsive to the faculty's varying comfort levels with the content.
Secondly, each module was organized with objectives and a checklist of readings,
activities, and discussion prompts. Lastly, to honor the time and focus required of
the faculty members, a stipend was granted upon completion of the course.

The CT mini-course included four modules, as shown in Figure 5.3. Each module included lesson objectives, a checklist of activities to complete, and a discussion question as an opportunity to share learnings and check for understanding.
Activities included readings from the book or other resources, recorded presentations, and online CT/CS experiences (e.g., completing Code.org lessons).

Intro to CT/CS	*CT in Action*	*Exploring CT*	*Inclusive & Effective CS Methods*
• Foundational CT and CS knowledge • CT/CS as a critical literacy • CT/CS language development	Hands-on, face-to-face stations: • Build It - physical computing (MakeyMakey, robotics) • Block It - blocks programming (Scratch, Made with Code) • Unplug It - activities that do not require a computer	• Developing deeper understanding of the CT pillars • Making connections to other disciplines such as humanities, math, and science • Hands-on activities with Code.org and Google's CT for Educators course	• Using pedagogy to address bias and inequities in CT/CS education • Introducing K12 CS framework and CSTA standards

FIGURE 5.3. CT Mini-Course Modules

Module 1: Introduction to CS/CT

The first module was constructed to provide foundation knowledge of CS/CT. Using common definitions and CS language helped to build an understanding that extends across all CT/CS work. The module also provided an explanation of why CS/CT is a critical literacy that all learners should have access to across grade levels and content areas.

Module 2: CT in Action

The CT in Action module occurred in a face-to-face three-hour session as part of an SOE end of the year retreat. The CT in Action session was designed to be experiential, engaging, and hands-on. Three CT stations called, Unplug It, Block It and Build It, provided the overarching structure and allowed time for participants to experiment with the foundational pillars of CT as they moved through each station. The stations were prepared with all the necessary materials and directions to function as stations that allowed for creativity and collaboration. An intentional focus on collaboration with peers provided a safe learning space to explore and problem solve under the guidance, support, and encouragement of the TeachCS@CSS team.

Module 3: Exploring CT

Module 3 builds on Modules 1 and 2, taking a deep dive into the foundations of CT and how they each could be integrated into specific content areas. To provide context for other content areas this module incorporated work that had previously been created in Google's CT for Educators course. For educators who were ready for more hands on CS application, the module provided an opportunity to engage with Code.org's Accelerated Intro to CS Course.

Module 4: Inclusive and Effective Methods for Teaching CS

Module 4 addressed how unconscious bias can impact K–12 education, pedagogy for teaching CS, and K–12 standards and frameworks. Through online experiences and in collaboration with members from MIT's Teaching Systems Lab during a SOE retreat, Education faculty unpacked how stereotype threat and unconscious bias may surface in the CS classroom using case studies and simulations (equity teaching practice spaces). Module 4 also provided opportunities to review and unpack pedagogy that supports CS as well as review examples and models from the Krauss and Prottsman text in preparation for the SOE faculty and adjuncts to create CT/CS lessons.

Lessons Learned From Phase I

After the Education faculty participated in the online PD modules, the TeachCS@CSS team collected data during on-going discussions at department meetings where faculty shared their experience with the PD. In addition, the project evaluator surveyed faculty participants. Faculty who chose to not participate in the project shared their reasons and apprehensions as well.

- Reflections and survey data demonstrated that shared ownership was paramount. Education faculty "buy-in" became of utmost importance in order to support the progress of the project. Additionally, providing opportunities for faculty to communicate and provide feedback in a safe environment with the TeachCS@CSS team helped create a collaborative and inclusive space for learning. The TeachCS@CSS team reviewed written and oral feedback on the PD experience and utilized this for project improvement.
- CT/CS champions emerged among faculty. These faculty champions openly supported the goals of the project at meetings and agreed to participate early in the curriculum writing phase. These early adopter faculty members provided additional support to the project goals.
- Having a course moderator facilitate the online PD course by being "present" and engaged was important. As faculty progressed through the modules at different paces and new faculty members were hired, responding to individual faculty member's work and questions required consistent attention.
- Survey data from the faculty revealed that although the stipend was appreciated, it was not a determining factor for faculty to participate.

Phase II—Curriculum for All Pre-Service Teachers

After providing PD to the Education faculty, the project focused on integrating the CT/CS content in the teacher preparation curriculum. The curriculum development focused first on two areas including foundation courses and content methods courses. The PD course modules were modified and strengthened based on feedback from the Education faculty. The modules were then mapped and placed in the teacher preparation foundation courses such as technology labs, introduction courses to American education, assessment, exceptional learners, and field experiences. The undergraduate and graduate programs approached the placement and format of the content in slightly different ways, however, the content was the same for all programs. Next, CS/CT integrated lessons were developed and placed in the content methods courses.

All of the Education faculty were invited to participate in the curriculum development process and those who participated (85%) were provided a stipend upon completion of developing and teaching the lesson in their respective course. The lessons were aligned with the CSTA standards and were openly shared across various licensure areas and programs. For example, a science lesson that utilized Sphero robots was used with all graduate and undergraduate licensure programs.

A coaching process, described in detail in Chapter 9 of this book, was used to facilitate the creation of these lessons. As part of the coaching process, an Education faculty member collaborated with a CS content expert (coach) to create CT/CS lesson plans and activities aligned with courses within the teacher preparation program curriculum. These collaborative curriculum design teams utilized a design sprint approach—a framework utilizing time constraints and design thinking phases to quickly generate a product (i.e., a lesson plan). This design sprint process helped answer critical questions through rapid prototyping and testing while reaching clearly defined goals and deliverables. The aim of the design sprint is to spark innovation, encourage student-centered thinking, and align teams under a shared vision for the focus of the instructional plans.

An example of one of the first lessons introducing teacher candidates to CT/CS is provided in Figure 5.4. This lesson, placed early in the curriculum, utilized components of Module 1 from the online PD course on CT. The objective of this

Time	First CS Lesson in Foundation Course Instructional Steps Slide Presentation Common Language Activity

10 min	**Anticipatory Set**
	Invisible Continuum Activity- Familiarity and comfort with CS. Describe an invisible line at the front of the room. One end is 1- you are very comfortable and other end of the line is 10 not comfortable at all. Using the following question prompts, teacher candidates physically move to the area on the line that best describes their comfort level on the question prompts.
	  1. How comfortable are you in your understanding of Computational Thinking?
	  2. What is your knowledge base on Computational Thinking?
	  3. How comfortable are you using the concepts of Computational Thinking in classroom setting?
	  4. Teacher candidates are able to empathize with one another and it opens a discussion on what do you know now after reading the first 3 chapters and what are you wanting to know more of by the end of this lesson.

60 min	**Instructional Activities**
	  1. Whole Group Discussion
	     ○ Define Computational Thinking (Quote from Wing)
	     ○ What is Computational Thinking?
	     ○ What is Computer Science?
	     ○ Making Connections
	  2. Common Language Activity
	     ○ Use the vocabulary and definition materials.
	  3. Participate in two unplugged activities
	     ○ Unplugged Activity 1: The Muddy City
	     ○ Unplugged Activity 2: The Orange Game
	  4. Choose one coding activity to participate in using Pair Programming Strategy.
	     ○ Code.org - Accelerated Course (Elementary-Middle School)
	     ○ Javascript.com by Code School

5 min	**Closure- Exit Ticket**
	  1. In what ways have you thought differently about CT?
	  2. How might you plan to include CT in future lesson plans or specific content areas?
	  3. In what ways have you thought differently about; decomposition, pattern matching, abstraction and algorithms (automation)?

FIGURE 5.4. Lesson: Introduction to Computational Thinking and Computer Science

first lesson provided the foundation of the CS for All movement and provided teacher candidates with an introduction to CT.

Lessons were also created for content methods courses such as science and social studies. Figure 5.5 provides an example of an elementary social studies methods lesson. The lesson was aligned with three Minnesota Standards of Effective Practice for New Teachers, including (1) Standard 1: Subject Matter; (2) Standard 3: Instructional Strategies; and (3) Standard 7: Planning Instruction. The intersection of these three standards with CS content provided an opportunity for teacher candidates to meet the required Minnesota-based American Indian tribes' social studies standards in grades 5 and 6, as students practiced how to plan for and use instructional strategies that support and model how CS content can be taught in social studies. One goal of this lesson was to demonstrate and model an integrated CS and content instructional approach instead of a CS stand-alone experience. The lesson also addressed critical equity concepts and approaches and asks teacher candidates to review and apply the CSTA standards to their instructional planning.

To support the dissemination, communication, and organization of the CS integrated lessons, the TeachCS@CSS project created a website, teachcs.css.edu. The website provides an opportunity to share the open-source TeachCS@CSS project internally and globally, providing information to members of the SOE as well as other teacher education programs and stakeholders. The website continues to be expanded and new information is added as the project changes and grows. Eventually, the website will include access to the online PD course discussed earlier. In addition, the project created a program schema to provide curriculum mapping for the CT/CS lessons throughout the teacher preparation program. These program schemas helped to ensure that CT/CS lessons were introduced and reinforced throughout the program.

To provide feedback on Phase II of the project, the TeachCS@CSS project evaluator surveyed the undergraduate and graduate teacher candidates after they participated in the revised curriculum. The survey data from the teacher candidates showed that 64% (n=25) of those who participated in the survey indicated they were either "a little knowledgeable" or "not very knowledgeable" about CS concepts when they *started* the program. While only 16% indicated that they were "knowledgeable" when they *started* the program. The teacher candidate survey data showed a dramatic difference after their participation in the revised curriculum with 84% indicating that they were "extremely knowledgeable', "very knowledgeable," or "knowledgeable" about computer science concepts. The data suggest that the revised curriculum had a positive impact on the teacher candidates' perception of computer science concepts.

To gather other stakeholder information about the project, faculty member, Long, gathered reflective anonymous feedback from the undergraduate Elementary Education Degree Completion Program students about their experience with the CS/CT modules and lessons. Several of these reflective statements shared

Elementary Social Studies CS Lesson Plan

Time	Instructional Steps and Learning Tasks
10 Min.	Review 4 pillars of computational thinking matching the pillar to the definition. Computational Thinking (CT) has four distinct parts: Decomposition, Pattern Recognition (Pattern Matching, Abstraction and Algorithms (Automation). Project this lesson plan to model for teacher candidates as well as to share the objective, assessments, and process. Teacher candidates will choose one lesson from a previously created lesson plan from the Native American Unit created for this class. The objective is to purposefully integrate computational thinking into the lesson. Read and review Krauss & Prottsman (2017) pp.45-83 (with pp. 137-140 as optional inspiration).
15 Min.	Select one of the lessons previously created for the Native American Unit to integrate with computational thinking strategies from the reading. Discuss alignment among CT, social studies standards, instructional strategies, and assessment. Investigate the CSTA K-12 Standards, which can be found here: CSTA Standards

45-60 Min	With a peer, provide time to work on the lesson plan that you have converted to a google doc.
	1. Start with Objective/Standard/Assessment alignment.
	2. Then move to the procedural portion of the lesson plan.
	  • Select an appropriate standard, and add it to the lesson plan. NOTE: Use Krauss & Prottsman's words as inspiration and to generate ideas.
	  • Revisit the learning objective and target from the lesson to re-word if necessary, given the new standard CT added.
	  • In the Instructional Strategies and Learning Tasks portion of the lesson, add or change information to reflect the focus on Computational Thinking
	  • Be mindful of the transitions, accommodations, differentiation, materials used, and higher order thinking questions planned within the lesson.
	Bold all changes made
	This could be extended to complete for homework and then shared at the next class session. Another option is to post on blackboard for peers to share and comment.
	  • Submit this revised lesson in Blackboard.
	CS Information for detailed assignment instructions.
	
	Closure:
	Share the revised lesson plan with another group. Google folder to upload lessons to share with everyone.
	Praise- something specific, Question- what question do you have, Polish - what is something they may want to revise

FIGURE 5.5. Lesson: Elementary Social Studies

below demonstrate the students' positive experience and ideas about how they believe they could use the CS content with their future K12 students. One student stated; *"I have more positive thoughts about computational thinking because it doesn't involve strictly using technology. Rather, it's using problem-solving and critical thinking to answer questions."* Another student shared, *"I could plan hands-on activities integrating CT to also help with community building. They would be good morning meeting activities."* One student summed up her experience stating, *"Computational thinking is not that scary and it is actually related to things that we use in our daily lives."* A review of the reflective statements suggests that students were able to see connections to other areas of the K–12 curriculum and were also reassured that the content is something they could teach.

Lessons Learned From Phase II

- The TeachCS@CSS team experienced and observed challenges with scheduling support with adjunct faculty through the PD and the coaching process. Adjunct faculty have less flexibility often due to other demands on their time.
- Survey data, reflections, and discussions with faculty revealed varied comfort levels, content knowledge, and time commitment from faculty and these aspects played a factor in creating lessons and participation in the coaching model.
- Building a sustainable coaching model proved to be an important consideration, especially for new Education faculty and adjuncts due to the time commitment for all stakeholders.
- Survey data and course reflections suggest that teacher candidates are eager for more CT/CS information and resources.

Phase III — PD and Co-Design with K–12 School Partners

Teacher candidates need opportunities to apply educational theory and pedagogical approaches in the K12 classroom to practice and improve their teaching competencies. The TeachCS@CSS project understood the need to provide teacher candidates with opportunities to teach CS/CT integrated lessons so that they could build experience and confidence in teaching this unfamiliar content area. At The CSS, teacher candidates are required to complete field experiences in three semesters in K–12 schools before student teaching. As part of these experiences, teacher candidates are required to create and teach lessons, applying new ideas from foundation and methods courses. Cooperating teachers in the schools fulfill a critical role in providing essential mentoring and support to teacher candidates. Normally, cooperating teachers serve as the content and pedagogical expert during these field experiences. However, because CS and CT are new concepts for most cooperating teachers, the TeachCS@CSS project decided to collaborate with partner schools who would be willing to pilot field experiences where teacher candidates could teach CS/CT integrated content.

Four various types of K–12 partner schools were identified as part of the TeachCS@CSS project to provide opportunities to pilot the teaching of CT/CS integrated lessons in field experiences. As part of this partnership, the schools agreed to collaborate to offer PD in CS and CT to their cooperating teachers where teacher candidates would be placed for their field experience. Two K–12 partner schools are located near the Duluth main campus, and two schools are located in the Twin Cities area near extended campuses. These four schools were approached based on the SOE's successful history of working with schools and their willingness to work with the project. One partner school, a public middle and high school, had previous experience hosting many teacher candidates in field experiences. In another case, an Education faculty served as a board member for a private high school. Another elementary public charter school was recommended due to its focus on STEM. And, due to the College's long-time commitment to serving the Native American population in the Duluth area the project team approached and secured a partnership with a rural tribal K–12 school.

The project team was mindful of the differences in each school and worked individually and in collaboration with their teachers and administrators to provide PD that met the needs of their teachers. The PD sessions held with the partner schools were grounded and informed by the PD experiences with the Education faculty and were modified based on the needs and feedback from the school partners. Typically, the initial PD session consisted of pre-workshop preparation where teachers were asked to read an article about CT and the importance of broadening participation in CS. Next, the TeachCS@CSS team facilitated sessions at the partner school where teachers participated in small and whole group discussions regarding the CT definition and CT pillars. Teachers then participated in the CT in Action stations described earlier in this chapter. To close the PD session, a critical reflection and discussion activity was provided to encourage teachers to think about how CS/CT could be taught in their classrooms.

In addition, the project team shared the SOE field experience information and protocols with the cooperating teachers at the partner schools. This information provided general field experience expectation information, including the responsibilities of the teacher candidates. The TeachCS@CSS team also hosted webinars with cooperating teachers and field supervisors about supporting teacher candidates in the field. In particular, the project team discussed the new expectation for teacher candidates to be able to teach CS/CT integrated lessons. This information included protocols for scheduling lesson observations and recommendations for providing reflective feedback.

While PD was provided to many teachers in the partner schools, it is important to note that not all teacher candidates were able to conduct their field experiences in partner schools. Instead, we placed a small pilot group of teacher candidates at each partner school. The project's goal of the field experience pilot was to learn what design and implementation elements were most effective and least effective or challenging. In this way, Phase III of the model could be strengthened before implementing the new CS/CT integrated field experiences on a larger scale.

Once the teacher candidates were identified and matched with a cooperating teacher, additional support and planning were provided by the project team and CS coaches. The following stakeholders participated in planning the pilot field experience: cooperating teacher(s), tech integration specialist, teacher candidate(s), CS content coach, and field experience supervisors. Planning meetings were held at each of the four partner schools in order to customize the experience to fit the context for each teacher candidate and classroom. These planning meetings provided an opportunity to build community, brainstorm possibilities for lessons, and developing logistics and timelines. To provide additional instructional support to teacher candidates, brief check-ins between the teacher candidate and the CS content coach provided opportunities to create lessons that integrated CS/CT in the content area.

While a great deal of time and effort was spent to plan and collaborate with stakeholders, in practice there were challenges that were not anticipated. Specifically, it proved challenging to schedule meetings where all stakeholders could attend. Therefore, some of the stakeholders were not as informed about the process as planned. Secondly, due to a variety of factors, that included finding a common time to meet in the timeframe the teacher candidate needed to teach their lesson, the lesson may not have been observed by the field supervisor as planned. Lastly, field supervisors did not receive enough training to understand CS/CT in order to provide effective feedback to teacher candidates regarding their lessons.

As part of the pilot, the teacher candidates who delivered CT/CS lesson plans in their field experiences provided feedback about the project as part of a reflection activity. Teacher candidates shared what new knowledge they gained as well as questions and their emotional response to the experience. Examples of feedback from several teacher candidates included:

- I have more positive thoughts about computational thinking because it doesn't strictly involve using technology. Rather, it's using problem solving and critical thinking to answer questions. I can now plan hands-on activities integrating CT even in building community within the classroom. I am not so terrified about the terms (decomposition, pattern matching, abstraction, and algorithm) because we are making connections naturally when we solve problems.
- It's more about the thought process than about computer.
- By participating in the CS in Action activities in class, I have noticed that I am thinking more intentionally about what and how I am teaching instead of simply having students complete a task.
- It is important to understand and engage in practices that address my implicit biases and microaggressions that I have as a teacher. All students should have access to all subject areas. Students shouldn't feel like their culture or a stereotype keeps them in a certain subject area or out of a certain subject area. Subjects should be equitable.

These compelling reflections demonstrate the impact of the revised teacher preparation curriculum on teacher candidates. Reflective statements such as these have helped to inform the direction of the project and suggest that teacher candidates who had the opportunity to participate saw the value in the project, understood equity issues in CS, and saw opportunities to integrate CT content. However, observations from CS coaches indicated that more work needs to be done to address a deeper understanding of CT content and how teacher candidates can strengthen their lessons to better align with CSTA Standards.

Lesson Learned From Phase III

- Survey data, course reflections, and project debriefing sessions suggest that while the TeachCS@CSS model planned and implemented critical stakeholder field experience planning meetings, the face-to-face format for these meetings is not sustainable due to the time commitments and scheduling difficulties. Considerations for future planning may include utilizing web-based conferencing to accommodate schedules.
- The TeachCS@CSS project team understands the need to collect more data to inform what aspects of the coaching model are crucial to support the teacher candidates in field experiences.
- Teacher candidate survey data and lesson observation feedback revealed that providing more opportunities for teacher candidates to interact with CT/CS material across the curriculum as well as practice teaching CS integrated lessons may be beneficial.
- Lesson observation feedback from CS content coaches revealed that it was sometimes difficult to determine the cause of the field experience challenges teacher candidates experienced. For example, in some cases teacher candidates may have struggled with the CS/CT content and this may have caused challenges with managing the class procedures and student behaviors.

NEXT STEPS

An analogy the TeachCS@CSS team often used was, "We are building the airplane as we are flying it." Currently, there are no models of teacher preparation programs in the U.S that aligned with the goals of TeachCS@CSS. While a few U.S teacher preparation programs have infused CS into their curriculum, typically this has occurred in the secondary mathematics and science licensure areas or in a stand-alone educational technology course (Yadav et al., 2017; see also Chapters 2 and 7). The SOE at the CSS is the first to integrate CT/CS across all licensure levels, K–6, 5–12 (e.g., social science, communication arts, mathematics) and K–12 (e.g., Spanish), and content areas. Therefore, the TeachCS@CSS team needed to create new program models, processes, and templates that guided the work of the project. In addition, the team built a repository of documents, hosted on the project's website, that supports the design and provides examples of products such as lesson plans and program schemas.

As described earlier, the TeachCS@CSS project was designed and implemented utilizing three phases. Components of these phases and the products, such as the online PD in CT, are ever-evolving and require a process for continual improvement that consists of design, implementation, and feedback cycles. As the project progresses, the Education faculty and TeachCS@CSS team are aware of the following components that need to be addressed.

- The CSTA and Minnesota Standards of Effective Practice for New Teachers need to be further unpacked and TeachCS@CSS stakeholders need to engage in curriculum mapping and crosswalks to determine potential gaps as well as create a robust scope and sequence.
- Adjustments need to be made to address the known CT/CS curriculum gaps and to strengthen scaffolding for the content in the teacher preparation curriculum.
- The TeachCS@CSS team needs to ensure that the vision and mission of the project is clearly articulated to all stakeholders and becomes part of the "regular course of doing business."
- The TeachCS@CSS team needs to better understand the role of Shulman's (1986) Pedagogical Content Knowledge (PCK), which speaks to the specialized pedagogy that may be required to effectively teach a content area. PCK includes teacher interpretation of the content, understanding of student misconceptions, and assessment (see Chapter 4 for a more detailed discussion on PCK). While long-established content areas such as mathematics have a body of research to support PCK, there is little in the area of K12 computer science content, including how to support teacher candidates.
- The role of field experiences in teaching CS needs to be explored further. Teacher candidates need to move from theory to actual practice in order to develop effective and equitable teaching strategies (Darling-Hammond & Bransford, 2007).
- The role of coaches for teacher candidates in field experiences needs future exploration. Pierce & Buysee (2014) note that implementing new teaching practices from PD with the support of a coach, may increase the likelihood of adoption from 20% to 80%. The team would like to explore this concept further.
- Additionally, an exploration of the observation and evaluation tools that teacher preparation programs utilize to assess teacher candidates need to be examined. Are the current tools sufficient or are others needed to fully capture CT/CS as it is integrated in lessons and field experiences?
- The project team has identified a need to further explore what is the appropriate amount of CT/CS content knowledge that Education faculty and

teacher candidates need to integrate the subject into their lessons. What is the best way to measure this knowledge?

While there are many complexities, barriers, and areas that require further research and attention in how to best support teacher candidates to address CT/CS in teacher preparation, it is important that these barriers do become reasons for moving forward. Teacher candidates, who experience a curriculum such as TeachCS@CSS, have an opportunity to become advocates and change agents in their future classrooms and schools and will be better prepared to address the equity gap in CS education.

REFERENCES

Computer Science Teachers Association (CSTA). (2013). *Bugs in the system: Computer science teacher certification in the U.S.* https://csteachers.org/documents/en-us/3b4a70cd-2a9b-478b-95cd-376530c3e976/1

Computer Science Teachers Association (CSTA). (2017). *CSTA K12 standards.* https://www.csteachers.org/page/standards

Council of Chief State School Officers (CCSSO). (2016). *Interstate new teacher assessment and support consortium* (INTASC). http://programs.ccsso.org/projects/interstate_new_teacher_assessment_and_support_consortium/

Darling-Hammond, L., & Bransford, J. (2007*). Preparing teachers for a changing world*: *What teachers should learn and be able to do.* Jossey-Bass.

Darling-Hammond, L., Hyler, M. E., & Gardner, M. (2017). *Effective teacher professional development.* Learning Policy Institute.

DeLyser, L., Goode, J., Guzdial, M., Kafai, Y., & Yadav, A. (2018). *Priming the computer science teacher pump: Integrating computer science education into schools of education.* CSforALL.

Erickson, L. B., & Wentworth, N. (2010). *Tensions in teacher preparation : Accountability, assessment, and accreditation* (Vol. 1st ed). Emerald Group Publishing Limited.

Garet, M. S., Porter, A. C., Desimone, L., Birman, B. F., & Yoon, K. S. (2001). What makes professional development effective? Results from a national sample of teachers. *American Educational Research Journal, 38*(4), 915–945. doi:10.3102/00028312038004915

International Society for Technology in Education (ISTE). (2016). *ISTE standards for students.* https://www.iste.org/standards/for-students

Krauss, J., & Prottsman, K. (2016). *Computational thinking and coding for every student: The teacher's getting started guide.* Corwin.

Metzler, M. (2009). The great debate over teacher education reform escalates: More rhetoric or a new reality? *Journal of Teaching in Physical Education, 28*(3), 293–309. http://search.ebscohost.com.akin.css.edu/login.aspx?direct=true&db=s3h&AN=42734548&site=eds-live&scope=site

National Science Foundation. (n.d.). https://www.nsf.gov/news/special_reports/csed/cs-forall.jsp

Pierce, J., & Buysse, V. (2014). *Effective coaching: Improving teacher practice and outcomes for all learners* (Rep.). WestEd National Center for Systematic Improvement. doi: https://ncsi-library.wested.org/resources/57

Shulman, L. S. (1986). Those who understand: Knowledge growth in teaching. *Educational Researcher, 15*(2), 4. doi:10.2307/1175860

Wing, J. M. (2006). Computational thinking. *Communications of the ACM*, 49, 33–35. doi:10.1145/1118178.1118215

Yadav, A., Stephenson, C., Hong, H. (2017). Computational thinking for teacher education. *Communications of the ACM, 60*, 55–62. doi: 10.1145/2994591. https://cacm.acm.org/magazines/2017/4/215031-computational-thinking-for-teacher-education/fulltext

CHAPTER 6

TEACHING TEACHERS

A Computer Science Methods Course

Michelle Friend

In order to meet the needs of schools to provide high quality computer science education for all students in elementary and secondary schools, computer science teachers must be prepared. While future teachers can learn content from computer science courses, colleges of education must provide methods courses that support teachers' development of pedagogical skills and pedagogical content knowledge. This chapter describes a CS Teaching Methods Course developed at the University of Nebraska at Omaha (UNO) as an exemplar of one approach to preparing computer science teachers.

Keywords: Pedagogy, Pre-service Teachers, CS Teaching Methods

INTRODUCTION

As pressure to provide computer science (CS) in K–12 schools grows, an increasing number of states are creating CS teaching endorsements—the certification that allows public school teachers to teach CS. While content area courses already exist to prepare these future teachers in computing, colleges of education must

Preparing Pre-Service Teachers to Teach Computer Science: Models, Practices, and Policies,
pages 113–128.

create specialized CS methods courses or determine how to address the specialized methods of teaching CS within existing methods courses.

This chapter describes a CS Teaching Methods Course developed at the University of Nebraska at Omaha (UNO). In Nebraska, computer science is a supplemental credential: pre-service teacher candidates (or in-service teachers) with a different primary discipline can add the CS credential by taking five computing courses and the CS Teaching Methods Course. This chapter first presents the system of teacher credentialing, then describes features of the course including goals, format, and assignments. Throughout the chapter, pre-service teachers enrolled in the class will be referred to as "candidates," while "students" is reserved for the K–12 students who these candidates teach.

BACKGROUND

Teacher Certification

In the United States, the regulation of education occurs largely at the state level. Each state determines the requirements for teachers to gain a teaching credential, also known as a teaching endorsement or teaching license, which gives teachers the legal right to teach in public schools. There are most commonly two types of teaching credentials: multi-subject and single-subject. A multi-subject credential certifies a teacher to work in a self-contained classroom across all disciplines. These are most commonly elementary classrooms. Although in practice an elementary teacher may work with a team, and specialize in one or more subjects, the credential ensures competence with all major areas—mathematics, English, social studies, and science. A single-subject credential certifies a teacher to work in a departmentalized class usually found in middle and high school, grades six through 12. Teachers are certified to teach only the specific discipline(s) found on the credential, such as mathematics, English, or one or more sciences. A third type of credential is the PK–12 (pre-kindergarten through twelfth grade) credential which certifies the teacher to teach all grades. This is most common in non-core subjects, including art and music.

Teachers may seek a second endorsement area, such as a mathematics teacher who seeks out a science or business credential. These additional credentials can enhance a teacher's ability to get a job, because of the flexibility of being able to teach multiple subjects. In some disciplines this is quite common. For example, physical education teachers are often also certified to teach health. In some states, each science is an independent credential; for example, a chemistry teacher may also seek certification as a biology or physics teacher.

There are also supplemental certifications—certifications added on to another certification, but that cannot be the primary endorsed discipline. In Nebraska, the endorsement to teach CS is a supplementary endorsement that certifies the holder to teach computing from PK–12.

The Path to Certification

Pre-service teachers in any area must be prepared both with a strong grounding in content and also with a strong pedagogical foundation. The most common way to become a teacher is through a teacher preparation program at a college or university. These programs determine a plan of study for pre-service teacher candidates that ensures they meet the state licensure requirements. Teacher preparation programs typically require candidates to take a number of content courses from disciplinary experts, as well as education courses covering general teaching topics such as lesson planning, classroom management, and teaching diverse learners. One of the final courses in a teacher preparation program is a course in teaching methods in the discipline (e.g., Abell et al., 2010; Hazzan et al., 2011). This course is critical in providing teacher candidates with a foundation in pedagogical content knowledge (Shulman, 1986), the integration of how to best teach the subject at hand to the students present.

EXEMPLARS: CS TEACHING METHODS COURSE

Pre-service teacher candidates at the University of Nebraska at Omaha (UNO) who wish to teach CS must receive an "Information Technology" (IT) supplemental endorsement. Although titled information technology, the endorsement is rigorously focused on CS. A PK–12 endorsement, it is designed to prepare CS teachers to teach all levels from kindergarten through AP Computer Science. This endorsement is added on to a primary endorsement in another subject (e.g., business, mathematics, or history). Thus, for their primary endorsement, candidates are required to take content courses in their primary subject area, as well as at least three general education courses, including developmental psychology, lesson planning, and a general teaching methods course. They also have to take additional computer science content and pedagogy courses.

The IT supplemental endorsement requires candidates to have completed five CS content courses and a CS teaching methods course. All candidates must take *CS Principles* and *Introduction to Computer Science I,* and *Introduction to Computer Science II*, which cover programming, data structures, algorithmic design, and problem solving. For the remaining two courses, candidates have a choice of several CS electives including *Introduction to Web Development, Programming on the Internet, Networking*, and *Cybersecurity.*

In addition to the CS teaching methods course, candidates concurrently enroll in the teaching methods course for their primary endorsement area. Through the primary methods course, candidates complete a practicum experience, where they spend approximately 50 hours in a classroom under the supervision of a classroom teacher, and are expected to teach (and video record) at least four lessons. Candidates in the *CS Teaching Methods Course* are required to provide a video of themselves teaching a lesson related to CS to students, usually recorded as one of the four lessons for their primary methods course. Candidates generally have some latitude in creating the lesson, but they must fit it into the curriculum of the course. Some effort is made to place candidates in practicum experiences where they can gain CS teaching experience, though this is not always possible. For example, a candidate whose primary endorsement is in business will likely be placed with a mentor teacher who teaches both business and CS classes. However, not all schools offer CS, and due to space and organization limitations, students may not have the opportunity to teach in a CS class. Because CS can be integrated into other content areas, the professor and candidate work together to design appropriate lessons for the candidate to get practice teaching computing concepts when it is not possible for the candidate to have a pure CS experience.

One feature of this *CS Teaching Methods* course is that it is available to both undergraduate pre-service teacher candidates and to graduate students adding the IT endorsement. Because of this cross-listing, it is taught as a hybrid, where students meet in person four times for three hours, completing the rest of the work online, in accordance with the design of the graduate teaching education program.

CS Teaching Methods Course Syllabus—Overview

Teachers must acquire three areas of knowledge, skills, and dispositions to be effective: (a) knowledge of learners and how they learn and develop within social contexts; (b) knowledge of subject matter and curriculum goals; and (c) an understanding of teaching in light of the content, learners, and context (Bransford, Darling-Hammond et al., 2005, pp. 10–11). In the UNO program, knowledge of subject matter itself is provided through the CS content courses, but understanding diverse learners (Carter & Darling-Hammond, 2016), pedagogical content knowledge (Hubbard, 2018; Shulman, 1986), and how to design learning experiences to align with curricular goals (Bransford, Derry et al., 2005) are covered in the *CS Teaching Methods* course. In order to support candidates in developing an understanding of these areas, there are seven learning outcomes associated with the course:

1. Become familiar with CS curricula and standards
2. Become familiar with multiple pedagogies useful in conveying CS concepts
3. Be proficient in recognizing and addressing issues of equity and access in computing
4. Differentiate instruction and use culturally responsive practices to enhance student learning
5. Design effective assessments of students' knowledge of computational topics and monitor student progress to inform instruction
6. Incorporate current research-based learning theory and instructional strategies to support student learning
7. Systematically and critically examine teaching practices of self and others

The course is organized around five curriculum units which address these outcomes: (1) curriculum & standards, (2) pedagogies, (3) assessment, (4) equity, access, & differentiation, and (5) pedagogical content knowledge & misconceptions.

Although to some extent the framework (Bransford, Darling-Hammond, et al., 2005) is individually addressed in different units, the reality is that all units touch upon all aspects of teaching and learning. For example, knowledge of learners and contexts are included in the equity unit, knowledge of subject matter and learning goals are included in the curriculum & standards unit, and knowledge of teaching is included in the remaining units. The course is further guided by the *How People Learn* framework as described in National Research Council (2000), in which candidates must learn to reflexively be knowledge-centered, learner-centered, community-centered, and assessment-centered in order to effectively support student learning.

The first two units—curriculum & standards and pedagogies—are introduced simultaneously, at the beginning of the course. Each of the remaining units is centered around a subsequent class meeting and continues for several weeks, encompassing a related project, reading, and online discussion.

Unit 1: Curriculum & Standards

The curriculum & standards unit is fairly brief. The goal is to ensure that candidates are grounded in the state and national standards they will be expected to teach, and have an introduction to various curricula available for addressing those standards. This is generally a review since throughout their other teacher education coursework, candidates are well aware of state standards and how to write lesson plans that address standards as learning outcomes. Further, because of the CS content courses, including the CS Principles course, candidates are familiar with at least some CS curricula. Through discussion, candidates are asked to reflect upon how the curricula meet the learning goals, and how curricula address goals in different ways, in order to develop the ability to critically think about how curriculum enacts learning goals and how it can be effected by teachers. They are also asked to self-assess against the CS Educator Standards (CS Educator Standards, 2019) and reflect on how to gain mastery.

Unit 2: Pedagogies

The idea of pedagogies specific to teaching CS is introduced early in the course and continues throughout, especially as each course meeting includes candidates engaging as learners with a pedagogy they may not have previously encountered. Candidates participate in the activity, then discuss it as a teaching strategy, reflecting on how they might use it, and how students might engage and learn from the activity.

One pedagogical activity occurs at the opening of the first class: the "First Day" Role Play (Levine, n.d.). These role plays are an opportunity for candidates to understand object-oriented programming by acting as objects. In the First Day Role Play, each candidate is given a card that tells them what kind of object they are and what behaviors they can act out. For example, a candidate may receive a card titled "You are an Acrobat" followed by the instructions "When you are asked to **clap**, you will be given a number. Clap your hands that many times." The "You are a Calculator" card has an instruction, "When you are asked to **add**, you will be given two numbers. Reply (verbally) with their sum. Note that you can only add two numbers—not just one (or none) and not three or more." The "You are a FancyAdder" card has an instruction, "When you are asked to **add**, you may be given many numbers. Find a calculator and ask the calculator to add the first two. Then ask the calculator to add that sum and the next number. Continue until you have a sum of all the numbers. Reply verbally to your 'boss' with the sum." A list is created on the board of the candidates and what kind of object they are, and the instructor—acting as the driver—calls on candidates and gives them commands, such as "Jamie, clap 3." This is an engaging opportunity to build community and help candidates (and the instructor) learn each other's names in a computing context. It also introduces programming concepts including state, data passing, polymorphism, and multiple instances. Throughout and at the end of the activity, candidates are asked to reflect on what is going on, to ensure they understand the analogy between the activity and programming, and also to introduce vocabulary. For example, candidates immediately notice that the FancyAdder has a different add routine than the Calculator, and quickly understand that different objects can have different implementations of the same function. At the end of the activity, there is a discussion about how to implement it in class, a reflection on what went well and could have gone better, and what the curricular and learning goals of the activity were.

As their reading assignment during the first unit, candidates respond to articles about kinesthetic learning activities in CS (e.g., Begel et al., 2004; McConnell, 2005). In order to support high quality teaching, the project for this unit is to research an evidence-based teaching strategy, and to synthesize findings into a handout or infographic that introduces the strategy to other teachers. Students share their handouts with each other. Topics have ranged from traditional CS pedagogies like pair programming, in which two students work together in a structured way with one directing and one typing (Braught et al., 2011) to traditional education pedagogies like reciprocal teaching, in which one student leads small group discussion (Hattie, 2008, pp. 203–204; Palincsar & Brown, 1984) and accountable talk, a style and guide to leading rich student discussions where students engage with each other and provide evidence for their ideas (Michaels & O'Connor, 2012). Candidates are supported in finding a topic, particularly through resources such as *Visible Teaching*, a series of meta-reviews of effective educational research (Hattie, 2008) and CS education pedagogy reviews (e.g., Lathrop, 2010).

Unit 3: Assessment

The unit on assessment centers around the idea of open-ended assignments and rubrics. It introduces candidates to the idea of evidence-centered design in creating assessments (Pellegrino, 2014) and equitable grading practices (Feldman, 2018). Although the use of rubrics is a best practice (Brookhart, 2013), many candidates are more familiar with checklist-style grading and closed-ended computing exercises than the open-ended projects that promote true student creativity and engagement. This unit also provides an opportunity to discuss a variety of issues around assessment. Candidates are usually already familiar with formative assessment (use of assessment to inform instruction), but they are pushed to think about as many ways to systematically collect information on how their students are doing as possible (e.g. structured discussions where all students speak, observations, pre-learning quizzes, etc.). Candidates are introduced to the Zone of Proximal Development (ZPD) (Vygotsky, 1978), or the difference between what a learner can do without help and what they can do with help. They investigate how teachers—and other students—can support student learning, and that there is a difference between a form of help that increases learning versus someone doing the work for a learner. This leads naturally to the challenges of assessing collaborative work and the introduction of a variety of approaches including the idea of using collaborative work only for learning and not for assessment (Feldman, 2018). The project for this unit is to design or modify an assignment and create a rubric to assess student work.

Unit 4: Equity, Access, and Differentiation

Equity, Access, and Differentiation are topics that students are generally already familiar with, both from previous teacher education courses and also because of the widespread discussions and reporting about lack of diversity in computing. Although the Omaha Public Schools are the most diverse in the state, many candidates are most familiar and comfortable with gender equity as the major issue they will face as teachers. In addition to referring to published resources such as *Stuck in the Shallow End* (Margolis et al., 2008) that introduce candidates to the impact of inequity and implicit bias in schools, candidates are also introduced to the idea of 'hidden minority' students they may encounter, such as students who are homeless or have learning differences that might affect their learning and performance. One assignment is to create a *CT Bin* to add to a repository of activities; this assignment is described in more detail below. Because this unit occurs late in the semester, the required project is a video lesson and reflection. Candidates must plan a lesson and video record themselves teaching it to students. The videos are posted so that other candidates can see them. Candidates must reflect on their own video and give feedback to other students as well. The reflection focuses on how the candidate differentiated and used formative assessment to modify instruction.

Unit 5: Pedagogical Content Knowledge & Misconceptions

Although candidates have been learning pedagogical content knowledge (PCK) throughout the semester, in the final unit, PCK is introduced as a term and concept (Shulman, 1986). PCK is explained as synthesis of teachers professional knowledge base, which includes knowledge of assessment, pedagogy, content, curriculum, and students (Gess-Newsome, 2015), enacted through teacher practice. Because Shulman envisioned PCK as interacting strongly with student misconceptions, and because much of the CS education literature relating to PCK examines misconceptions, most of the assignments focus on CS misconceptions. Candidates brainstorm and read about common misconceptions identified in CS (e.g., Kaczmarczyk et al., 2010; Simon et al., 2006). Candidates are introduced to concept cartoons and assigned to create a concept cartoon for CS, discussed in more detail below.

Sample Assignments

The course is largely project-based, providing candidates the opportunity to practice the skills they will need as CS teachers. In addition to projects, students are also required to read and respond to articles about CS teaching, largely from the Special Interest Group in Computer Science Education conference. In-class time focuses on experiencing CS pedagogy and on discussion, primarily of typical experiences and challenges in CS classes. For example, many practicing teachers do "code-alongs" where they lead students in live programming, yet that is a challenge because students struggle to stay on pace with the instructor—some get lost while others race ahead. Candidates can brainstorm how to address these issues, discuss ways to avoid running into them, and in general work through common challenges in teaching CS before experiencing them.

Some of the assignments, particularly the video lesson and teaching strategy handout, are straightforward and common across teaching methods courses. Three assignments—the CS Autobiography, the Concept Cartoon, and the CT Bin—are unique and described in more detail.

CS Autobiography

In the CS Autobiography, candidates are asked to write about their experiences with CS. This assignment is based on work in mathematics education (Allen & Schnell, 2016; Lawler & Gargroetzi, 2017). The assignment is due by the end of the first week of class; in the hybrid schedule, this means candidates submit the assignment before the first class meeting. Full credit is given to students who complete the assignment. Figure 6.1 shows a screen shot of the assignment from the course Learning Management System.

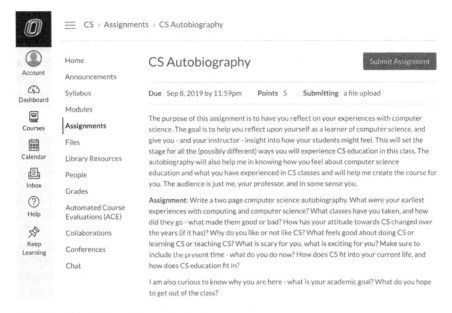

FIGURE 6.1.   CS Autobiography Assignment

This assignment has multiple purposes. First, as described in the prompt, it helps build community and gives the instructor a sense of who is in the course, their preparation and experiences with computing, and their feelings about CS. The instructor reports generally on the responses during the first class, noting similarities across the class, which can give candidates a sense of community with each other as well. A second benefit is that candidates are introduced to the CS Autobiography as a pedagogical tool. As described in Allen and Schnell (2016), there are a variety of ways to use this assignment with younger students, including allowing artistic expression that can be displayed in the classroom, and can be further revisited at the end of the year so students can see their growth as learners. The third benefit is as a form of data. Analysis of the autobiographies demonstrates interesting trends regarding the identities of prospective computer science teachers.

The autobiographies are long, and because candidates have a reasonable expectation of privacy, none are reproduced in whole here. However, there are themes and examples appropriate for sharing. Over two years of collecting autobiographies, nearly all candidates describe using computers during their childhoods. About half the candidates have vivid memories of playing computer games, which range based on their ages. Many of the candidates describe dying of dysentery in *Oregon Trail*. One candidate wrote, "My CS world was blown away when we got a Commodore 64 for Christmas. Now that was amazing, we were able to not only play games but type out documents and do some basic computer programing. However it was mainly used for game play." Younger candidates describe more recent technologies such as Nintendo game stations. Candidates also frequently describe programming and tinkering as introductions to an interest in CS. One candidate's autobiography described this introduction:

> I first got interested in Computer Science when I was in high school. I was always interested in learning programming and making things on the computer. So my sophomore year of high school I took my school's first level programming class and each year after took the subsequent. The classes covered BASIC, C++ then Java my final year.

For some of the candidates, their own interest in computing was what motivated their desire to become a CS teacher, but many were motivated either by providing meaningful CS experiences for their students. For example, one in-service teacher responded to the prompt talking about his/her students: "After teaching a Fundamentals of Information Technology class for two years, I decided I wanted to give my students a better knowledge of technology and encourage more students to student computer science."

Candidates' attitudes tended to break into two distinct sets. Many of the candidates describe high interest and high self-efficacy in CS. These are candidates who have been highly successful in learning computing, describing programming projects and success in CS classes, usually long before embarking on the CS teaching endorsement. Some students describe a much more troubled path. They may also have high interest, but describe various challenges in finding success—frustrations in being able to do what they want, lack of confidence or even experience of failure in computing classes. These low-confidence candidates also describe social issues—the perception of CS as nerdy, especially earlier in their lives, and also fears that they would not be able to keep up with technically advanced students:

> I am really nervous for this endorsement in Computer Science. A lot of the students in my other class I am taking teach AP Computer Science, they know several coding languages, they build computer programs, they know about algorithms, processes, and problem solving skills. I am extremely intimidated about writing a computer program. I also feel that the information or topics sometimes discussed in computer science or far out of my grasp of understanding. I am not confident in my analytical skills, programming skills, or even problem-solving skills. I also am afraid once I have this endorsement I will have to teach programming classes at my school, and I will be learning right with the kids!

The professor shares these themes with the candidates so that they can be reminded that they will likely have a similarly diverse set of students in their own classes, and must attend to the needs of all students—from those who have high anxiety to those who have high confidence and prior experiences.

Concept Cartoons

Concept cartoons have their genesis in science education (Keogh & Naylor, 1999). A concept cartoon is a single-panel cartoon that surfaces misconceptions (Naylor, 2000) (see Figures 6.2 & 6.3). In the center is an image representing a single concept. Around the central image are cartoon figures, each expressing an idea about the central concept. One of the ideas is correct and the others represent common misconceptions. Concept cartoons can easily be used to prompt student thinking about the central idea. Ideally the cartoons are used in classroom discussions, with students choosing which character they agree with and giving reasons why. Not only does the ensuing discussion act as a formative assessment to understand student thinking, but by relying on evidence to support their beliefs, students generally will resolve on the correct choice. Concept cartoons can be used to promote discussion between groups of different sizes. For example, as a whole class activity, the different perspectives can be assigned to corners of the classroom, with students moving to the corner that matches their thinking, then discussing or debating the sides and moving as they change their minds (e.g., Edwards & Flores, 2018). Alternatively, small groups can discuss and come to agreement. In the case of CS, depending on the central idea, it can be possible to ultimately write code to demonstrate the correct answer.

While it is obvious that concept cartoons can be an engaging way to prompt discussion and surface misconceptions in CS as they are in science, there is not a collection of CS concept cartoons. Thus, one assignment in the CS Teaching Methods Course is to create concept cartoons that could be used in candidates' classes. The project is introduced in class, where candidates are given examples such as those shown in Figures 6.2 and 6.3, and discuss them as students would. Then candidates are directed to create their own concept cartoons. Candidates

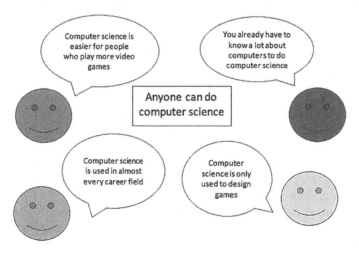

FIGURE 6.2. Concept Cartoon in Computer Science—Sample 1

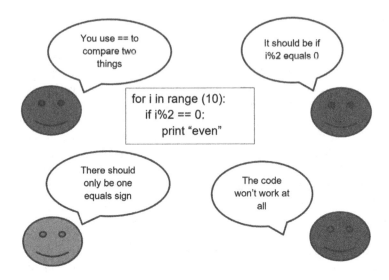

FIGURE 6.3. Concept Cartoon in Computer Science—Sample 2

who are not artistically inclined and do not want to use stick figures or smiley faces are encouraged to use templates available from the Science Learning Hub, the University of Waikato (http://sciencelearn.org.nz) which also has a description of the activity and example science cartoons. The cartoons are evaluated based on whether there is a single correct answer, at least two misconceptions represented, and whether the cartoon responses address the central concept.

Computational Thinking Bins

Computational Thinking (CT) Bins are standalone, unplugged activities that pre-college students can complete alone or in small groups. This activity emerged out of two foundations. First, professors in the College of Education at UNO had created STEM Bins—standalone activities covering a variety of science topics. Each activity is located in a plastic bin, and the assorted bins are used for outreach activities. They are easy to transport and each activity is designed so that students can engage with the activity independently, increasing the impact of outreach since there are not intense needs for adult oversight over activities. Many activities are kinesthetic and interactive, such as building bridges with popsicle sticks or creating a small structure out of blocks and then creating engineering drawings of different perspectives of the structure. Others are more thought-provoking, such as an activity where a variety of unusual kitchen tools are displayed and students must identify their likely uses before checking against an answer key.

The second genesis of the CT Bins was a need for similar activities that focused on CS and computational thinking, especially for outreach activities such as CS Education Week. Once the first set of bins was created, teachers were interested in using them, both as curricular activities and also as easily-implemented substitute teacher lesson plans. Thus the bins were extended to include not only instructions for students, but also information for teachers, including a content-based explanation of the activity and a description of how to use it with students (beyond just putting the bin on the table and letting students go).

Because of the nature of creating this kind of independent computational thinking activity for students, this became an assignment in the CS methods course. Candidates are introduced to the existing set of bins (*Computational Thinking Bins*, n.d.) and complete some of the activities in class. Then they brainstorm other topics and activities that could be created into bins. Candidates can work individually or in pairs or small groups to create bins. A rubric was used to assess bins (see Table 6.1).

TABLE 6.1.   Rubric to Assess CT Bins

Criteria	Target	Approaching Target	Below Target	Points
Topic	The bin has a single purpose that is clearly communicated and straightforward to understand. The purpose or topic is strongly connected to computing.	It is hard to figure out the topic or purpose of the activity—there are multiple possibilities or it seems undirected. There is a weak connection to computing.	It is nearly impossible to figure out the topic or purpose of the bin. There is no connection to computing.	30
Usability	Students can complete the activity without oversight or instruction from a teacher. The activity is appropriately challenging for students of the identified grade level—not too childish or too hard	Students can engage with the bin independently but may need teacher support to complete the activity. The bin is developmentally inappropriate for students of the identified grade level.	Students cannot reasonably complete the activity independently. The activity is likely to be impossibly difficult or so easy as to be boring for students of the identified grades.	50
Teacher Instructions	The teacher instructions are clear, complete, and fully explained for a novice teacher.	All sections of the teacher materials have been filled out, but a novice teacher would have difficulty understanding what to do. The documentation is incomplete.	The teacher instructions are incomplete with missing parts. Even an experienced teacher would have difficulty understanding the materials.	20
Complete	The bin has all required parts. There is a solid example of what to do. The instructions are correct.	The bin is missing small parts, but can still be used and understood, with difficulty.	The bin is unusable, but has a reasonable start.	10

Although the outcome of this assignment, in terms of creation of CT Bins as a resource, has been extremely successful, the assignment itself has not been as successful as would be ideal. There are myriad great ideas available to teachers, particularly through the internet. Thus, the most common project submission is a modification of an existing activity. In terms of future CS teachers learning how to teach CS well, it is not clear that modifying existing activities for future use by others is the best use of course resources. Some candidates have created completely new activities. In terms of class outcomes, this is an excellent result, but writing clear instructions is hard, and the usability of fully unique bins is lower than bins resulting from modified activities. This is clearly a case where a use-modify-create framework would work best (Lee et al., 2011), but it is not clear that the framework is the best use of limited course time. Thus the assignment stands at this time as an option for students in the methods course, while the use of the bins themselves is one of the pedagogies covered as a class activity.

NEXT STEPS

As the need for highly qualified CS teachers in K–12 grows and as states create pathways for teacher credentialing, an increasing number of universities will be called upon to create CS teaching methods courses. The description of the UNO offering can be used as an example for programs that want to create similar courses.

Unlike other disciplinary areas such as mathematics and science which have a long history of teacher preparation (Cochran-Smith & Villegas, 2016), there is little existing research about CS teacher preparation (Armoni, 2011). In particular, we lack information about the efficacy of different models, how to address important teacher learning outcomes, or even precisely what are the upcoming innovations in CS education. For example, science has grappled with the move from "cookbook science" to an inquiry-based focus with students learning about the nature of science (Osborne, 2014). While some controversies, such as addressing inequity in computing opportunities (e.g., Margolis et al., 2008), have surfaced, it is not clear that we have successfully determined how to prepare teachers to interact with students without bias.

Next steps for teacher preparation, then, require that more schools offer CS teacher preparation programs. These programs should be designed not only to prepare teachers of other subjects, but also career-changers, who know CS content but need to be fully prepared to teach (Delyser et al., 2018). These programs need to be the subject of high-quality research, to understand how to best prepare teachers, especially teachers with a variety of prior experiences and attitudes about computing. In the meantime, programs can continue building on existing models, both from other disciplines like mathematics and science, and also programs such as the CS teacher preparation program at UNO.

REFERENCES

Abell, S. K., Appleton, K., & Hanuscin, D. L. (2010). *Designing and teaching the elementary science methods course. Designing and teaching the elementary science methods course*. Routledge. https://doi.org/10.4324/9780203859131

Allen, K., & Schnell, K. (2016). Developing mathematics identity. *Mathemtics Teaching in the Middle School, 21*(7), 398–405.

Armoni, M. (2011). Looking at secondary teacher preparation through the lens of computer science. *ACM Transactions on Computing Education, 11*(4), 1–38. https://doi.org/10.1145/2048931.2048934

Begel, A., Garcia, D. D., & Wolfman, S. A. (2004). Kinesthetic learning in the classroom. *Proceedings of the 35th SIGCSE Technical Symposium on Computer Science Education—SIGCSE '04* (p. 183). https://doi.org/10.1145/971300.971367

Bransford, J., Darling-Hammond, L., & LePage, P. (2005). Introduction. In L. Darling-Hammond & J. Bransford (Eds.), *Preparing teachers for a changing world* (pp. 1–39). Jossey-Bass.

Bransford, J., Derry, S., Berliner, D., & Hammerness, K. (2005). Theories of learning and their roles in teaching. In L. Darling-Hammond & J. Bransford (Eds.), *Preparing teachers for a changing World* (pp. 40–87). Jossey-Bass.

Braught, G., Wahls, T., & Eby, L. M. (2011). The case for pair programming in the computer science classroom. *ACM Transactions on Computing Education, 11*(1), 1–21. https://doi.org/10.1145/1921607.1921609

Brookhart, S. M. (2013). *How to create and use rubrics for formative assessment and grading*. ACSD.

Carter, P. L., & Darling-Hammond, L. (2016). Teaching diverse learners. In D. H. Gitomer & C. A. Bell (Eds.), *Handbook of research on teaching* (5th ed., pp. 593–637). American Educational Research Association.

Cochran-Smith, M., & Villegas, A. M. (2016). Research on teacher preparation: Charting the landscape of a sprawling Field. In D. H. Gitomer & C. A. Bell (Eds.), *Handbook of research on teaching* (5th ed., pp. 439–548). American Educational Research Association.

Computational Thinking Bins. (n.d.). https://www.unomaha.edu/college-of-information-science-and-technology/computer-science-education/community-engagement/ct-bins.php

Computer Science Teachers Association. (2020). *Standards for CS teachers*. https://csteachers.org/teacherstandards

Delyser, L. A., Goode, J., Guzdial, M., Kafai, Y., & Yadav, A. (2018). *Priming the computer science teacher pump: Integrating computer science education into schools of education*. https://www.computingteacher.org/

Edwards, J., & Flores, A. (2018). Four corners in learning mathematics with technology. *Ohio Journal of School Mathematics, 78*, 45–51.

Feldman, J. (2018). *Grading for equity*. Corwin Press.

Gess-Newsome, J. (2015). A model of teacher professional knowledge and skill including PCK. In A. Berry, P. Friedrichesen, & J. Loughran (Eds.), *Re-examining pedagogical content knowledge in science education*. Routledge.

Hattie, J. (2008). *Visible learning: A synthesis of over 800 meta-analyses relating to achievement*. Routledge.

Hazzan, O., Lapidot, T., & Ragonis, N. (2011). Design of a methods of teaching computer science course. In *Guide to teaching computer science: an activity-based approach* (pp. 229–234). Springer-Verlag. https://doi.org/10.1007/978-0-85729-443-2

Hubbard, A. (2018). Pedagogical content knowledge in computing education: A review of the research literature. *Computer Science Education, 28*(2), 117–135. https://doi.org/10.1080/08993408.2018.1509580

Kaczmarczyk, L. C., Petrick, E. R., East, J. P., & Herman, G. L. (2010). Identifying student misconceptions of programming. *Proceedings of the 41st ACM Technical Symposium on Computer Science Education—SIGCSE '10*, 107–111. https://doi.org/10.1145/1734263.1734299

Keogh, B., & Naylor, S. (1999). Concept cartoons, teaching and learning in science: An evaluation. *International Journal of Science Education, 21*(4), 431–446. https://doi.org/10.1080/095006999290642

Lathrop, S. D. (2010). *Teaching techniques for advanced computer programming.* United States Military Academy.

Lawler, B. R., & Gargroetzi, E. C. (2017). Mathematical autobiography as a window into sociopolitical teacher identity. In *Proceedings of the sixth annual Mathematics Teacher Education Partnership conference* (pp. 88–95). Washington, DC.

Lee, I., Martin, F., Denner, J., Coulter, B., Allan, W., Erickson, J., Malyn-Smith, J., & Werner, L. (2011). Computational thinking for youth in practice. *ACM Inroads, 2*(1), 32. https://doi.org/10.1145/1929887.1929902

Levine, D. (n.d.). *Role playing in an object-oriented world.* Retrieved May 10, 2019, from http://www.cs.sbu.edu/dlevine/RolePlay/roleplay.html

Margolis, J., Estrella, R., Goode, J., Holme, J. J., & Nao, K. (2008). *Stuck in the shallow end: Education, race, and computing.* MIT Press.

McConnell, J. (2005). Active and cooperative learning: Further tips and tricks (Part I). *Inroads—the SIGCSE Bulletin, 37*(2), 27–30. https://doi.org/10.1145/1138403.1138426

Michaels, S., & O'Connor, C. (2012). *Talk Science Primer.*

National Research Council. (2000). *How people learn: Brain, mind, experience and school.* (J. D. Bransford, A. L. Brown, & R. R. Cocking, Eds.). The National Academies Press. https://doi.org/10.17226/9853

Naylor, S. (2000). *Science concept cartoons.* Millgate House.

Osborne, J. (2014). Teaching scientific practices: Meeting the challenge of change. *Journal of Science Teacher Education, 25*(2), 177–196. https://doi.org/10.1007/s10972-014-9384-1

Palincsar, A. S., & Brown, A. L. (1984). Reciprocal teaching of comprehension-tostering and comprehension-monitoring activities. *Cognition and Instruction, 1*(2), 117–175.

Pellegrino, J. W. (2014). Assessment as a positive influence on 21st century teaching and learning: A systems approach to progress. *Psicologia Educativa, 20*(2), 65–77. https://doi.org/10.1016/j.pse.2014.11.002

Shulman, L. S. (1986). Those who understand: Knowledge growth in teaching. *Educational Researcher, 15*(2), 4–14.

Simon, B., Chen, T., Lewandowski, G., Sanders, K., & Mccartney, R. (2006). Commonsense computing: What students know before we teach (Episode 1: Sorting). In *Proceedings of the 2nd International Computing Education Research Workshop* (pp. 29–40). Canterbury, UK.

Vygotsky, L. (1978). *Mind in society: The development of higher psychological processes.* Harvard University Press.

CHAPTER 7

REDESIGNING EDUCATIONAL TECHNOLOGY COURSEWORK TO FOSTER PRE-SERVICE TEACHER LEARNING OF COMPUTATIONAL THINKING IN CONTENT AREA INSTRUCTION

Hui Yang and Chrystalla Mouza

In this chapter, we describe a pedagogical approach aimed at preparing pre-service teachers to integrate computational thinking into K–8 education. We present the re-design of an educational technology course for pre-service teachers which introduces computing tools and pedagogies specific to incorporating computational thinking concepts with disciplinary content and pedagogical knowledge in K–8 settings. Data were collected from 57 pre-service teachers over the period of one semester. Specifically, a total of 171 lesson plans developed by pre-service teachers through three separate lesson planning tasks were collected and analyzed qualitatively. The analysis utilized a coding scheme that focused on identifying specific computational thinking concepts represented in lesson plans. Findings indicated that each lesson planning task supported different computational thinking concepts. The concepts of

Preparing Pre-Service Teachers to Teach Computer Science: Models, Practices, and Policies, pages 129–151.
129

data and problem decomposition were more frequently represented in participants' lesson designs followed by algorithmic thinking, simulation, and automation. Implications and next steps are discussed based on the analysis.

Keywords: Computational Thinking, Educational Technology Coursework, Lesson Plans, K–8 Education

INTRODUCTION

The deep and growing role of technology in all academic disciplines makes it necessary to help all students acquire a deeper understanding of computing by drawing on computer science (CS) principles (National Academies of Sciences, Engineering, and Medicine, 2017). This objective has been described in the literature under the term computational thinking (CT). Broadly speaking, CT involves the use of CS concepts and cognitive processes to solve problems within specific disciplines, including problem decomposition, abstraction, algorithms, data, and automation (Anderson, 2016; Barr & Stephenson, 2011). For example, students can use CT in science to collect and classify data, in English to decompose articles and identify patterns, and in music to create and manipulate compositions through programming. As such, CT is a fundamental cognitive skill that should be an integral part of everyone's education (National Research Council, 2010; Wing, 2006). Indeed, both the Common Core State Standards and the Next Generation Science Standards in the United States identify CT as a scientific practice. Similarly, the National Educational Technology Standards for Students from the International Society for Technology in Education (ISTE) include CT as a skill needed to engage and thrive in a digital world. The ISTE standards are designed for use by educators across a variety of curricular disciplines and with students of different ages (ISTE, 2016).

While there is growing support to help K–12 students develop CT skills (e.g., Atmatzidou & Demetriadis, 2016; Mouza et al., 2017), preparing enough teachers to integrate CT into their disciplines remains an enormous challenge (DeLyser et al., 2018). In a recent survey of the field on pre-college computing education, Blikstein (2018) found that teacher development was a central concern expressed by computing education experts, who emphasized the need to prioritize the preparation, professional development, and retention of teachers. To date, a number of efforts have focused on preparing in-service teachers to deliver specific computer science curricula such as Exploring Computer Science and Computer Science Principles. While these efforts are critical in preparing practicing teachers, pre-service education has the potential to create a more sustainable pipeline of well-prepared teachers similar to other disciplines (Guzdial, 2017). Specifically, teacher educators are in a unique position to help pre-service teachers integrate CT within specific disciplinary contexts because they have a deeper understanding of their discipline and can illustrate how CT concepts relate to subject matter and pedagogy (Yadav et al., 2017). According to Yadav et al. (2014) such integration is essential if we are to prepare pre-service teachers who are able to apply CT in their future classrooms.

In this chapter, we describe a pedagogical approach aimed at preparing pre-service teachers to integrate CT into K–8 education. We first present the redesign of an educational technology course for pre-service teachers which introduces computing tools and pedagogies specific to incorporating CT with disciplinary content and pedagogical knowledge in K–8 settings. According to Yadav et al. (2017), educational technology courses offer a natural fit for helping pre-service teachers integrate CT within their discipline, particularly when they make CS principles explicit. Subsequently, we address the following research questions:

1. In what ways do pre-service teachers enrolled in an educational technology course connect specific CT concepts with content and pedagogy in three different lesson planning tasks?
2. What are pre-service teachers' perceptions around the use of CT in their future classrooms after each lesson planning task?

BACKGROUND

In this section we describe the theoretical framework and prior work related to our study.

Framework of Technological Pedagogical Content Knowledge in Relation to CT

Theoretical models of teacher knowledge traditionally focus on Shulman's framework which includes content knowledge (CK), pedagogical knowledge (PK) and pedagogical content knowledge (PCK) (Shulman, 1987). Building upon these ideas different views on how to position teacher knowledge in relation to CT have been proposed (e.g., Angeli et al., 2016; Yadav et al., 2016). Some views focus on what has been called CS-Pedagogical Content Knowledge (CS-PCK), which primarily identifies knowledge required to teach CS content (Saeli et al., 2011; Yadav et al., 2016). While these efforts are valuable, they do not explicate the type of knowledge needed to embed CT into subject matter, particularly by generalist teachers in K–8 settings (Mouza et al., 2017).

The Technological Pedagogical Content Knowledge (TPACK) framework provides a promising lens for studying teacher knowledge in relation to CT. TPACK builds on Shulman's (1987) seminal scholarship on pedagogical content knowledge—knowledge at the intersection of content and pedagogical knowledge. Mishra and Koehler (2006), described TPACK in relation to digital technology broadly, but not in relation to CT. Specifically, they proposed that TPACK centers on the nuanced interactions among content knowledge (CK), technology knowledge (TK), and pedagogical knowledge (PK) to form a synthesized body of knowledge that supports effective use of technology within specific subject domains (Mishra & Koehler, 2006). Given that digital tools play a central role in CT-related concepts and practices (Bower & Falkner, 2015), the TPACK framework may provide a useful lens for examining CT in classroom teaching and learning. To embed CT in classroom instruction, pre-service teachers need to acquire technological knowledge (TK) related to computational tools. They also need to make connections to existing disciplinary content as well as general and content specific pedagogy (PK and PCK). The ability to bring together the individual domains of technology, content, and pedagogy can help teachers support the effective use of CT-related tools and concepts within specific disciplines.

Although the TPACK framework can provide a useful frame for considering teacher knowledge in relation to CT, it does not provide practical recommendations on how to develop this body of knowledge among pre-service teachers. To facilitate the practical adoption of the TPACK framework, Harris and Hofer (2009) proposed a 5-step curricular-based technology integration approach consistent with the ways in which teachers plan lessons. This approach asks teachers to (a) choose their learning goals, (b) make pedagogical decisions, (c) select activity types, (d) select assessment strategies, and (e) select tools/resources. In this chapter, we describe how we utilized the 5-step approach described above in order to support pre-service teachers as they designed lessons that embedded knowledge of CT concepts, tools, and practices with content and pedagogy.

Pre-Service Teacher Preparation for Computational Thinking

Research on the preparation of pre-service teachers in relation to CT remains significantly under-developed though some studies have started to emerge (Mouza et al., 2018). These studies have examined among others, understandings and attitudes towards CT (e.g., Chang & Peterson, 2018; Yadav et al., 2014), integration of CT in mathematics and science content (e.g., Gadanidis et al., 2017; Jaipal-Jamani & Angeli, 2017), and intentions to integrate CT with subject matter (e.g., McGinnis et al., 2019).

Chang and Peterson (2018) compared pre-service teacher outcomes in relation to CT as a result of their participation in two different course designs focusing on technology integration. In the first design (Design A), 44 pre-service teachers were introduced to CT through an unstructured play-like exposure to CT tools followed by reflection. In the second course design (Design B), 15 pre-service teachers engaged in a more systematic introduction to CT and the role of computing in society, in addition to the unstructured play with CT tools. Analysis of course reflections collected from 44 and 15 pre-service teachers respectively, indicated that participants gained awareness related to CT and acknowledged its value and relevance. Yet they offered different conceptualizations of CT with many situating CT as a problem-solving process or as content specific to CS only. Participants in the second course design exhibited a deeper understanding related to the use of CT in their future classrooms

Focusing specifically on the integration of CT in mathematics, Gadanidis and colleagues (2017) developed a course for K–6 elementary school pre-service teachers to facilitate the development of conceptual understanding of mathematics and mathematics teaching with CT. The course was offered through a hybrid format over a period of 9 weeks and focused on the role of CT in relation to geometry, probability, patterning, and algebra, as well as measurement and number sense. Face-to-face sessions consisted of hands-on learning using digital tools and coding platforms to support mathematics teaching and learning. Online activities focused on readings and collaborative knowledge construction around the use of CT in mathematics topics as well as reflection on the role of CT in mathematics (e.g., identifying coding as a form of mathematical process). Data were collected through online discussions and reflection assignments from 143 pre-service teachers while participating in the course in order to examine both learning and attitudes towards CT in mathematics. Results indicated that participants were able to recognize the role of CT in mathematics, engage with coding, find cross-curricular connections of coding, and acknowledge the role of CT in society. Further, although participants initially expressed concerns about coding, by the end of the course the majority expressed a positive attitude in learning how to code and teach mathematics through coding.

In science, Jaipal-Jamani and Angeli (2017) introduced robotics construction kits in a 12-weeks science methods course for pre-service teachers. Specifically, pre-service teachers engaged with four programming tasks that involved writing algorithms and debugging programs. Data were collected from 21 pre-service teachers and included a pre and post assessment of science content knowledge, pre and post questionnaires on interest and self-efficacy towards robotics, and a pre and post questionnaire on robotics and coding knowledge. Results from these assessments revealed that engaging pre-service teachers in learning robotics positively influenced their interest and beliefs towards teaching with robotics, their science knowledge, and their CT skills. The authors argued that these findings have promise related to the role of robotics activities as an instructional strategy that could help enhance pre-service teachers' interest and self-efficacy towards CT and science concepts.

Similarly, McGinnis and colleagues (2019) developed a curricular module on CT that was integrated in a senior level elementary science methods course. The CT module included an introduction to CT as a core science and engineering practice consistent with NGSS, CT challenges through robotics activities, and CT integration in elementary science through citizen science (e.g., Cornell Lab of Ornithology's Celebrate Urban Birds). Data were collected from 37 pre-service teachers through a variety of sources that included: (a) pre and post drawings accompanied by explanations on participants' understandings of CT and their views of how CT could be integrated into science teaching; (b) written online reflections describing their thoughts and feelings towards CT and anticipated benefits/challenges of CT integration; and (c) lesson plans that asked participants to design, teach, and reflect upon a CT-integrated science or engineering lesson. Results indicated that pre-service teachers expressed an intention to integrate CT in their teaching and described that opportunities to integrate CT in science would benefit their young students due to the use of technological tools to teach CT and the ability to make science more fun and engaging. Nonetheless, pre-service teachers provided varied reasons for integrating CT in their practices and in their actions to integrate it in their classroom science lesson plans. Further, pre-service teachers varied in the scope and accuracy of their lesson planning and instruction of CT.

Methodologically, these studies typically utilized pre and post surveys, questionnaires, and to a lesser extent computational products and instructional design tasks, such as lesson plans. Involving pre-service teachers in the process of designing lessons that integrated CT with specific disciplinary content was found to be a fruitful exercise, with the potential to support participants' learning and future application of CT in practice (McGinnis et al., 2019). Furthermore, the use of lesson plans themselves provided evidence for the integration of CT in content-based instruction. In this work, we capitalized on using lessons plans as a means to documenting pre-service teachers' understanding of CT in the context of their participation in a redesigned educational technology course.

METHODS

Context of this Work

The Elementary Teacher Education (ETE) program that served as the foundation of this work is a four-year undergraduate teacher education program in the United States. Graduates of the program are eligible for both elementary (K–5) and middle school (6–8) teacher certification. The program curriculum is divided into three areas: (a) the general studies courses, which help develop subject matter knowledge; (b) the professional studies courses (e.g., methods), which prepare pre-service teachers for their future classroom; and (c) the concentration courses, which help develop expertise in a middle school content area. Additionally, the program curriculum is designed to provide pre-service teachers with a range of field experiences in a variety of classroom settings. These experiences culminate with student teaching, where pre-service teachers assume increased teaching responsibilities over a period of a full semester.

Integrating Technology in Education Course

Integrating Technology in Education is a required 2-credit hour course for all pre-service teachers, taken during their junior or senior year. This 14-week course introduces technologies available for use in classroom content areas, pedagogical considerations with these technologies, and teaching and learning practices that combine the use of technologies with content and pedagogy (Mouza & Karchmer-

Klein, 2015). In previous semesters, the course focused exclusively on technology integration independent of CT. Specifically, the course employed an integrated pedagogical approach which juxtaposed the educational technology course with methods courses and a 3-week field experience in authentic classrooms (see Mouza et al., 2014). This integrated approach enables preservice teachers to connect knowledge of technology acquired in their educational technology coursework with both content and pedagogy (Niess, 2012). For the purpose of this work, the course was redesigned to support the development of pre-service teachers' knowledge of CT and the ways it can be integrated with specific content and pedagogy. To accomplish this goal, we targeted three distinct components of the course related to CT concepts, tools, and practices.

The first component of the course focused on the increased use of CT vocabularies to help enhance pre-service teachers' understanding related to CT in K–8 settings (Barr & Stephenson, 2011). In particular, we adopted the CT concepts and definitions provided by the Computer Science Teachers Association and the International Society for Technology in Education (CSTA & ISTE, 2011). These CT concepts and definitions include: (a) *problem decomposition*: breaking down complex problems into more manageable parts; (b) *algorithmic thinking*: using a precise sequence of steps or instructions to solve problems; (c) *abstraction*: reducing complexity to define a main idea/applying abstraction to develop models of natural or artificial phenomena; (d) *data collection, analysis and representation*: accessing, evaluating, and representing data using words, images, or models; (e) *automation*: using digital tools to automate solutions; (f) *parallelization*: making things happen at the same time/organizing resources to simultaneously carry out tasks that help achieve a common goal; and (g) *simulation*: representing a process.

The second component of the course was similar to other studies reported in the literature (e.g., Chang & Peterson, 2018; McGinnis et al., 2019) and sought to provide pre-service teachers with opportunities to experience a variety of computational tools that can be used to support students' development of CT knowledge and skills. The computational tools introduced in the course (e.g., Scratch visual programming, concept mapping software, Internet resources, and web 2.0 tools) are available for use in a variety of classroom content areas (e.g., literacy, mathematics, science, and social studies). Similar to the work of Gadanidis et al. (2017), the course was offered in a hybrid format, whereby some of the sessions were conducted online and some face-to face. During the face-to-face sessions, participants had opportunities for hands-on learning where they experienced a variety of low-tech and high-tech tools that support CT (e.g., board games, electronics, and robotics) (Resnick et al., 2009). Table 7.1 provides an overview of the computational tools utilized in the course and their relationship to CT concepts, tools, and practices.

The third component of the course focused on providing explicit instructional design scaffolding for the development of CT-infused lessons. Specifically, pre-service teachers engaged in the design of three lesson planning tasks following

TABLE 7.1. CT-related Tools, Practices, and Concepts Introduced Through the Redesigned Course

CT-related Technology	Activity & Related Practices (CT Concepts, Tools & Practices)	CT Supported Concepts/Skills
Interactive Whiteboards (Weeks 1–2)	Identify two interactive whiteboard resources that support key CT skills: Simulation (e.g., a resource that can be used to represent a phenomenon such as prey and predator relationship); Sequencing (a resource that could be used to sequence events); Data (e.g., a resource that could be used to represent data such as a graph; a resource that could be used to organize information)	Simulation Abstraction Algorithmic Thinking Data
Programming Hour of Code Scratch (Weeks 4–6)	CS unplugged (activity done without computers to introduce algorithms) Hour of Code: Completion of a Grades 2–8 activity Introduction to Scratch Programming: Scratch is an object oriented programming language Review lessons that support the use of Scratch: ScratchED Design of a learning activity in a content area that involves Scratch Programming/Reflection	Algorithmic Thinking Problem Decomposition Simulation Abstraction
Concept Mapping Tools (Weeks 8–9)	Design of a learning activity that uses concept mapping in a content area to support student development of CT skills, such as decompose a mathematical problem, model abstraction (e.g., life cycle of a butterfly), sequence events in a story or plan essay execution.	Problem Decomposition Algorithmic Thinking Simulation Abstraction
Data (Week 10)	Introduction to Internet Research including use of keywords, boolean logic and operators and evaluation of online content	Problem-Decomposition Simulation Abstraction
Collaboration tools (Week 12–13)	Select and read an article on multiple approaches to developing CT: board games, robotics, programming. Use of a collaborative presentation tool (e.g., Voicethread) to present the reading to classmates.	Problem Decomposition Algorithmic Thinking Simulation Abstraction
Maker Tools (Week 14)	Exploration of low-tech, high-tech computational tools including robotics, board games for coding, and circuits. Reflection on the use of computational tools in K–8 settings	Problem Decomposition Algorithmic Thinking

Note: No classes or assignments are given during the 3-weeks pre-service teachers are in their field placements.

the 5-step approach presented by Harris and Hofer (2009). This strategy helped pre-service teachers to start lesson planning by first considering the content and pedagogy and then identifying the computational tools and practices that could help CT student development. There are three lesson planning tasks throughout the course; two are hypothetical (i.e., pre-service teachers design but not implement the lessons in real classrooms). The third task, called case development, represents an implementation of a CT-infused lesson in an authentic classroom. The three lesson planning tasks are described below.

Lesson-Planning Task 1: Programming

The programming lesson planning task asked pre-service teachers to develop a lesson plan that incorporated Scratch programming software within a content area. To achieve this goal, pre-service teachers first examined and explored various resources (e.g., Scratch projects, teaching resources) through multiple platforms (e.g., ScratchEd community). Subsequently, they defined a content-specific learning goal and developed a lesson plan that integrated programming with curriculum content. All pre-service teachers were provided with a series of scaffolding prompts aligned with the TPACK framework (Harris et al., 2010) during their lesson planning process. The writing prompts centered on two main components. The first component guided pre-service teachers to identify lesson goals and make pedagogical decisions. These prompts included the following:

- Consider the pedagogical decisions you'll need to make to develop this lesson idea. How will you introduce Scratch to your students?
- What activity types will students engage with to learn the concept?
- In what ways will you assess student learning?

The second component aimed at scaffolding pre-service teachers' reflection. It included prompts that asked participants to explain how their lesson designs supported students' content understanding as well as the development of CT knowledge and skills These prompts included the following:

- How will programming help your students achieve the identified learning goal?
- How will the lesson support the development of students' CT skills?
- What was your experience with Scratch?

Lesson Planning Task 2: Concept Mapping

The concept mapping lesson planning task asked pre-service teachers to design a lesson plan that incorporated a concept mapping tool of their choice in a content area. Similar to the programming lesson plan, participants first explored various types of concept mapping tools, identified a learning goal within a content area of their choice (e.g., science, mathematics, social studies, English), and developed a lesson plan that integrated concept mapping in a core curricular area while explicitly attending to the ways in which lesson goals and tools supported student development of CT. To scaffold lesson development, a series of planning and reflection prompts was again provided that paralleled those of the programming task.

Lesson-Planning Task 3: Case Development

The case development task served as the course capstone allowing pre-service teachers to progressively design, implement, and reflect on lessons that support the development of CT knowledge and skills among K–8 students. Unlike the first two lesson-planning tasks, however, case development asked participants to implement their lesson in an authentic classroom setting and reflect on the experience. Specifically, pre-service teachers designed a lesson that integrated computational tools (e.g., Scratch, concept mapping, etc.) within a content area to support students' CT knowledge and skills. The final product was a 1,000-word reflective case report consisting of pre-service teachers' responses to several prompts organized around two major components; (a) case narrative: *How did you introduce the lesson to students? What happened during the actual implementation of your lesson?*, and (b) case reflection: *How did the lesson support the development of students' CT skills? What are two things you will remember about this lesson for future planning?* (see Mouza & Karchmer-Klein, 2013).

TABLE 7. 2. Coding Scheme for Participants' Lesson Plans

CT Concept	Description	Example
Problem Decomposition	Decomposing problems or concepts into more manageable parts.	Students used the base ten blocks to decompose the numbers by their place values in order to solve addition and subtraction problems (Lesson Planning Task 2).
Algorithmic Thinking	Using sequencing or steps to solve problems or to complete tasks.	Students planned a Scratch project step by step to present the battles of the Civil War (Lesson Planning Task 1).
Abstraction	Applying abstraction to develop models or define main ideas.	Students summarized the main idea of a story and represented the main idea by creating a Scratch animation (Lesson Planning Task 1)
Data	Accessing, evaluating, analyzing and representing data using words, images or models.	Students evaluated and represented data through an online research project (Lesson Planning Task 3).
Automation	Using digital tools to automate solutions.	Students created a Metric Converter using Scratch (Lesson Planning Task 3).
Parallelization	Organizing resources simultaneously to carry out tasks that help achieve a common goal or make things happen at the same time.	N/A
Simulation	Representing a process.	Students represented the process of the water cycle using a concept mapping tool (Lesson Planning Task 2).

Data Collection and Analysis

Data for this chapter were collected from 57 K–8 pre-service teachers enrolled in the course during one semester. Each participant completed the three lesson planning tasks described above, which resulted in a total of 171 lesson plans. The lesson plans were analyzed based on coding instructions provided by Saldaña (2015). The first author and a graduate research assistant first selected a sample of participants (N=10) and independently examined their lesson plans across all three tasks to identify CT representations. The researchers then shared and compared their coding results (initial inter-rater reliability 92.6%) to develop a coding scheme related to CT concepts and their representation among the lesson plans (see Table 7.2). Finally, the first author independently coded the lesson plans based on the coding scheme shown on Table 7.2. In this chapter, we first present the subject matter and grade level addressed by the 171 lesson plans. Subsequently, we present the number of instances that each CT concept was represented in each lesson planning task.

RESULTS AND EXEMPLARS

Table 7.3 presents an overview of the content areas represented in participants CT-integrated lessons and the grade level addressed. As seen in Table 7.3, all content areas were represented but not equally across the lesson planning tasks. For instance, for the first lesson-planning task participants focused primarily on using programming with mathematics. In contrast, the majority of the participants focused on literacy for the second lesson planning task and science for the third lesson-planning task. Further, most participants designed their lessons for stu-

TABLE 7. 3. Overview of the Content/Grade Across the Three Lesson Planning Tasks

	Task 1: Programming Lesson Plan	Task 2: Concept Mapping Lesson Plan	Task 3: Case Report
Content Area			
Mathematics	49%	9%	18%
Science	17%	21%	40%
Social Studies	12%	30%	30%
Literacy	21%	40%	9%
Technology	-	-	3%
Grade Level			
K -2nd Grade	35%	27%	30%
3rd –5th Grade	59%	61%	70%
6th–8th Grade	5%	12%	0% (no case reports focused on students in grades 6–8)

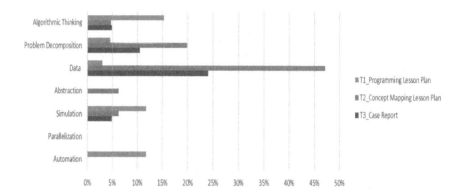

FIGURE 7.1.   CT Practices Reflected in the Three Lesson Planning Tasks

dents in grades 3–5 because at the time of the study they were placed primarily in elementary classrooms for their field experience.

Further, our analysis indicated that each lesson planning task supported different components of CT as shown in Figure 7.1. For instance, the CT concepts of algorithmic thinking, simulation, and automation were more prominently represented in lesson planning task 1 while the CT concepts of data and problem decomposition were clearly represented in lesson planning tasks 2 and 3. As seen in Figure 7.1, the CT concept of parallelization was not represented in participants' lesson plans while the CT concept of automation was only evident in the programming lesson plans.

Below we provide some examples that illustrate how different CT concepts were represented in pre-service teachers' lesson-planning tasks. We also present reflections from pre-service teacher participants on each lesson planning task related to the computational tools used and their perceptions around the use of CT in their future classrooms.

CT concepts: Algorithmic Thinking & Automation in Programming Lesson Plan (Task 1)

In this example we present how a participant, named Molly, integrated CT concepts of algorithmic thinking and automation in a 4th grade lesson on writing. Molly's lesson focused on guiding students into developing detailed narratives and representing the main ideas of their stories using the programming platform Scratch. To achieve the lesson goals, Molly envisioned implementing the lesson for three instructional days. On day one, Molly planned to introduce Scratch to students, placing an emphasis on the programming elements they may need to represent a story. This introduction to programming included a whole class demonstration on specific programming functions in Scratch. On day two, Molly planned to have students work in pairs to create a story which would be later represented on Scratch. In particular, Molly provided a graphic organizer for each student group to plot their story addressing essential writing elements. On day three, Molly planned to provide each student group with a laptop to create a Scratch project representing their writing product. Molly planned to assess students' work by focusing on both the writing (e.g., how students sequenced elements of their story) and computational products developed in Scratch. As Molly explained in her reflection, this lesson could support students CT primarily in algorithmic thinking (e.g., creating the Scratch story following sequential orders) and automation (e.g., programming their story in Scratch). This example showcases one approach to using programming tools like Scratch, within a specific discipline to promote both students' writing skills and CT understandings.

When asked to reflect on their own experience with programming in Scratch most pre-service teachers noted that they found Scratch easy to use and were able to get a better understanding of how programming can be integrated with subject matter to support student development of CT. Some excerpts from the 57 participants' responses are listed below. These excerpts illustrate that participants began to identify Scratch as a programming tool with the potential to support content in various disciplines and not simply to teach about coding:

- My experience with Scratch was effective and successful. I was able to work on my own to figure out how to incorporate motion, sound, pictures, shapes, etc. Scratch had games based on subjects and topic areas of choice. I was able to explore different programs that people came up with on Scratch and look at how they completed the programming for it. This gave us a better idea of what we would need to do in the future if we wanted to use Scratch again.
- The first time I have ever heard of Scratch was through this class. Before that, I had no idea what it was. I enjoyed working with Scratch in class, and through researching ways to incorporate it into a lesson for this assignment. Since we used Scratch to create fun animations in class, I thought that was the only purpose of Scratch—to create fun little games for children. I didn't realize that Scratch could be used with content as well.
- It took me a while to get all of the sprites, backgrounds, and effects to work for me the way I wanted them to, but eventually everything fell into place! It's not the most sophisticated Scratch product but I am very proud of how my first time working with it turned out! This is a very valuable tool that I think more people should learn about! (see Figure 7.2).

Some preservice teachers, however, were skeptical about the implementation of programming tools as a means to promote CT in their future classrooms. Their concerns were mostly related to the technical skills required of them and their students in using programming. Specific excerpts are listed below:

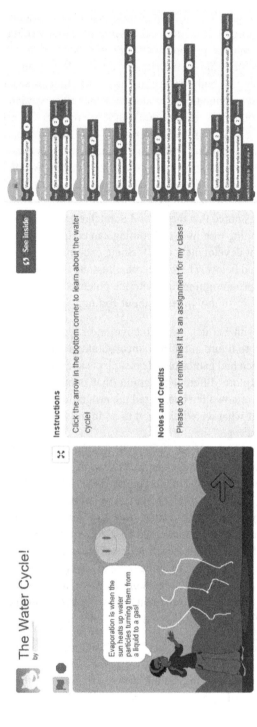

FIGURE 7.2. The Scratch Project Created by the Pre-Service Teacher (left) That Integrates CT Concepts (i.e., Simulation) With Science Content (i.e., Water Cycle) and the Project Code (Right).

- Through my exploration of the Scratch website, I came across many different Scratch activities that I could use in future lesson plans. I think that Scratch is easy to use—just press the green flag, and follow the directions of the activity. However, it is difficult to create your own Scratch activity—for me at least. I'm sure with enough practice I will become more comfortable and be able to create activities to go along with my future lessons.
- I thought Scratch was a fun way to teach students how to code without all of the complicated steps. I do wonder though if normal classroom environments have the time to introduce it and use it on a regular basis.

Data and Abstraction in Concept Mapping: Lesson Planning Task 2

As illustrated in Figure 7.1, most concept mapping lesson plans addressed CT concepts related to data, abstraction, and problem decomposition. Naomi's concept mapping lesson illustrated these concepts in the context of a third-grade literacy lesson. Naomi planned on launching the lesson by having students read the *Cinderella Disney* tale followed by the *Domitila* tale. Upon completing their reading, Naomi planned to provide students with a graphic organizer to recount the story. As a last step, Naomi planned on providing each student with an iPad where they could use a concept mapping app to compare and contrast the two stories (e.g., cultures of the stories) using their written notes (e.g., Figure 7.3 shows a hypothetical student example created by Naomi). In this example, Naomi integrated knowledge of a concept mapping tool to foster students' reading comprehension as well as to develop CT in the areas of abstraction (e.g., distill main ideas of the stories) and data (e.g., organizing, comparing, and representing information from two stories).

Participants (like Naomi) not only infused CT into their concept mapping lessons, but also identified CT vocabulary while reflecting on how the designed lessons contributed to the development of students' CT. For instance, they were able to precisely articulate how their concept mapping lessons supported students' development of CT, particularly in the areas of decomposition, data, and abstraction. Reflecting on the use of concept mapping as a means to supporting student development of CT other participants noted:

- I used concept mapping to create a sample concept map on *The Crayon Box that Talked* (see Figure 4—left). Concept mapping helps my students achieve the learning goal set for them because it helps them analyze and briefly explain their knowledge of the characters, main events, big problem, solution to the problem, plot, setting, themes, moral of the story, etc. The end products will allow me to formatively assess their learning, so that I can engage in additional instruction with those students who face challenges. The CT skills supported by my lesson include *decomposition* and *abstraction*. Decomposition is supported because my students are tasked with making a concept map that involves having them break down the

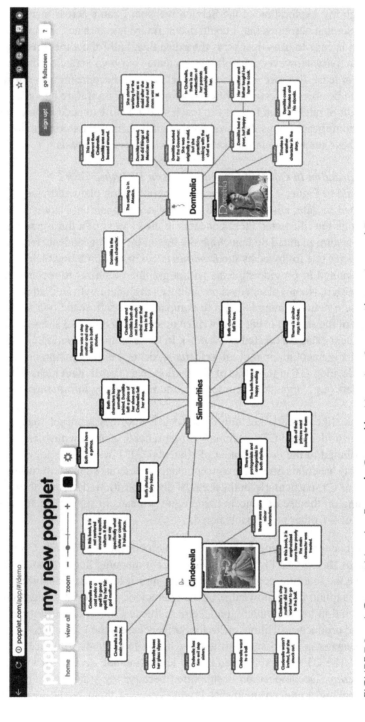

FIGURE 7.3. A Concept Mapping Example Created by Naomi to Support Abstraction and Data

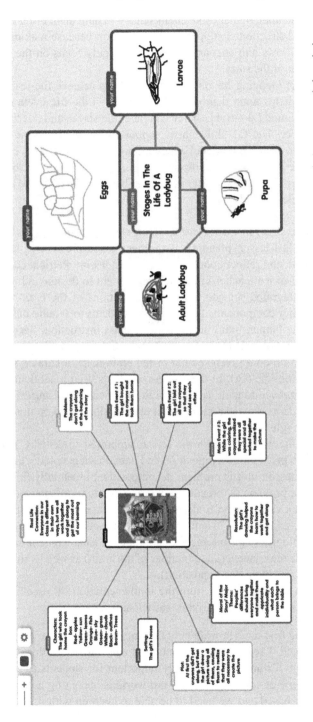

FIGURE 7.4. Concept Mapping Examples That Support Student Development of CT (decomposition and abstraction—left and abstraction—right)

story into smaller, manageable chunks that will help them bring everything together. Abstraction is supported by the lesson because making the concept map allows and encourages students to only focus on the important information of the story.

- My concept mapping lesson will help students achieve the learning goal because it helps them demonstrate the stages in the life cycle of a ladybug (see Figure 7.4—right). They can label the stages and put them in the correct order. The CT skill that is supported by this lesson is modeling *abstraction*. This is a model of a general principle of the life cycle pattern. In this case it is a ladybug life cycle. It is taking something abstract and representing it using the model in order to better understand the patterns in the life cycle of a ladybug.

Problem Decomposition in Case Development: Lesson-Planning Task 3

As noted, the last lesson planning assignment asked pre-service teachers to design, implement, and reflect upon a CT-integrated lesson. Patricia collaborated with another pre-service teacher in her field placement to design and implement a 3rd grade CT-integrated science unit on the functions of the brain. This unit included three major components. First it guided students to acquire basic knowledge related to the human brain through whole class instruction. Second, it engaged students into an online research activity where they worked in small groups to gather information on a given section of the brain using a curated set of web resources (e.g., brainline.org). In the process, students used a handout to record research findings related to their assigned brain functions (see Figure 7.5). Third, each group of students created a multimedia presentation based on their research findings using Google Slides.

Reflecting on the ways in which the lesson supported students' CT development in relation to problem decomposition and data, Patricia noted: "the CT skill supported in this lesson unit is problem decomposition; essentially finding solutions to a complex problem by breaking the problem into more manageable parts and analyzing data collected to find patterns." The case of Patricia provided a meaningful instantiation of CT in authentic classroom settings. Patricia integrated CT-related technologies (e.g., Internet) to facilitate students' content understandings towards a science concept (i.e., functions of the brain) as well as students' CT development (i.e., problem decomposition).

Reflecting on lessons learned from the implementation of lessons that supported student development of CT, other participants noted:

- After seeing first-hand how quickly the students caught on to programming using Scratch, I really think that students can start using this software at an early age. I think it is extremely important for students to be familiar with this type of software because our world is becoming more and more technology based and we need to be able to keep up with it. In my future

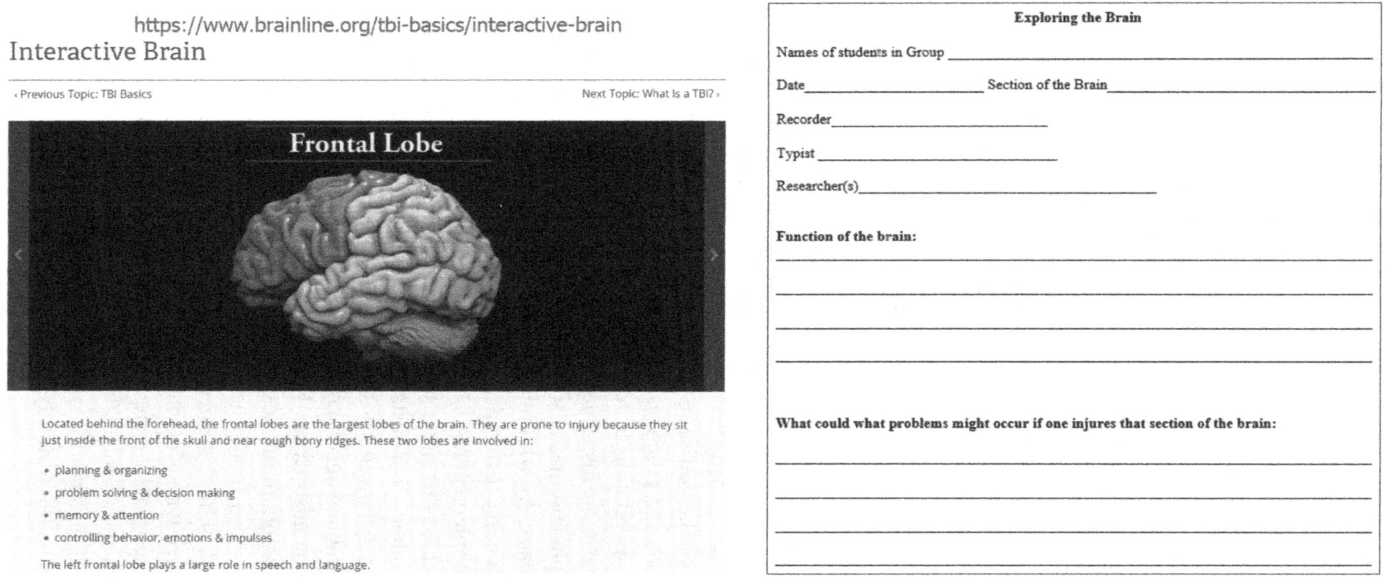

FIGURE 7.5. Instructional Scaffolding Provided in Patricia's Lesson for the Completion of the Online Research Assignment.

Exploring the Brain

Names of students in Group_____

Date_____ Section of the Brain_____

Recorder_____

Typist_____

Researcher(s)_____

Function of the brain:

What could what problems might occur if one injures that section of the brain:

https://www.brainline.org/tbi-basics/interactive-brain

Interactive Brain

‹ Previous Topic: TBI Basics   Next Topic: What Is a TBI? ›

Frontal Lobe

Located behind the forehead, the frontal lobes are the largest lobes of the brain. They are prone to injury because they sit just inside the front of the skull and near rough bony ridges. These two lobes are involved in:

• planning & organizing
• problem solving & decision making
• memory & attention
• controlling behavior, emotions & impulses

The left frontal lobe plays a large role in speech and language.

classroom, I plan to implement computational tools such as Scratch in my daily lessons. By doing this, I am not only getting the students more engaged and interested in what I am teaching, I am also furthering their CT skills in programming. When implementing this technology is not possible during my lesson, I could still apply CT concepts in my teaching. I can ask the students to record the correct order in which they do tasks and then ask them why this order is so important (algorithmic thinking).

- Based on my experience, I think it is important to more fully integrate CT into my students' daily activities. For example, when doing a science activity, I could have students anticipate the order in which they would carry out an experiment (algorithmic thinking). Additionally, conducting computer science unplugged activities like Harold the Robot, would familiarize my students with the way in which computers follow instructions, thereby developing their CT skills.

NEXT STEPS

This chapter presented one pedagogical approach to helping pre-service teachers acquire knowledge that enables them to infuse CT with computational tools, content, and pedagogy. In particular, we presented a redesigned educational technology course, offered by our teacher preparation program to support pre-service teachers as they developed their own understanding of CT and its role in K-8 settings. As part of the course redesign, we focused on introducing foundational CS concepts, tools, and practices that help promote pre-service teachers' knowledge of CT and its relation to technology, content, and pedagogy. Importantly, we placed emphasis on fostering pre-service teachers' CT enactment through a series of lesson planning tasks scaffolded by writing and reflection prompts and continuous feedback. As with other studies in the field, our work examined pre-service teachers' course materials, such as lesson plans and case studies to identify evidence of CT implementation.

Findings indicated that pre-service teachers utilized certain CT concepts more frequently than others. For instance, most pre-service teachers focused on the CT concept of data. Fewer pre-service teachers attempted to integrate CT concepts related to problem decomposition and algorithmic thinking and only a small number focused on abstraction. Further, the CT concept of automation was only addressed in the programming lesson plans. This finding is similar to other studies in the field which also found that pre-service teachers focused primarily on the CT concept of data while enrolled in a science methods course (see McGinnis et al., 2019). We agree with McGinnis and colleagues that the CT concept of data is one that pre-service teachers are most familiar with through their coursework in both mathematics and science which may have influenced our outcomes. Further, the CT concept of data could be easily aligned with all computational tools explored in the course. Interestingly, pre-service teaches associated automation with programming and thus this concept was absent from other lesson plans. Finally, the concept of parallelization was absent from participants' lesson plans. Upon reflecting on our own instruction, it was clear that parallelization was not addressed in any of the course modules and, therefore, it is not surprising that participants were unable to make connections with it during their lesson planning.

Our work presented pre-service teachers' learning outcomes from this course in designing, enacting, and reflecting on lesson plans that integrated CT concepts with technology, content, and pedagogy. Examination of lessons plans indicated that participants were better equipped to apply CT knowledge and skills with technological tools such as concept mapping rather than programming environments, like Scratch. Noticeably, a certain number of pre-service teachers reported that learning to program was challenging, which raised concerns related to the integration of programming into their future lessons. Accordingly, future research could benefit from examining more closely whether the affordances of computational tools influence pre-service teachers' ability to connect CT with disciplinary content and pedagogy. Further, future research should focus more explicitly on the application of these ideas in authentic classroom contexts. Most of the existing work asks pre-service teachers to develop hypothetical lesson designs that they are not asked to implement. Given that pre-service teachers do not get to widely observe CT practices in their field placement classrooms yet (Mouza et al., 2017), it is important that they have opportunities to apply their learning in real contexts.

In terms of next steps, it is also important that pre-service teacher preparation for CT moves beyond one-shot approaches in distinct courses (e.g., educational technology). Rather, future efforts should focus on integrating CT with disciplinary methods courses and field experiences (e.g., Yadav, et al., 2017). Lucarelli et al. for example (see Chapter 5, this volume), discuss an approach to infusing CT across their teacher preparation program by focusing on the professional development of teacher educators. For pre-service teachers to successfully apply CT in practice, we must provide extensive opportunities to develop and apply this knowledge across a variety of disciplines and contexts.

REFERENCES

Anderson, N. D. (2016). A Call for computational thinking in undergraduate psychology. *Psychology Learning & Teaching, 15*(3), 226–234.

Angeli, C., Voogt, J., Fluck, A., Webb, M., Cox, M., Malyn-Smith, J., & Zagami, J. (2016). A K–6 computational thinking curriculum framework: Implications for teacher knowledge. *Educational Technology & Society, 19*(3), 47–57.

Atmatzidou, S., & Demetriadis, S. (2016). Advancing students' computational thinking skills through educational robotics: A study on age and gender relevant differences. *Robotics and Autonomous Systems, 75*, 661–670.

Barr, V., & Stephenson, C. (2011). Bringing computational thinking to K–12: What is involved and what is the role of the computer science education community? *ACM Inroads, 2*(1), 48–54.

Blikstein, P. (2018). *Pre-college computer science education: A survey of the field.* https://services.google.com/fh/files/misc/pre-college-computer-science-education-report.pdf

Bower, M., & Falkner, K. (2015). Computational thinking, the notional machine, pre-service teachers, and research opportunities. *Proceedings of the 17th Australasian Computer Education Conference* (ACE2015) (pp. 37–46), Sydney, Australia.

Chang, Y. h., & Peterson, L. (2018). Pre-service teachers' perceptions of computational thinking. *Journal of Technology and Teacher Education, 26*(3), 353–374.

Computer Science Teacher Association, & International Society for Technology in Education. (2011). *Computational thinking. Teacher resources.* http://csta.acm.org/Curriculum/sub/CurrFiles/472.11CTTeacherResources_2ed-SP-vF.pdf

DeLyser, L. A., Goode, J., Guzdial, M., Kafai, Y., & Yadav, A. (2018). *Priming the computer science teacher pump: Integrating computer science education into schools of education.* CSforAll.

Gadanidis, G., Cendros, R., Floyd, L., & Namukasa, I. (2017). Computational thinking in mathematics teacher education. *Contemporary Issues in Technology and Teacher Education, 17*(4). https://www.citejournal.org/volume-17/issue-4-17/mathematics/computational-thinking-in-mathematics-teacher-education

Guzdial, M. (2017, April). Phone interview with Paulo Blikstein.

Harris, J., Grandgenett, N., & Hofer, M. (2010). Testing a TPACK-based technology integration assessment instrument. In C. D. Maddux, D. Gibson, & B. Dodge (Eds.), *Research highlights in technology and teacher education* (pp. 323–331). Society for Information Technology and Teacher Education (SITE).

Harris, J., & Hofer, M. (2009). Grounded tech integration: An effective approach based on content, pedagogy, and teacher planning. *Learning and Leading with Technology, 37*(2), 22–25.

International Society for Technology in Education. (2016). *National educational technology standards for students.* http://www.iste.org

Jaipal-Jamani, K., & Angeli, C. (2017). Effect of robotics on elementary preservice teachers' self-efficacy, science learning, and computational thinking. *Journal of Science Education and Technology, 26*(2), 175–192.

Lucarelli, C., Long, J., Rosato, J., Treichel, C., & Benedict, H. (2021). Creating change agents: A teacher preparation model that prepares all teachers to facilitate computer science concepts. In C. Mouza, A. Yadav, & A. Ottenbreit-Leftwich (Eds), *Preparing pre-service teachers to teach computer science: Models, practices, and policies* (pp. 91–112). Information Age Publishing.

McGinnis, R. J., Jass Ketelhut, D., Mills, K., Hestness, E., Jeong, H., Cabrera, L. (2019). *Preservice science teachers intentions and avoidances to integrate computational thinking into their science lesson plans for young learners.* Annual International Conference of the National Association of Research in Science Teaching (NARST), Baltimore, Maryland, April 3, 2019.

Mishra, P., & Koehler, M. (2006). Technological pedagogical content knowledge: A framework for teacher knowledge. *Teachers College Record, 108*(6), 1017–1054. https://doi.org/10.1111/j.1467-9620.2006.00684.x

Mouza, C., & Karchmer-Klein, R. (2013). Promoting and assessing pre-service teachers technological pedagogical content knowledge in the context of case development. *Journal of Educational Computing Research, 48*(2), 127–152.

Mouza, C., & Karchmer-Klein, R. (2015). Designing effective technology preparation opportunities for preservice teachers. In C. Angeli and N. Valanides (Eds.), *Technological pedagogical content knowledge: Exploring, developing, and assessing TPCK* (pp. 115–136). Springer.

Mouza, C., Karchmer-Klein, R., Nandakumar, R., Yilmaz-Ozden, S., & Hun, L. (2014). Investigating the impact of an integrated approach to the development of preservice teachers' technological pedagogical content knowledge (TPACK). *Computers & Education, 71*, 206–221. doi: 10.1015/j.compedu.2013.09.020.

Mouza, C., Marzocchi, A., Pan, Y., & Pollock, L. (2016). Development, implementation and outcomes of an equitable computer science after-school program: Findings from middle school students. *Journal of Research on Technology in Education, 48*(2), 84–104.

Mouza, C., Yadav, A., & Leftwich, A. (2018). Developing computationally literate teachers: Current perspectives and future directions for teacher preparation in computing education. *Journal of Technology and Teacher Education, 26*(3), 333–352.

Mouza, C., Yang, H., Pan, Y. C., Yilmaz Ozden, S. Y., & Pollock, L. (2017). Resetting educational technology coursework for pre-service teachers: A computational thinking approach to the development of technological pedagogical content knowledge (TPACK). *Australasian Journal of Educational Technology, 33*(3), 61–76.

National Academies of Sciences, Engineering, and Medicine. (2017). *Assessing and responding to the growth of computer science undergraduate enrollments.* The National Academies Press. https://doi.org/10.17226/24926 .

National Research Council. (2010). *Report of a workshop on the scope and nature of computational thinking.* National Academy of Sciences.

Resnick, M., Maloney, J., Monroy-Hernández, A., Rusk, N., Eastmond, E., Brennan, K., & Kafai, Y. (2009). Scratch: programming for all. *Communications of the ACM, 52*(11), 60–67.

Saeli, M., Perrenet, J., Jochems, W. M. G., Zwaneveld, B., Nederland, O. U., & Centrum, R. D. M. (2011). Teaching programming in secondary school : A pedagogical content knowledge perspective. *Informatics in Education, 10*(1), 73–88. http://doi.org/10.1145/2016911.2016943

Saldaña, J. (2015). *The coding manual for qualitative researchers.* Sage Publications Ltd.

Shulman, L. S. (1987). Knowledge and teaching: Foundations of the new reform. *Harvard Educational Review, 57*, 1–23. https://doi.org/10.17763/haer.57.1.j463w79r56455411

Wing, J. M. (2006). Computational thinking. *Communications of the ACM , 49*(3), 33–35.

Yadav, A., Hong, H., & Stephenson, C. (2016). Computational thinking for all: Pedagogical approaches to embedding a 21st century problem solving in K–12 classrooms. *TechTrends 60*, 565–568. DOI: 10.1007/s11528-016-0087-7

Yadav, A., Mayfield, C., Zhou, N., Hambrusch, S., & Korb, J. T. (2014). Computational thinking in elementary and secondary teacher education. *ACM Transactions on Computing Education, 14* (1), Article 5. https://doi.org/10.1145/2576872

Yadav, A., Stephenson, C., & Hong, H. (2017). Computational thinking for teacher education. *Communications of the ACM, 80*(4), 55–62.

CHAPTER 8

PREPARING SECONDARY EDUCATION MATHEMATICS TEACHER CANDIDATES FOR AP COMPUTER SCIENCE PRINCIPLES

A Two-Course Design Model[1]

Rebecca Odom-Bartel, Jeremy Zelkowski, and Jeff Gray

Through a combined inter-disciplinary effort from the College of Education's Secondary Education Mathematics Teacher Education Program (SEMA TEP) and the College of Engineering's Computer Science (CS) department, the University of Alabama (UA) is currently developing a curriculum design model that prepares SEMA teacher candidates to teach Advanced Placement (AP) Computer Science Principles (AP CSP). This effort addresses the challenges associated with expanding the teach-

[1] The project described in this chapter was supported in part by National Science Foundation CSforAll grant #1738849. Opinions are those of the authors and may not reflect those of the National Science Foundation.

Preparing Pre-Service Teachers to Teach Computer Science: Models, Practices, and Policies, pages 153–169.

er candidate pipeline of future CS high school educators in the state of Alabama. Specifically, the project explores a two-course sequence and associated activities that form a pathway for increasing the pool of future educators who are prepared to teach the AP CSP course without deep pre-existing content knowledge. The approach leverages an existing research-practitioner partnership with local in-service AP CSP teachers who support SEMA teacher candidates being trained to offer AP CSP in the future. In this chapter, we discuss our model and implementation with respect to how the project can be adapted for efforts in other states.

Keywords: Computer Science Education, Preservice Teacher Education, Program Design, Teacher Candidates, AP Computer Science Principles

INTRODUCTION

Over the past decade, interest in K–12 computer science (CS) has increased at a remarkable rate. According to the College Board (2018), the number of high school students in the United States taking an Advanced Placement (AP) CS exam in 2008 (19,829 total exams; 15,014 for AP CSA and 4,815 for AP CSAB) grew by 560% in 2018 (130,904 total exams; 60,040 for AP CSA and 70,864 for AP CSP), and the number of middle school and elementary school students introduced to CS has seen similar, if not larger, increases in student participation. Furthermore, many local education agencies (LEAs) and state departments of education are facing the need to respond to new legislation that requires CS to be introduced into all schools. For instance, the passage of Alabama HB 216 on May 29, 2019, helped Alabama to satisfy the nine Code.org policies that make CS foundational (Code.org, 2019b), including the requirement that every K–12 school offer a CS course in grades 6–12 and integration of CS into every K–5 grade (Taylor, 2019).

This national growth in the U.S. has created a unique challenge with respect to the content preparation needs of tens of thousands of educators who are introducing CS into their schools. Most K–12 educators have little to no content background in CS prior to professional learning experiences in the subject area. A core challenge is the development of professional learning programs that address both the lack of content, as well as provide pedagogical depth in order to expedite the growing demand for new K–12 CS educators.

The large majority of efforts to bring CS to K–12 classrooms have focused on training in-service educators (i.e., those who are already teaching, typically certified or approved to teach in an area other than CS). Our own concentration over the past five years has targeted AP CS Principles (AP CSP) while training the first wave of in-service teachers within our own state (Gray et al., 2015; Gray et al., 2017), as well as a national online course with over 2,100 in-service educators who desired to learn more about CSP (Gray et al., 2016), which was prior to the first AP CSP exam. From our efforts to prepare a new wave of CS educators, we have identified multiple challenges in training in-service educators who have little to no previous content knowledge, including: (a) retention issues, which may require additional teachers to be trained when a teacher leaves a particular school; (b) the lack of time in summer and school year schedules to offer the depth needed to produce more than novice teachers in the field, and to cover important topics beyond core CS content and pedagogy, such as perspectives on equity and inclusiveness; (c) expecting teachers to add additional responsibilities to their already overloaded schedules; and (d) informing administrators and counselors about how to provide support to the unique environment that is AP CS (e.g., developing a culture of equitable access to CS courses offered at each school).

We believe that a more sustainable approach toward recognizing the importance and continued growth of K–12 CS education is to begin the process of infusing CS content and pedagogy courses within a pre-service course of study (i.e., new pathways for students in teacher preparation programs enrolled at Colleges of Education) (Delyser et al., 2018). In fact, institutions of higher education across Alabama have been given the charge to lead the future vision of K–12 CS teacher preparation. The HB 216 legislation that recently passed mentions "pre-service" on 10 separate areas, and stipulates "requirements for institutions of higher education to provide pre-service coursework that leads to certification in computer science." The legislation also provides four pathways for certification that include: (a) Double major (CS & Secondary Education)—a pathway that is much less likely to scale, due to salary differences among the two majors; (b) certification through passing the ETS 5652 Praxis test in CS with a cut-score of 149; (c) a permit-based option that establishes certification for a single course, provided an educator completes the professional learning from an endorsed provider (e.g., completing an AP CSP training from a College Board endorsed curriculum provider); or (d) an alternative certification for those in industry who desire to teach CS.

BACKGROUND

There are existing CS pre-service or teacher candidate training models that have been implemented recently. For example, the UTeach model (Pérez & Romero, 2014) was developed, implemented at multiple institutions, and has produced over 5,278 K–12 STEM educators from across 23 states from 1997 through 2019 (UTeach, 2019). However, the supermajority of UTeach graduates are mathematics and science teachers, there are few CS educators. The UTeach model allows students to receive a core STEM degree while obtaining a teaching certificate within four years. One difficulty in attracting STEM majors to teacher education has been disparities between starting STEM salaries versus teaching salaries (e.g., at least double in STEM careers than teaching). As a further issue, most states require a major in the teaching field for secondary disciplines (e.g., mathematics, history). In some states, teacher candidates double major in secondary education and their subject discipline. Thus, to add CS curriculum into an existing secondary education teacher preparation program, whether traditional, UTeach, or some other program model, is nearly impossible without extending time to program completion. Hence, our project examined a pathway to *add on* expertise towards the teaching of a CS course while completing a mathematics teaching credential program.

There are 47 states that allow high school CS coursework to count as a mathematics graduation elective (Code.org, 2017, 2018, 2019a), including Alabama. The National Council of Teachers of Mathematics (NCTM) supports such an endeavor with two conditions in their position statement: (a) Mathematics educators continue to teach mathematics skills, concepts, and problem solving strategies; and (b) the inclusion of CS courses should not hinder students' ability to be college and career-ready in mathematics (NCTM, 2016). With these conditions in mind, CS and Secondary Education Mathematics (SEMA) faculty developed a shared, goal-oriented partnership to add the AP CSP teaching preparation of SEMA teacher candidates at the University of Alabama (UA) through a two-course sequence and summer experience.

This chapter summarizes our experiences in developing a two-course pathway that prepares SEMA students to have a permit-based course certification for AP CSP, with the potential to be certified fully in CS through the ETS 5652 Praxis exam. We further present the results of the first two cohorts, certification eligibility, and early teaching opportunities. In the next section, we present our exemplar model followed by the methods of implementation, while reporting initial outcomes of our collaborative grant project across the College of Education and the College of Engineering that is sponsored by the National Science Foundation.

THE UNIVERSITY OF ALABAMA EXEMPLAR MODEL

Approximately 30–35 SEMA teacher candidates enroll in the CS 104: CS Principles course annually (Sophomores and Juniors, typically). A subset of students (currently, an average of 11–12 per year) are recruited to the second course in our project's pathway course (CS 492: CS Curriculum for Math Ed) who consider CS as an option they would consider teaching alongside mathematics (Gray et al., 2020). Both courses are official courses in The University of Alabama CS department.

First Pathway Course: CS 104

The CS 104 course is primarily a content-equivalent course for AP CSP; high school students who receive a 3 or above on the AP CSP receive credit for CS 104 at The University of Alabama (UA). The course objectives follow closely with the College Board's AP CSP Curriculum Framework. Students work through computational thinking practices and concepts outlined by the College Board and are assessed using instruments comparable to those in a high school AP CSP course. The two overarching assessments for the AP CSP Exam are currently the Create Performance Task (CPT) and End of Course Exam. In CS 104, the End of Course Exam is replaced by two Examinations and multiple lecture quizzes. Although the new 2020 AP CSP Curriculum Framework removed the Explore Performance

Task (EPT), the CS 104 course will keep an EPT-like assignment in future editions of our course.

CS 104 students are required to examine a computing innovation that has impacted their lives or their future careers. Students must research the innovation to uncover the computational process behind it. An example of an EPT student submission can be found in the artifacts repository folder referenced at the end of the chapter. This example, in particular, highlights the level of detail students are required to research, specifically the need to understand and explain how data is transmitted, transformed, and stored. To prepare students for the CPT, a series of five programming assignments require the students to work individually or as a group. Each homework requires students to develop a program using iterative design methods, implementation and testing, and collaboration with each other, the instructor, and outside resources, as needed. Examples of the homework assignments can be found in the artifacts repository folder referenced at the end of the chapter. These examples include pictorial renderings of student code, which would be a similar method if the student was attempting to submit for an official AP Examination score.

Second Pathway Course: CS 492

The new CS 492 course is for those who already have CS content preparation (e.g., CS 104). This second course covers several topics that are designed to give students a deeper insight into the *why* and *how* of the AP CSP course (rather than the *what* that is covered as content in CS 104). The CS 492 course introduces the following topics: (a) equity and diversity in CS (Margolis & Goode, 2016); (b) the AP CSP Curriculum Framework with focus on the Five Big Ideas of Computing (prior to 2020, the course taught the prescribed seven Big Ideas before a change by the College Board to the AP CSP Curriculum Framework); (c) an understanding of national and state CS standards; (d) a survey of the specific AP CSP curriculum materials offered by many of the College Board endorsed curricula providers; (e) several readings on CS education and CS vocabulary expansion; (f) deeper exploration into the pedagogy of teaching computer programming; and (g) a summary of other CS curricula, such as Exploring Computer Science (n.d.) and Bootstrap (2019). Students also have an opportunity in the course to listen to virtual presentations by national CS education experts and to participate in classroom observations of AP CSP courses at local high schools.

Course assessments include (a) practice AP CSP exam questions; (b) a semester project equivalent to the AP CSP Create Performance Task; (c) student-led development of AP CSP lesson plans based on one of the Five Big Ideas of AP CSP; (d) an essay focused on student reflections during clinical observations; and (e) a secondary research project designed to familiarize students with currently used CS curricula such as Code.org CS Discoveries, Beauty and Joy of Computing (BJC), Bootstrap, and Exploring CS. Our CS 492 students also have an opportunity to attend a College Board sponsored AP Summer Institute (APSI) for AP

CSP, and attend the CSTA conference or SIGCSE conference. Students are also encouraged to join an intensive five-week summer online workshop comprised of student colleagues and in-service teachers from Alabama for Praxis Preparation that covers all material on the ETS 5652 exam. We offer a special section of the *Foundations of CS for Teachers: Praxis Prep* online course by WeTeach CS (University of Texas-Austin), with discussion boards and biweekly meetings for both our SEMA students and also in-service teachers who want to join in their preparation for the exam. The results of the Praxis preparation effort have been highly successful (Odom-Bartel et al., 2020). A resource folder (http://bit.ly/uac-s2cdmodel) includes assignments for both courses and some selected examples of student work (with student permission).

MAKING THE EXEMPLAR MODEL WORK

Overview of Secondary Mathematics Program Design

Our secondary mathematics (SEMA) teacher preparation programmatic design includes three successive mathematics methods course semesters, specifically designed to take novice teacher candidates to unit-planning prepared interns (e.g., full-time student teaching), one of very few programs nationally to align to and meet the recommendations of the multiple professional organizations for mathematics teacher preparation (AMTE, 2017; CBMS, 2012; MTEP, 2014). During three semesters, teacher candidates complete a set of capstone mathematics courses specifically designed for their depth of mathematical content knowledge as it relates to the secondary content they will teach through connections of other undergraduate mathematics courses (e.g., analysis, modern algebra, discrete math, linear algebra, calculus). Teacher candidates also complete a structured set of clinical experience hours in mathematics classrooms for a total of 200 hours in three semesters before their full-time student teaching internship.

Incorporating CS Education into the SEMA Program Design

As part of a teacher candidate's mathematics major, an introductory CS course is required. For many years, the primary course satisfying this requirement was the first in-major programming course for CS majors, with many SEMA students lacking any prior programming experiences in high school or college. In 2015, we recognized how a new CS course would better serve mathematics teacher candidates by allowing the AP equivalent CSP course to serve as this CS math major requirement. Our CS 104 was one of two national university-hosted pilot courses commissioned by the College Board in 2012–2013 as a CSP pilot prior to the actual AP course offered in 2017 (the other university pilot in this time period was at the University of Wisconsin-Madison—http://www.csprinciples.org/home/pilot-sites). The CS 104 course fits within the existing mathematics teacher preparation program easily by providing the option of completing the course as part of the mathematics major without additional program requirements.

Building the Two-Course Sequence

In addition to the CS content-specific CS 104 course, we also considered how a sequence course (CS 492—CS Curriculum for Math Education) that is focused on the CS content of the AP CSP course, curriculum standards, and pedagogical practices would fit within the SEMA teacher candidate schedule. We found semester-2 (spring Junior year) was the least filled semester, which traditionally is comprised of only 13 semester credit hours and a 60-hour clinical field experience. A late afternoon start time (5pm) also allowed those who were full-time student teachers in the spring semester to attend the course. Teacher candidates electing to pursue the CS experience can fit the course in their Junior or Senior year alongside either a Junior year clinical experience or major internship experience.

The process for developing this two-course sequence was not easy. It required three departments (CS, Math, and Secondary Education) to align course offerings scheduled at times that permitted teacher candidates enough flexibility in school-based clinical settings and complete their appropriate existing program coursework requirements.

The CS 104 course is one of the first university courses in the nation that was mapped as the AP equivalent for CSP. The University of Alabama was one of the first universities to officially recognize AP CSP and provide a formal statement of mapping from qualifying scores to credit for a university course. The CS 104 course covers the AP CSP Curriculum Framework, including the Five Big Ideas, Learning Objectives, and Essential Knowledge topics. The CS 104 students also submit homework corresponding to the official AP CSP Create Performance Task. SEMA teacher candidates experience the AP CSP course as if they were students completing the AP CSP course. These experiences include:

- *Computing Essentials:* Students are given the opportunity to learn and experience the essential foundations of computer programming by writing simple programs using a blocks-based language (e.g., Snap!).
- *Computational Thinking:* Students are introduced to methods of computational thinking and required to develop and refine their computational thinking abilities in small programming assignments, essays, and data research.
- *Global Impact:* Students begin to see how CS relates to their own and their students' daily lives.

This experience sets the stage in the sequence course to begin the curriculum planning and implementation as a future AP CSP teacher.

In the sequence course, CS 492 students learn about the motivating reasons behind the inclusion of topics in the curriculum and begin to develop sample lesson plans focused on the learning objectives of AP CSP. Table 8.1 presents an organized look and overview of the key topical course areas while Figure 8.1 depicts the community building within the CS 492 course.

Delivery	National	State	Local
Face to Face	**Workshop:** Led by an AP CSP Development Committee Board Advisor	**Workshop:** Led by AP CS Content Specialist from Alabama's Code.org Regional Partner **Discussion Session:** Host State Department of Education Administrator for Computer Science Education	**Classroom Observations:** Supervised by Local CSP Teachers during AP CSP Course
	National Conference Session: Impacting Mathematics Teacher Education, Initiating Critical Conversations about Computer Science & Math	**Discussion Session:** Host Governor's Office of Education and Workforce Transformation, Education Policy Advisor, and Coordinator **Workshop:** Led by Educational Technology State Administrator	**Discussion Session:** Host Local Area CSP Education Teachers Symposium
Virtual Meeting	**Discussion Session:** Host National Leader in Equity and Inclusion for CS Education **Discussion Session:** Host Code.org Director of State Government Affairs	**Collaborative Meetings:** Host in-service and teacher candidate online bi-weekly summer webinars in preparation for Praxis II CS exam	
Professional Development		**Professional Development:** Enrollment in the Alabama CSP APSI	

FIGURE 8.1. Community Building Activities During the CS 492 Course and Afterwards

TABLE 8.1. CS 492 Curriculum Framework and Core Topical Areas

Core Topical Area	Directive Literature	Description of Course Assignments and Learning Goals
Diversity and Equity in CS Education	Margolis, 2008	Students examine portions of key literature in CS equity research and place them in the context of their own teaching philosophies. Throughout the course, students are expected to reference these key topics and ways they would address them in their curriculum. Examples include student created lesson plans that specifically address concerns surrounding under-represented minorities in CS, observation write-ups where students examine demographics and current curriculum delivery techniques.
CS K–12 Standards	CSTA, 2018	Students are introduced to the portfolio of K–12 CS standards, including efforts by CSTA and the CS K–12 Framework, as well as the Alabama Digital Literacy and Computer Science (DLCS) standards that were passed by the Alabama State Board of Education in March 2018. Students develop artifacts for their own teaching portfolio that include CS standards integration with state and national math standards, and areas where CS topics introduce new concepts. Examples include a two sequenced unit lesson plan that addresses one of the Five Big Ideas of CSP, observation write-ups that require students to identify standards both nationally and at the state level, and multiple classroom discussions of standards and how they align with local, state, and national requirements.

TABLE 8.1. Continued

Core Topical Area	Directive Literature	Description of Course Assignments and Learning Goals
Problem Solving through Computational Thinking	CSTA, 2018; NCTM 2014, 2016	Computational thinking practices explored along with the development of critical problem solving strategies using computational approaches. Examples include working through the Create Performance Task for the AP CSP Examination, developing alternative solutions to programming practices, and creating additional learning paths for pre-existing lesson plans.
AP CSP Curriculum Framework and Performance Tasks	Wiggins & McTighe, 2006	A detailed exploration into the Five Big Ideas of AP CSP, along with their associated Key Understandings, Learning Objectives, and Essential Knowledge statements. The students read essays on Understanding by Design as they explore the AP CSP Curriculum Framework. They also examine student samples of AP CSP Create Performance Tasks and perform a mock reading based on the existing AP CSP rubric for the Create Performance Task. A final activity of the course requires the students to create two of their own sample lesson plans based on two separate AP CSP Learning Objectives. Students discuss scaffolding and mock assignments that integrate with their lesson plan.
Building a Network of Support and Mentorship	CSTA, 2018; NCTM, 2012; 2014	Within the timeline of course delivery, students are introduced to several local, state, and national partners in CS Education. Partners share new initiatives, resources, and support for educators throughout their tenure as CS educators. Students become aware of local and state mentorship opportunities and connect with other educators on the same path. This interaction provides a solid foundation for the students to grow within the CS Education community and strengthen the already existing CS Educator Network in the state and region.

Note: CS 492 utilizes CSTA, NCTM, and requisite pedagogical literature in the design of single course preparation for teaching AP CSP by Secondary Mathematics Teacher Candidates upon entering the teaching profession as a mathematics teacher.

RESULTS

Making AP CSP Curriculum Attractive to SEMA Teacher Candidates

Currently, CS Education is situated tightly with Mathematics Education, which makes recruiting mathematics teacher candidates a primary goal. As mentioned previously, there is a shortage of mathematics teacher candidates nationally, therefore, making CS Education attractive to SEMA teacher candidates as an additional expertise is imperative toward growing CS Educational Initiatives. We have taken several approaches to build our teacher candidate pool:

- AP CSP is taught within the contextualization of mathematics topics that would be of interest to SEMA teacher candidates

- Broadened understanding of how CS Education can benefit student outcomes, as well as help strengthen mathematical practices of students (Yadav, et al., 2017)
- Provide resources to school administrators, counselors, and SEMA teacher candidates on how to develop CS education courses in their own school districts
- State sponsored tuition reimbursement potential through Alabama Math and Science Teacher Education Program (AMSTEP)
- Continue to build a community of practitioners by involving current teacher candidates with recruitment of next year's teacher candidates

Seamless Integration of CS into a SEMA Teacher Candidate Program

Secondary Mathematics Teacher preparation programs are under intense pressure to produce enough mathematics teachers to meet the demands of schools, with respect to quantity and quality of in-demand educators. The preparation of mathematics teachers is primary while the addition of the AP CSP experience is secondary. For our project to make the CS option a reality in our nationally recognized SEMA program, three things had to intersect (See Figure 8.2). First, SEMA, CS, and Mathematics department faculty had to collaborate on course scheduling which included offering the CS course in the evenings one night a week to accommodate enrollment by student teaching interns in their final SEMA semester. Second, assignments had to be structured on a timeline in the CS course that would not heavily conflict with the edTPA (Teacher Performance Assessment)

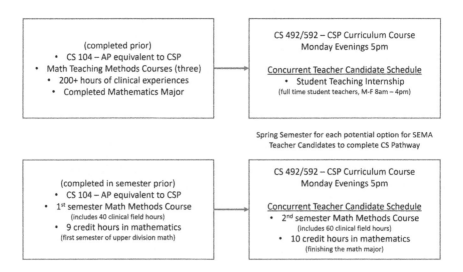

FIGURE 8.2. Two Optional Pathways for SEMA Teacher Candidates in CSP Preparation

portfolio for interns and other major assignments for non-interns in their course-work. Lastly, an expectation of cross-collaborative commitments between faculty were needed to help shape the development and improvements of the CS course.

After the first year of implementation, participants provided experiences in the post-course interview. The first quote below comes from a graduate who had the opportunity to be hired at a school to teach mathematics and also a CSP class. She said, "If I hadn't been given the opportunities this past year with CS, I don't know where I would be today. Having this CS background helped me get a job at a once-in-a-lifetime school and I could not be more thankful! So far, I have really enjoyed teaching CS [in addition to math]. I teach the non-AP version of CSP at my school [first year teaching], and so I felt very comfortable going into the course with my prior knowledge. While there are things that I still struggle with (like pacing), I think my kids are learning a lot and exploring the subject along with me. We do labs almost every week and I try to add in some CS unplugged projects every once in a while to keep them engaged. Everything I've used so far I've gotten from the APSI or from the [CS 492/592] course last spring."

This student was a highly engaged mathematics teacher candidate during her program, scoring above the third-quartile on her observations of students being engaged in the Standards for Mathematical Practices assessed with the Mathematics Classroom Observation Protocol for Practices (Gleason et al., 2017). She said during a national presentation, "teaching CSP has allowed me to learn more about what the Mathematical Practices look like in real applications of the mathematics I teach. It has improved my ideas about the NCTM Mathematical Teaching Practices" (NCTM, 2014). This student also passed the ETS Praxis test 5652 with a very high score and is one of the first certified CS teachers in Alabama from our pathway, teaching CSP as a first year teacher and now AP CSP as a second year teacher. She also teaches a Python course and preparing to offer her first AP CSA course.

Another student who graduated and attended the APSI said, "I was excited to attend the conference (e.g., APSI) especially as a beginning teacher. The APSI encouraged me in that other veteran teachers were just as prepared or even less prepared than me to teach AP CSP. In general, I was more prepared to teach [math or CS] after the APSI because I was given the chance to collaborate with other teachers during my summer and make positive connections. Being able to attend the APSI this summer really made me less nervous about teaching CS this year. It was nice to walk into a room every morning with people who were also still learning and others who were there to share their experiences and tips with each other. Leaving the APSI, I had new teachers to contact if I needed help, an experienced professional to call when I needed her, and many resources that have made my transition into teaching CS easier than I could have imagined!"

Although these two students provided rich detailed responses, they represent the greatest outcomes or possibilities of our model to provide mathematics teacher candidates the opportunity to engage in teaching AP CSP as a first-year teacher

Cohort Year	Students (n=)	Program Status	APSI or Praxis II Path	Passed Praxis II?	Teaching/ Taught CS?	Still interested in teaching CS?
Spring '18	11	9 graduated	3 of 7 APSI	2 of 2	2 of 3	5 yes
		0 still in program	n/a	n/a	n/a	n/a
		2 discontinued*	n/a	n/a	n/a	unknown
Spring '19	10	7 graduated	6 of 6 Praxis II	5 of 6	0 of 6	6 yes
		0 still in program	n/a	n/a	n/a	n/a
		3 discontinued*	1 of 1 Praxis II	1 of 1	n/a	unknown
Spring '20	9^	8 graduated	7 of 7 Praxis II	7 of 7	1 of 8	7 yes
		1 still in program	1 of 1 Praxis II	1 of 1	n/a	1 yes
		0 discontinued	n/a	n/a	n/a	n/a

Note: APSI or Praxis II column denotes pathway to qualifying to teach CSP. Passed Praxis II column denotes teacher candidates who sat for the Praxis II 5652 exam and whether they passed or not. Teaching CS? Indicates if candidates upon graduation are teaching CS or have taught CS as early career teacher. ^Spring 2020 participants, one graduated and is teaching CS but elected not to take the CS Praxis, rather is permitted to teacher CSP and only wants to teach CSP. One of 8 in 2020 cohort elected to continue in math education only program but not pursue CS Praxis II testing.

FIGURE 8.3.   Descriptive of Current Status of SEMA CS Participants in CSP Sequence

alongside mathematics. Figure 8.3 presents the *up-to-date* status of participants in our project.

Overall, we see that in Figure 8.3 that 25 of 30 SEMA teacher candidate participants still have interest in teaching or are teaching AP CSP after the two-course sequence. Fourteen of 15 teacher candidates have passed the Praxis II exam as of July 2020. Under Alabama law and new certifications, once teacher candidates have their Secondary Math teaching license, they will immediately be able to apply and add the CS teaching credential via the Praxis II passed exam. We acknowledge that five students discontinued, of which, two had academic issues, two elected to withdraw from the university for personal reasons, and one changed majors out of a teaching major. Lastly, we have a few SEMA teacher candidates or graduates, who indicated that focusing on mathematics teaching solely was more important to them as an early career teacher than dually looking at teaching mathematics and CS. We are hopeful, later in their careers, that CS may enter their consideration and at least be advocates for CS if their school does not offer it. Their background experiences from our project will be valuable to their school given the new legislation that requires every high school to offer an authentic CS course.

NEXT STEPS FROM INITIAL RESULTS

There are four primary actions that we have identified as our next steps for moving our project forward. First and foremost, we need to establish a continued community of practice for the graduates of our pathway during their first few years of teaching to help them remain aware of opportunities from the community at large (e.g., the Alabama CSTA chapter) with respect to support for their teaching of CS in middle grades and AP CSP in high school. As part of an earlier NSF project, we established a community of practice (a Piazza discussion forum) for all Alabama secondary school CS teachers. All of our pre-service teacher candidates are invited to join this community of practice. Second, we would like to see how this program model effectively prepares teacher candidates to successfully implement a CS curriculum early in their careers for student success. Third, we are studying the effects of our program design in recruitment and engaging teacher candidates to effectively advocate for CS in their future schools. Lastly and most optimistically, we look to lead on how dual certification in a primary discipline can add CS teacher credentialing as a pre-service preparation that results in two teaching disciplines in the secondary grades.

Using the information we gained over the past two years of the two-course pathway, we feel there are several takeaways:

1. A key component of any additional CS pre-service curricula needs to address the current alignment with our state's Digital Literacy and Computer Science (DLCS) standards that were approved March 2018. During our two project years, our state standards were adjusted and changed, which required a continuous update to the curriculum we created for CS 104 and CS 492.

2. Adding material related to the middle school Computer Science Discoveries (CSD) into the current pathway sequence felt overloaded and there is room for additional course development focusing on CSD.

3. Although we think that the two course sequence and additional experiences fully prepares teacher candidates to teach an AP CSP course, we believe it does not prepare SEMA students to fully teach an AP CSA course. Additional coursework is needed to add AP CSA preparedness to teacher candidate portfolios.

4. We have created a pilot experiment to prepare both in-service teachers and our SEMA teacher candidates with a preparatory experience for the ETS 5652 Praxis test (Odom-Bartel et al., 2020). The outcomes are very promising (e.g., all of the teacher candidates who have taken the Praxis have passed and will be eligible for certification for CS upon their issued first teaching license in mathematics). As we move forward, we will continue to add additional prep material and expand the opportunities for CS certification.

With these next-steps and takeaways in mind, we believe that more research should be dedicated to CS Education over the next decade, specifically looking at how much pre-service preparation is needed to fully prepare CS Educators for all levels of secondary education. Additionally, should these pre-service initiatives be molded into pre-existing programs of Education or developed as stand-alone CS Educator programs? One thing we are confident about from our experience in this project is that interdisciplinary collaboration between Education and Computer Science is imperative for a sustainable CS Educator program (Delyser et al., 2018).

Along with collaboration between three departments (Computer Science, Secondary Education, Mathematics), our working relationship with the Alabama State Department of Education, University Provost office, and numerous non-profit CS Education organizations helped tremendously in achieving our success. To build off this success, we hope to achieve the following: (a) gain further collaboration between the College of Engineering and the College of Education, (b) identify additional funding resources to incentivize SEMA students into taking on additional coursework, (c) explore options to place our course pathway online to support teacher candidates at other universities and support in-service teachers across our state, and (d) find a more permanent home for the teacher preparation program.

SUMMARY

We have drawn three significant conclusions for mathematics teacher educators and the CS teacher education community. First, there are many mathematics teacher preparation programs that cannot and should not consider such a daunting task of integrating CS education into mathematics teacher preparation. Many mathematics teacher preparation programs have only one mathematics methods course, one semester of clinical experience, and lack mathematical content courses focused on the recommendations of professional organizations. There are many mathematics teacher preparation programs that cannot secure full administrative support for the resources needed to meet the Association of Mathematics Teacher Educators (2017) standards, let alone the Mathematics Teaching Education Partnership (MTEP, 2014) gold-standard guiding principles, and/or complete the rigorous National Council of Teachers of Mathematics & The Council for the Accreditation of Educator Preparation (2012) specialized professional association process. Our mathematics preparation already is at top-tier achievement levels (Zelkowski et al., 2018; Zelkowski & Gleason, 2018) and has empirical evidence of direct effects of program impact. We encourage institutions to improve their existing mathematics teacher education program rather than taking on the large task of aligning CS, Math, and Math Education structures to achieve such a design and we caution to not decrease the quality of existing teacher preparation programs.

Second, teaching CS education may not be for all mathematics teachers, though we argue all mathematics teachers could benefit from the underlying skills that CS education provides (Yadav et al., 2017). Teaching CS requires a commitment from mathematics teachers to increase their own content knowledge, pedagogical knowledge, and technology knowledge in both mathematics and CS. With these thoughts in mind, the elective nature of the CS courses in our preparation program supports those who embrace this opportunity with passion and interest, a stark contrast from those who reluctantly take CS courses to fulfill a requirement. We believe this difference paired well with our goal of priming the pump of CS teachers.

Third, the demand for CS in K–12 schools is expected to continue to increase in the future. The readiness of teachers to embrace CS into all disciplines should be encouraged and there is a growing number of mathematics educators who seek to integrate CS into their school curriculum either as a stand-alone course or with content area focused courses.

In conclusion, we strongly encourage the field of mathematics teacher education, mathematics education, CS education, and teachers in general, to examine what is most beneficial for their students to pursue the opportunity of participating in engaged and meaningful mathematics and CS coursework. We must challenge the status quo and the traditional structures, particularly that of the American high school, as a means to provide more students with equitable opportunities in mathematics and CS by de-tracking and opening doors in these two fields.

Please visit our artifact repository for course materials we have developed and a selected few examples of student work: http://bit.ly/uacs2cdmodel.

REFERENCES

Association of Mathematics Teacher Educators (AMTE). (2017). *Standards for preparing teachers of mathematics.* https://amte.net/sites/default/files/SPTM.pdf

Bootstrap World. (2019). *Programming games with algebra, for every student.* https://www.bootstrapworld.org/

Code.org. (2017). *Hour of code impact.* https://code.org/about/evaluation/hourofcode

Code.org. (2018). *Where computer science counts.* Available at: https://code.org/action

Code.org. (2019a). *2019 State of computer science education equity and diversity.* https://advocacy.code.org/2019_state_of_cs.pdf

Code.org. (2019b). *Nine policy ideas to make computer science fundamental to K–12 education.* https://code.org/files/Making_CS_Fundamental.pdf

College Board. (2018). *AP data* [Data file]. https://research.collegeboard.org/programs/ap/data

Computer Science Teachers Association. (2018). *K–12 computer science standards.* Retrieved from: https://csta.acm.org/Curriculum/sub/K12Standards.html

Conference Board of the Mathematical Sciences (CBMS). (2012). *The mathematical education of teachers II (MET2).* American Mathematical Society and Mathematical Association of America.

Delyser, L., Goode, J., Guzdial, M., Kafai, Y., & Yadav, A. (2018). *Priming the computer science teacher pump: Integrating computer science education into schools of education.* https://drive.google.com/file/d/1DXgpLjl_k87TVpQ0cLusfdjnYySIgIjT/view

Exploring Computer Science. (n.d.). *ECS: Exploring Computer Science.* http://www.exploringcs.org/

Gleason, J., Livers, S. D., & Zelkowski, J. (2017). Mathematics classroom observation protocol for practices (MCOP²): Validity and reliability. *Investigations in Mathematical Learning, 9*(3), 111–129.

Gray, J., Corley, J., & Eddy, B. (2016). An experience report assessing a professional development MOOC for CS Principles, *ACM Technical Symposium on Computer Science Education (SIGCSE)* (pp. 455–460). Memphis, TN, March 2016.

Gray, J., Haynie, K., Packman, S., Boehm, M., Crawford, C., & Muralidhar, D. (2015). A mid-project report on a statewide professional development model for CS Principles, *ACM Technical Symposium on Computer Science Education (SIGCSE)* (pp. 380–385). Kansas City, MO.

Gray, J., Odom-Bartel, R. L., Zelkowski, J., Hamner, K., & Rogers-Farris, S. (2020). A pre-service pathway for preparing future AP CS Principles teachers. In Heckman, S., Monge, A., & Cutter, P. (Eds.). *Proceedings of the 51st ACTM Technical Symposium on Computer Science Education* (pp. 1127–1132). Association for Computing Machinery.

Gray, J., Roberts, M., & Corley, J. (2017). Getting principled: Reflections on teaching CS Principles at two college board university pilots, *ACM Technical Symposium on Computer Science Education (SIGCSE)* (pp. 249–254). Seattle, WA, March 2017.

Margolis, J. (2008). *Stuck in the shallow end : Education, race, and computing.* The MIT Press.

Margolis, J., & Goode, J. (2016). Ten lessons for computer science for all. *Inroads, 7*(4), 52–56.

Mathematics Teacher Education Partnership (MTEP). (2014). *Guiding principles for secondary mathematics teacher preparation programs.* Association of Public & Land-grant Universities. http://www.aplu.org/projects-and-initiatives/stem-education/SMTI_Library/mte-partnership-guiding-principles-for-secondary-mathematics-teacher-preparation-programs/File

National Council of Teachers of Mathematics (NCTM). (2014). *Principles to actions: Ensuring mathematical success for all.* Author.

National Council of Teachers of Mathematics (NCTM). (2016). *Computer science and mathematics education position statement.* http://www.nctm.org/Standards-and-Positions/Position-Statements/Computer-Science-and-Mathematics-Education/

National Council of Teachers of Mathematics & The Council for the Accreditation of Educator Preparation. (2012). *Standards for mathematics teacher preparation.* https://www.nctm.org/Standards-and-Positions/CAEP-Standards/

Odom-Bartel, R. L., Fletcher, C., Owen, J., Gray, J., & Zelkowski, J. (2020). Preparing pre-service teacher candidates for the praxis exam: An innovative model of blended support. In Heckman, S., Monge, A., & Cutter, P. (Eds.). *Proceedings of the 51st ACTM Technical Symposium on Computer Science Education* (p. 1298). Association for Computing Machinery.

Pérez, M., & Romero, P. (2014). Secondary STEM teacher preparation as a top priority for the university of the future. *The Journal of the World Universities Forum, 6*(4), 21–36.

Taylor, D. (2019). New law expands computer science in all Alabama schools. *Tuscaloosa News*, June 4, 2019. https://www.tuscaloosanews.com/news/20190604/new-law-expands-computer-science-in-all-alabama-schools

UTeach. (2019). *UTeach national expansion.* https://institute.uteach.utexas.edu/sites/institute.uteach.utexas.edu/files/uteach-national-snapshot_0.pdf

Wiggins, G. P., & McTighe, J. (2006). *Understanding by design.* Pearson Education, Inc.

Yadav, A., Stephenson, C., & Hong, H. (2017). Computational thinking for teacher education. *Communications of the ACM, 60*, 55–62. https://cacm.acm.org/magazines/2017/4/215031-computational-thinking-for-teacher-education/fulltext

Zelkowski, J., Campbell, T. G., & Gleason, J. (2018). Programmatic effects of capstone math content and math methods courses on teacher licensure exams. In W. M. Smith, B. R. Lawler, J. Strayer, & L. Augustyn, (Eds.), *Proceedings of the 7th Annual Mathematics Teacher Education—Partnership Conference* (pp. 91–96). Washington, DC: Association of Public Land-grant Universities.

Zelkowski, J., & Gleason, J. (2018). Programmatic effects on high stakes measures in secondary math teacher preparation. In L. Venenciano & A. Redmond-Sanogo (Eds.), *Proceedings of the 45th Annual Meeting of the Research Council on Mathematics Learning.* Research Council on Mathematics Learning.

PART III

UNIVERSITY AND STATE POLICIES FOR PREPARING
PRE-SERVICE TEACHERS TO TEACH COMPUTER
SCIENCE

CHAPTER 9

USING A COACHING MODEL TO SUPPORT COMPUTER SCIENCE PROFESSIONAL DEVELOPMENT FOR EDUCATION FACULTY

Jennifer Rosato, Heather Benedict,
Chery Lucarelli, Jill Long, and Christa Treichel

With the increasing demand for computational thinking and computer science (CT/CS) in K–12 schools, pre-service teaching programs are responding by adding CT/CS through required and elective coursework. However, most education faculty do not have a background in computing and need professional development and support to teach this new subject. The programs at the College of St. Scholastica developed a pre-service program model, TeachCS@CSS, which infused CT/CS across the curriculum for all pre-service teachers. Consequently, many of the education faculty needed not only computer science professional development, but also support in the process to integrate CT/CS in education courses. The TeachCS@CSS model includes professional development through a computational thinking mini-course and then support in the integration process through the use of coaching. Participants

Preparing Pre-Service Teachers to Teach Computer Science: Models, Practices and Policies,
pages 173–189.

in the coaching process found it valuable in developing their own understanding of CT/CS content and pedagogy and developed more confidence in their ability to teach CT/CS integrated with their disciplinary specialty. This chapter shares details of the coaching model and process, including the roles and expectations of the coach and the faculty, lessons learned and key components for success.

Keywords: Coaching, Education Faculty Development, Integrated Computer Science, Integrated Computational Thinking

INTRODUCTION

In 2013, the Computer Science Teachers Association (CSTA) released a report that described how and why computer science (CS) teacher certification processes face multiple challenges in the United States (CSTA, 2013). These challenges, in part, explain why only 75 teachers graduated from Title II teacher preparation institutions equipped to teach CS in 2017 (Code.org, 2017). At the same time, a study by Google and Gallup (2016) documented a high demand for CS education in the United States among parents, teachers, principals, and school superintendents in K–12 settings. With the current landscape in mind, it is not surprising that *Priming the Computer Science Pump* report claims there is a "critical need to provide teacher education programs that focus on pre-service teachers to meet the growing demand for teachers who are well qualified to teach computer science" (DeLyser et al., 2018, p. 14).

Clearly, there are challenges in preparing CS educators and a gap exists between the demand for CS instruction and the number of qualified educators. While change may be slow for resolving this pipeline challenge, pre-service teacher education programs are in a position to respond to this situation. This chapter highlights an example of a pre-service teacher education program at the College of St. Scholastica (CSS) that is designed to prepare educators to deliver CS education in K–12 settings. In particular, the chapter focuses on the use of coaching to support education faculty to deliver CS professional learning to future teachers: TeachCS@CSS.

The TeachCS@CSS model integrates computational thinking (CT) and CS across the curriculum for all teacher candidates in all licensure areas in the CSS teacher preparation programs (see Chapter 5). Because CT/CS is infused across the curriculum, *all* education faculty must be prepared to understand and teach CT/CS to teacher candidates independent of their discipline. Most education faculty, however, have little to no background in CT/CS. To equip them with the necessary background, the CSS provided education faculty with initial professional development through a blended CT/CS mini-course to help develop a baseline knowledge in the discipline. Through a mini-course designed for education faculty, CSS initially defined CT as "using special thinking patterns and processes to pose and solve problems or prepare programs for computation" (Krauss & Prottsman, 2017, p. 4). Other explanations and definitions were introduced by the end of the mini-course, including those provided in the K–12 Computer Science Framework (2016) and Jeannette Wing (2006).

The mini-course required about 25 hours to complete and was composed of four modules: (1) Introduction to CS and CT, (2) CT in Action, (3) Exploring CT, and (4) Inclusive and Effective Methods for Teaching CS. Included in the course were readings from the book by Krauss and Prottsman (2017), chosen for its focus on the needs of K–12 teachers and content for both elementary and secondary grades. Other course components included discussions, hands-on activities, and videos that were designed to provide an exploration of CT/CS concepts and practices. The first module laid the groundwork for the importance of CT and CS. The second module provided a set of hands-on activities in a fun and low stakes manner designed to reduce potential anxiety about CT/CS. The third module made connections to the ways in which CT/CS can be integrated in other disciplines. The final module introduced issues of equity in computing, pedagogical practices that can help to mitigate those issues, and connections to the larger CS education community (e.g. CSTA chapters and standards).

Since the mini-course only offered an introductory level of content, additional support was provided through a coaching process. While education faculty are experts in their content areas, courses, and the programs they teach in, coaches provided the CT/CS content expertise faculty needed at the beginning stages. For education faculty integrating CT/CS concepts in their courses, a coaching process provided support as they conceptualized, developed, taught, and refined their CT/CS lesson plans. Lesson plans generally addressed the integration of CT/CS with disciplinary content (e.g., science, language arts standards) and pedagogy.

Coaches were content experts in CT/CS with a substantial education background who could provide guidance on CS resources such as curriculum and standards. The coaching process used an iterative approach, grounded in design thinking, to progress through a series of milestones from the initial discovery session to the final product—a vetted lesson plan shareable with other education faculty.

The integrated model described above and in more detail in Chapter 5 was based on the idea that education faculty would take greater ownership of the program, the materials, and the student learning outcomes if they were involved in the design of the CT/CS curriculum, promoting a sustainable program. To ensure consistency and quality, coaches supported education faculty in this development. This chapter will share the importance of teaching integrated CT, details of the coaching model and process, including the roles and expectations of the coach and the faculty, early outcomes and lessons learned, and key components for success.

BACKGROUND

In this section, we first provide background information on how coaching is being utilized in K–12 schools, including specific examples of how it is being used to support the teaching of CS/CT. Next, we provide background information on teaching integrated CT. We also describe how CT fits into and aligns with our standards.

Coaching in K–12 Schools

Many will attest that roots of today's coaching began with the work of Dale Carnegie in his 1936 work *How to Win Friends and Influence People.* This work launched an entire industry for professional improvement and eventually evolved into the practice of professional coaching. In 1995 the International Coach Federation (ICF) was formed. According to the ICF, coaching in the professional (and business) context is "partnering with clients in a thought-provoking and creative process that inspires them to maximize their personal and professional potential" (About ICF, n.d.).

In education, different coaching philosophies have emerged such as cognitive coaching, which was co-developed by Arthur Costa and Robert Garmston beginning in 1984. Cognitive coaching is one of the most widely used forms of coaching in American schools today. In cognitive coaching, the coach's focus is "on mediating a practitioner's thinking, perceptions, beliefs, and assumptions toward the goals of self-directed learning and increased complexity of cognitive processing" (Costa & Garmston, 2002, p.5). Cognitive coaches are facilitators of thinking and the aim is to "produce self-directed persons with the cognitive capacity for high performance, both independently and as members of a community" (Costa & Garmston, 2002, p.16).

In 2007, Jim Knight published his book *Instructional Coaching: A Partnership Approach to Improving Instruction* resulting in a slow resurgence and eventual widespread adoption of professional coaching within K–12 districts. Instructional coaches, much like cognitive coaches, are skilled at facilitation of the reflective process. However, they also need to act as a resource and sometimes draw on their own expertise while collaborating with teachers (Knight, 2007). Both models of coaching include planning phases between coach and educator, observations of the educator, and conclude with reflective conversations with the educator. Where cognitive coaching relies primarily on educators to find the answers within themselves, instructional coaches also rely on model lessons, simplified explanations of proven teaching practices, content area expertise, classroom management strategies, content enhancement, and formative assessment (Knight, 2009). No matter the model, coaching allows teachers to apply learning from professional development experiences to the classroom; literature indicates that the support of a coach increases from 20% to 80% the likelihood of teachers implementing new practices (Pierce & Buysee, 2014).

With this new focus on coaching for K–12 teachers, there has been an emergence of placing instructional coaches within districts to help direct institutional change. These coaches have operated across multiple disciplines or have been specialized in such areas as literacy, Positive Behavior Interventions and Supports

(PBIS), and technology. In 2011, the International Society for Technology in Education (ISTE) published their first set of standards for coaches, also the same year they published their first set of standards for CS educators.

Coaching in the CS Context

Cognitive coaching involves teacher reflection on practice and establishes a professional learning community (Margolis et al., 2017), essential not only for CS teachers, but also for education faculty new to the discipline of CS. Coaches for CS are responsible for the process of coaching a teacher's decision-making process as well as serving as a content expert. In cognitive coaching, the main role of the coach is to support teachers in becoming more resourceful (Costa & Garmston, 2002). Margolis et al. (2017) found that "coaching helps to: (1) positively impact changes in pedagogy; (2) enrich teachers' CS content knowledge; (3) support educators especially in their first year of teaching a new CS course, and (4) break CS teacher isolation in schools" (p. 3). As part of the Exploring Computer Science (ECS) implementation in Chicago Public Schools (CPS), a peer coaching model was also adopted where new ECS teachers were paired up with ECS master teachers to work on the new teachers' practices (CS4All at CPS, n.d.).

Teaching Integrated Computational Thinking

CT in this work is seen from the standpoint of an integrated model because core academic standards are beginning to also take this integrated approach. Integration is the act of taking two seemingly separate disciplines and combining them together for a more holistic approach to learning content. The Next Generation Science Standards (NGSS, 2013), for instance, ask for the integration of CT with science content. Similarly, in Minnesota, the 2018 Legislative Statutes require technology and information literacy standards to be embedded across core-content areas. This is to be updated every 10 years by media specialists in Minnesota. The ISTE standards are also a core component of the CT integration effort, incorporating a CT standard for students. Along with the ISTE standards, the SAMR (Substitution, Augmentation, Modification, Redefinition) model (Puentedura, 2013) for technology integration is a potential framework for integrating CT as in some cases educators start with substitution, where a CT activity is embedded as a direct substitute for a tool that is already being used. The end goal, however, is to get to the Redefinition level, allowing for the teaching and learning to change in ways that were inconceivable prior to the integration.

Another approach to integration is through the arts. The Kennedy Center's definition for arts integration is "Arts Integration is an *approach* to teaching in which students construct and demonstrate *understanding* through an *art form*. Students engage in a *creative process* which connects an *art form* and another subject area and meets *evolving objectives* in both." This definition could easily be rewritten for CT as such: Integrating CT is an *approach* to teaching in which students construct *meaning* and demonstrate *understanding* through *computing*. Students engage in a *thought* process which connects computing and another subject area and meets *evolving objectives* in both. The Kennedy Center also positions that teachers are attracted to arts integration because (1) Arts integration practices are aligned with how students learn, and (2) Arts integration energizes teachers by providing increased professional satisfaction. It is hypothesized that integrating CT in a similar vein will have this same level of attraction to future educators. Another aspect of looking at it through this lens is to tie in the tenants of maker-centered learning and the idea that once students understand that the world we live in is a designed world, they understand that it is malleable. Empowered with this agency, they become the creators of the technologies we use, not just the consumers, possessing the potential of creating an equitable playing field in how technology is implemented in our lives.

CSTA in coordination with the K–12 CS Framework, takes an approach that breaks the standards down into concepts and identify practice(s) that align with the standards. In Minnesota, taking an approach similar to the technology and literacy standards, embedding the CSTA standards within other existing discipline-specific standards has the potential to be effective if the integration is done in a thoughtful manner. Working in a coaching relationship with education faculty is a starting point of inquiry to discover how best to connect CSTA standards with other academic areas. This integration has the potential to also address systemic equity and implicit bias issues within the teaching profession. In our model, the coaches drew upon resources such as the EngageCSEdu strategies provided by the National Center for Women in Technology (NCWIT), the SciGirls Seven Strategies for gender equitable teaching strategies, and Teaching System Lab's teacher practice spaces at the Massachusetts Institute of Technology to address implicit bias within the context of a STEM subject area. Each state has its own version of Minnesota's Standards of Effective Practice for teachers that should be considered when developing lesson plans for teacher candidates.

EXEMPLAR: TEACHCS@CSS

Description of the TeachCS@CSS Coaching Model

TeachCS@CSS decided to adopt coaching as a method for professional development as coaching provided continuous support to faculty in both lesson development and teaching practices as well as technical expertise and assistance in integrating CS/CT. The TeachCS@CSS team recognized the importance of establishing a coaching model as part of the professional development for the School of Education Faculty as well as teacher candidates. The CSS offers teacher preparation programs for initial licensure in a variety of areas in three delivery models at multiple sites within Minnesota (For a full review of programs, see Chapter 5).

For all programs, the School of Education has chosen to integrate technology throughout student coursework rather than offer a separate technology course. This approach is similar to other topics, such as equity, diversity, and inclusion which are also woven throughout the teacher education programs. While there is a specific course in both programs that discusses how to meet the needs of diverse learners, the topic is also incorporated in multiple courses. This integrative approach is indicative of why the CSS education program chose to add CS/CT throughout its curriculum, rather than offer a single stand-alone course.

To coordinate and change multiple courses in the curriculum, with content scaffolded from course-to-course, we felt it required many more faculty to buy-in to the need for CS and to develop materials for each course that they feel confident in teaching. This approach does offer the advantage of highlighting to students and faculty the interdisciplinary nature of CS and how it is woven into many aspects of modern life. This approach also addresses a fundamental equity concern—if every student is to learn CS, so must every teacher—and by extent, so must every education faculty. The TeachCS model provides shared ownership of the student-teacher outcomes and a path towards sustainability.

In the TeachCS@CSS coaching process, coaches partnered with the School of Education faculty to support them become self-directed learners by coaching them in the decision making process while they co-design lessons that integrate CT/CS concepts within their own content area. Coaches served as a resource for CT/CS content expertise. Faculty were treated as experts and professionals as they brought their own areas of expertise to the process. Coaches assisted faculty with finding natural intersections in their curriculum where CT and CS can be integrated. The coaching experience bridged critical intersections where learning and application meet. Coaches connected faculty with resources, co-designed lesson plans, and observed (sometimes co-taught) when faculty piloted their integrated lessons in undergraduate and graduate education courses. In this way, coaches also served to ensure that the new lessons developed by faculty were of high quality, that faculty felt supported in this learning endeavor, and that ultimately they felt confident to independently integrate this material for pre-service education students through their own self-directed learning.

Before a coaching cycle began, a faculty member was identified by the School of Education (SOE) leadership team either by self-selection or by invitation. The faculty members who agreed to participate in the coaching process identified a specific course to focus their CT/CS integration efforts. The initial lesson idea was passed by the project leadership team to ensure no duplication and an agreement was formed for further development and participation in the coaching process.

Background of Coaches
For this project, there were two coaches with a background in computing who supported education faculty. One coach was based on the main campus while the other one was near the Minneapolis-St. Paul campus. Each coach brought unique

skills and understanding to the project, but a common background in supporting educators to provide CS for all students was key to the process.

The first coach had a background in educational technology (M.Ed in Learning Technologies) providing professional development experiences to practicing K–12 teachers for about eleven years, seven of which included integrating CT into various content areas in collaboration with practicing teachers. The coach was certified in cognitive coaching and had experience coaching teachers directly at the K–12 level in lesson development around technology, CT, and innovative teaching practices. The coach also had a background in the arts (BFA in Drama) and had previous experience with serving as a technology coach on an arts integration project administered by Minnesota's Perpich Center for Arts Education in which they were able to draw parallels between art integration and the work being done with CT. In addition, the coach was a curriculum developer SciGirls Code: A National Connected Learning Model to Integrate Computing in STEM Learning with Middle School Girls funded by the National Science Foundation. This coach worked as a consultant on the project, external to the college and departments.

The second coach had a background in CS and information systems as a member of the Computer Information Sciences department at CSS (MA in Information Systems Management, BA in Biochemistry). During the past 10 years, this coach had collaborations with education faculty to offer professional development through programs such as Google's CS4HS, the NSF-Tapestry program, and the NSF CS10K project which aimes to prepare CS teachers. This coach had also offered summer camps and day-long events for K–12 students to learn CS, often targeting underrepresented groups, such as girls and rural students. While this coach did not have a formal background in coaching, she read key sections of the cognitive coaching book to strengthen coaching skills from working with teachers in other CS professional development experiences. This coach was internal to the institution and maintained professional peer relationships with the education faculty.

The Coaching Cycle

The formal coaching process started through a discovery conversation between the faculty member and the coach. The opportunity for conversation and shared understanding throughout the coaching cycle allows for community building which has the potential to reduce friction by shaping a culture that promotes learning. In the coaching cycle, the coach and the faculty first discussed the CT mini-course to ensure sufficient understanding of the content. They then discussed the nature of the content course selected for the development of CT/CS integrated lessons and chose one to two learning objectives for teacher candidates based on the content. The coach and the faculty member(s) then looked at their respective calendars and cooperatively decided on a timeframe of when the coaching cycle should take place while keeping the milestones shown in Figure 9.1 in mind. These milestones were adapted from cognitive coaching practices as applied to

Education faculty take ownership of the curriculum
Faculty develop deeper understanding of CT/CS
Longer process, ed faculty demands on time
Onboarding new faculty and adjuncts for coherency across sites & programs

Milestone 1—Rough Idea of Lesson Plan

The faculty member creates the learning objectives for the teacher candidates and a brief summary of their lesson idea or where they would like to go. At this stage, the coach suggests additional resources or learning that might need to happen to get the faculty comfortable with the CS content. The faculty works with the coach to create a learning plan and there may a bit of a back and forth conversation as they work through solidifying an idea.

Milestone 2—Creating a Rough Draft of the Lesson

The faculty member uses the CSS Education lesson plan template to outline lesson activities, refine objectives, and identify instructional resources that need to be curated or created. The lesson plan template aligns with the institutions' template used for student teachers but is augmented with specific elements for computational thinking and computer science including standards, equitable teaching strategies, and professional standards that educators need to meet. The coach provides feedback while suggesting additional resources or opportunities for the faculty to pivot their ideas. At this time it would be beneficial for the faculty member to also share their work with a colleague to get another perspective on the lesson. This could be a team member participating in the coaching or another trusted colleague.

Milestone 3—Finalizing the Lesson

The faculty member makes adjustments on the lesson based on feedback from the coach and creates instructional resources such as but not limited to presentation slides, handouts, and rubrics. These materials along with the lesson are with the coach for feedback and final adjustments are made before piloting the lesson.

Milestone 4—Lesson is Piloted in the Classroom

The faculty member pilots the lesson with teacher candidates. At this time, the coach observes the lesson and may co-teach if that arrangement is requested by the faculty member and arranged with the coach ahead of time. During the lesson, the coach takes notes about what is happening in the classroom for use during the lesson reflection (milestone 5). If another SOE faculty member will also be teaching the lesson, it can be helpful for them to observe as well. Faculty should take the lead

FIGURE 9.1. TeachCS@ CSS Coaching Model (continues)

on teaching in the classroom, however, the coach can be available as an in-class resource if needed.

Milestone 5—Lesson Reflection

The conversation starts with the coach asking the faculty a series of reflective questions about their experience teaching the lesson. This is meant to be a metacognitive process for the faculty member at first. Then the coach can tie in any observational notes into this process that may need to be addressed. Reflective questions could be given to the faculty member prior to the meeting.

Milestone 6—Lesson Refinement

Based on the observation notes and the reflection, the coach and the faculty member should identify any areas of refinement that may need to be addressed in the lesson so that it is ready for publication for sharing with other faculty internally and externally. At this point, the faculty member was interviewed by the external evaluator and/or complete an exit survey from a program supervisor (or coach).

Coaching Check-In Meetings

Each milestone may have one or more check in with a coach virtually or in-person. These do not need to be long meetings, with a typical duration of 15–30 mins after the initial discovery conversation, which is about an hour. The coach should work with the faculty member in reviewing the work that has been done, identifying next steps and creating one or two actionable items for moving forward. The social capital of having a coach is to keep a project moving forward.

FIGURE 9.1. Continued

the specific goal (developing and refining integrated lessons) of this project. The model and milestones were revised and clarified by the coaches through a reflective conversation with the project external evaluator.

Roles in the Coaching Model

Coach. Based on our experience, a coach should have expertise and training in education (CT/CS integration, knowledge of CS as a discipline, or teaching at the K–12 level) as well as coaching experience or training (understanding of collaboration, organization and communication skills, flexibility and adaptability, holding faculty participants accountable in a respectful and gentle way). Both coaches in this project had expertise in these areas. In addition, it was helpful to establish other roles. These roles are described below.

Supervisor. Based on our experience, there needs to be a supervisor. We recommend that the supervisor be someone from the School of Education's leadership team such as a Dean or Department Chair. In this project, the Dean served in this role. As a supervisor, the Dean was responsible for identifying faculty members who would participate in the work and ensure that the professional development was completed before the coaching cycle began. The Dean also worked with faculty members to identify the big picture time frame for completing the lesson development using the milestones described above as a guide. This was established by working backwards from when the lesson needs to be taught or during identified breaks depending on the faculties work preference. Finally, the expectations of the faculty were clearly communicated.

Curriculum Approval Team. We established a curriculum approval team that comprised of a subject matter expert in Education, CS, and Instructional Design. This team established a checklist that guided the approval process.

Faculty Participants. School of Education faculty or faculty who teach content area teaching methods courses and have completed the online professional development were the key participants for the coaching model. Participation in coaching required that faculty agreed to: (1) complete the professional development mini-course course, (2) develop a lesson by participating in the coaching cycle, (3) pilot the lesson (or supervise the lesson as it is taught by adjuncts), (4) finalize the lesson, and (5) complete an exit interview/survey.

Professional Development Providers and/or PD Moderators. There were also professional development providers/moderators that were internal and external to the project team. The coaches developed the initial training course but also invited outside experts from SciGirls to engage the coaching cohort around gender equitable teaching strategies in science. They also invited experts from MIT's Teaching Systems Lab to guide educators through a workshop on implicit bias that utilized the "Teacher Practice Spaces" developed at MIT (https://teachermoments.teachingsystemslab.org/equity).

Work Agreement and Commitment

In addition to clearly identified roles and other staff supports, there was a need for a clear set of expectations for the working relationship between the faculty member and the coach. Specifically, we expected timely communication, clear communication norms that enabled faculty to freely ask questions, and an agreed-upon timeline for the work. Finally, there was an overall understanding that as the work evolves there may be a need for flexibility and that the focus should be on the process and progression not perfection.

Faculty were expected to complete any pre-work required before engaging with the coach. The CSS team asked faculty to complete an online or blended CT mini-course for baseline content knowledge. In some cases, faculty needed to do pre-work before meeting with their coach. As part of the coaching process, faculty were expected to share their disciplinary expertise as well as their overall knowledge of the specific program in which they taught, as the coaches were not always familiar with programmatic level details. Further, faculty were responsible for communicating with their colleagues about their work for feedback and to engage in professional discourse. They wrote a detailed lesson plan so another person could implement the lesson in their own classrooms and willingly participated and supported the work of the project.

The coach initiated contact, provided constructive feedback, and created action items for faculty they were working with. The coaches established a supportive, non-evaluative environment. Further, the coaches connected faculty with CT/CS resources, including guidance on aligning lesson plans with the CSTA/ISTE standards. Finally, the coaches worked within the education program requirements (and sometimes barriers). As part of this program, both the coaches and the faculty followed the work agreement and commitments described in this section.

The Coaching Product

At the end of the coaching cycle, a lesson plan that had been implemented, refined, and reviewed by multiple stakeholders was produced that could be disseminated to other education faculty. All lesson plans developed as part of this program are hosted online at teachcs.css.edu for others to view and use under a Creative Commons license. The lesson plans generally addressed the integration of CT/CS with disciplinary content (e.g., science or language arts) and pedagogy. Lesson plan components included alignment with ISTE and CSTA standards as well as connections to Minnesota Standards of Effective Practice for Educators, learning outcomes, assessment, instructional materials, and an outline of the instructional plan. Additional components were also added to meet the needs of the target audience, including state educator standards addressed in the lesson. Initially, some lesson plans were designed more as exemplars for use in K–12 classrooms and needed refinement to meet the needs of other education faculty who would be utilizing them, including both full-time and adjunct faculty at CSS as well as those at other organizations.

TABLE 9.1. A Description of the Faculty and Interview Participants

Descriptor of the Faculty Interview Respondents	
Gender	2 male 6 female
Faculty status	2 adjunct 6 faculty
Faculty campus assignment	1 St. Cloud 3 St. Paul 4 Duluth
Pre-service program (Amy overlapped)	4 graduate 5 undergraduate
Instructional content area where CS was integrated	Children's Literature, Diversity and Inclusion, Elementary Education Methods, Math, Reflection/Professional Development, Science, Social Studies, Special Education, Technology

1.	What were you thinking about when you were working on integrating this material in your course?
2.	When you were thinking about teaching this content in your class, what concerns did you have?
3.	When you think about your students teaching this material in the field, what concerns do you have?
4.	What feedback can you offer about this coaching component?

FIGURE 9.2. Structured Interview Protocol Questions

Faculty Input

Eight interviews were conducted with faculty and adjuncts involved in the project (see Table 9.1 for more background information about the interview respondents). The external evaluator for the project conducted interviews beginning in October 2017 and continuing through January 2019. The external evaluator used a structured interview protocol (See questions in Figure 9.2.) and conducted 30-minute telephone interviews with individual faculty members. The coaches provided the external evaluator with faculty names and contact information once when the instructional planning was completed or a faculty member had taught the lesson at least once in the classroom. Subsequently, the external evaluator contacted the faculty by email to invite their participation in the interview process. Eight faculty members were contacted and all agreed to be interviewed. The study was approved in full by the Institutional Review Board at the CSS.

The qualitative interview content was analyzed using a thematic analysis approach where the data was treated inductively, explicitly, and realistically to respect and reflect the experiences of the faculty members (Nowell et al., 2017). Data for each question was first coded and then the codes were examined to identify shared patterns of meaning. These shared patterns became named themes that best captured the responses.

Results From Faculty

Interview data explain why an integration approach is essential and how the coaches supported faculty participants in this endeavor. Faculty described how the coaches supported them to achieve key accomplishments: (1) robustly aligning their instructional content with CS; and (2) designing integrated lessons that were aligned with both content and CS.

Integration

In the project, three of the eight faculty members were familiar with CS/CT but most were not. One faculty member reflected, "When I first did the [professional development] I thought, 'they picked the wrong person.' I was a fish out of water." Even though most faculty were not knowledgeable of CS/CT, all of them acknowledged the value of adding CS/CT content—not only for their pre-service education students but for future K–12 students who would receive the benefit of learning this material. Faculty also recognized they had little time in their classes to add new content but knew they could solve this problem by integrating CS/CT into existing course material. One faculty member summed up her motivation by saying, "When we integrate things, we get a richer program."

While integrating CS/CT content was perceived as valuable and necessary, most faculty needed support to make the integration happen in a way where they felt confident about the treatment of the CS/CT material. One faculty member explained her concerns early on in the process, "I was thinking about my own lack of knowledge and how that might affect the integration of it." This concern is not uncommon. In a study conducted by Israel et al. (2015), the authors found that K–5 elementary teachers were motivated to learn about computing but perceived that their lack of knowledge and experience would be a barrier to integration. Similar to the TeachCS@CSS project, they addressed this barrier by pairing K–5 teachers with a content expert who offered to co-teach and help teachers plan their instruction.

As described earlier in this chapter, coaching support was offered to faculty participating in the project. The one-on-one coaching addressed faculty's concerns about lacking CS/CT knowledge and expertise. The coaching also served as a safety net—faculty could learn about CS/CT, practice designing integrated lessons, and begin teaching these lessons in their pre-service education classes—all while being mentored by a CS content expert. As a faculty member noted, "Without the coaching, I wouldn't really know what to do. ...I still wasn't confident enough that I could do it myself." While this faculty member thought he would eventually be able to teach CS/CT content, at the beginning it was a challenge for him to understand how to integrate the material. When asked to specifically identify what the stumbling block was for him, he talked about not knowing what kinds of instructional activities might be appropriate for integrating CT into the class. Even though the course already incorporated some technology components, he explained, "Without some good coaching, I think it would have been a little intimidating or [I would have been] a little bit in the dark about what works."

When other faculty members shared their concerns about designing lessons with CS/CT content, they explained their desire for "seamless" integration. As one faculty explained, "I don't want this to be another thing I've crammed into my class. It's about rebranding an activity rather than adding a new one. How do we make this not look like a smorgasbord of ideas but make it seamless and integrated?" Another faculty member explained it like this, "Tech is purposeful...not because it's cool. How can this be infused in a purposeful way because it enhances learning? If someone tried to do this without the modules and just reading the book, a lot would be lost. You still have to wrap your mind around what it means. It needs to be part of your coursework, not another thing. It needs to be layered in. Not window dressing. Not about 'wow' optics but about how you teach."

Similar to the faculty involved in this project, K–12 teachers and administrators have identified that limited instructional time is a barrier to teaching CS/CT (Google & Gallup, 2015). Across many educational settings, school staff must find a balance in delivering the mandated curriculum, preparing students for state assessments, and incorporating additional district initiatives. While integrating CS/CT into the existing curriculum is challenging, it can be done in a manner that addresses CS/CT and the instructional content area with integrity (Israel et al., 2015). The Priming the CS Teacher Pump report declared, "The best way for computer science is to be integrated it into other subject areas, such as mathematics, science, and literacy" (DeLyser et al., 2018, p. 32). These contributions supported the integration of CS into non-CS instructional content to ensure that students of all ages and abilities are exposed to and have the opportunity to engage with CS/CT in a meaningful way.

Alignment and Standards

While the integration of CS content is one way to deliver instructional content in schools, teachers and administrators often do not have state standards to help guide the development of integrated coursework that includes CS content. In the absence of state standards for CS, where do teachers go to determine what do students at each grade level need to learn and be able to do? The coaches and faculty in this project relied heavily on the standards developed by CSTA and ISTE for assistance when designing lessons.

When designing their lessons, many faculty shared that they were concerned about aligning CS/CT standards with their content standards and were often aware that they felt out of their depth. Fortunately, faculty were supported by their coach to navigate this territory that felt unfamiliar to them. During the interviews, faculty described the standards work as a partnership—they brought the expertise with the content standards for their course and their coach brought the expertise with the CSTA or ISTE standards. "I always start with the standards. ...she [the coach] was very well versed in the CS standards, I knew my standards and then we could talk about the connections between the two." Another faculty member said she and the coach brainstormed together about the connections they should be making before they developed the lesson. This quote from a faculty member described the planning process and how she felt about her capacity to work with the standards: "The goal is that the lesson is anchored in standards (I know ISTE) but the CSTA ones are really vast and the strands, there are a lot of them. I worried about that. I knew the content and the pedagogy for [content area] and ISTE but wanted to make strong connections to the CSTA standards to weave in CS and CT thinking. [The coach] spent a lot of time guiding me through the CSTA standards and helping me."

The coaches brought the ability to see the bigger picture in the project and helped faculty to plan robust, comprehensive lessons. One faculty eloquently explained: "The designer should focus on aligning the content with the standards embedded in the course. You've got to assess it as well. [The coach] was good at that, the CS stuff, and could see the integration. Never suggested things outside of my focus, kept me focused, brought me back to aligning with my standards. [The coach] is good, has teaching experience, she was focused on aligning objectives, activities, and assessment. She's good at that and I appreciated that because she kept me honest if I got off track."

NEXT STEPS

The coaching process with the education faculty raised some questions yet to be answered, identified during a debriefing process led by the external evaluator. One key question is how to adapt the coaching process for use with teacher candidates as they deliver lessons with integrated CT/CS content in schools. During this project, several teacher candidates piloted designing and implementing CT/CS lessons as part of a field experience course. The coaches were able to provide similar support to these teacher candidates as they did for faculty; however, in order for this to be scalable for all teacher candidates, education faculty supervising field placements will need to incorporate the coaching process as part of their supervision.

There is also a need to identify how, when, and if the coaching process should be concluded with each individual, yet allow for coaching support as needed while the faculty become more confident in delivering lessons. Faculty expressed a desire to continue their learning about CT/CS and how best to teach students, but that was outside the scope of the coaching process. Further, with faculty at several campuses and students at many different schools during field experiences, coaching support that can be provided remotely would help to sustain and scale the project. The model will need to be adapted to meet the needs of a faculty-teacher candidate audience and the existing systems currently used in the teacher preparation programs.

Further refinement of the coaching model so that it can be disseminated and used at other institutions will need to include more direction and guidance for the coaches themselves, including enhancements to the coaching process documents and potentially a coaching course. Long-term, developing the capacity of education faculty to provide CS coaching support internally (both with new faculty and with teacher candidates) will help to sustain a coaching program without relying on consultants external to the college or department.

REFERENCES

About ICF. (n.d.). https://coachfederation.org/about

Code.org. (2017). *Recommendations for states developing computer science teacher pathways.* https://code.org/files/TeacherPathwayRecommendations.pdf

Computer Science Teachers Association (CSTA). (2013). *Bugs in the system: Computer science teacher certification in the U.S.* https://csteachers.org/documents/en-us/3b4a70cd-2a9b-478b-95cd-376530c3e976/1

Costa, A. L., & Garmston R. J. (2002). *Cognitive coaching: A foundation for renaissance schools (2nd ed.).* Christopher-Gordon.

CS4All at Chicago Public Schools. (n.d.). ECS peer coaching. http://www.cs4all.io/programs/ecs-peer-coaching

DeLyser, L., Goode, J., Guzdial, M., Kafai, Y., & Yadav, A., (2018). *Priming the computer science teacher pump: Integrating computer science education into schools of education.* CSforALL.

Google Inc. & Gallup Inc. (2015). *Searching for computer science: Access and barriers in U.S. K–12 education.* https://services.google.com/fh/files/misc/searching-for-computer-science_report.pdf.

Google Inc. & Gallup Inc. (2016). *Trends in the State of Computer Science in U.S. K–12 Schools.* https://news.gallup.com/reports/196379/trends-state-computer-science-schools.aspx#.

Israel, M., Pearson, J., Tapia, T., Wherfel, Q. M., & Reese, G. (2015). Supporting all learners in school-wide computational thinking: A cross-case qualitative analysis. *Computers & Education*, 82, 263–279. doi:10.1016/j.compedu.2014.11.022.

K–12 Computer Science Framework. (2016). http://www.k12cs.org.

Knight, J. (2007). *Instructional coaching: A partnership approach to improving instruction.* Corwin Press.

Knight, J. (Ed.). (2009). *Coaching: Approaches and perspectives.* Corwin Press.

Krauss, J., & Prottsman, K. (2017). *Computational thinking and coding for every student: The teacher's getting-started guide.* Corwin Press.

Margolis, J., Ryoo, J., & Goode, J. (2017). Seeing myself through someone else's eyes: The value of in-classroom coaching for computer science teaching and learning. *ACM Transactions on Computing Education,17*(2), Article No.6. doi:10.1145/2967616

NGSS Lead States. (2013). Next Generation Science Standards: For states, by states. http://www.nextgenscience.org/

Nowell, L. S., Norris, J. M., White, D. E., & Moules, N. J. (2017). Thematic analysis: Striving to meet the trustworthiness criteria. *International Journal of Qualitative Methods, 16*(1), 1–3. doi:10.1177/1609406917733847

Pierce, J., & Buysse, V. (2014). *Effective coaching: Improving teacher practice and outcomes for all learners* (Rep.). WestEd National Center for Systematic Improvement. doi: https://ncsi-library.wested.org/resources/57

Puentedura, R. R. (2013, May 29). SAMR: Moving from enhancement to transformation [Web log post]. http://www.hippasus.com/rrpweblog/archives/000095.html

Ryoo, J. J., Goode, J., & Margolis, J. (2015). It takes a village: Supporting inquiry- and equity-oriented computer science pedagogy through a professional learning community. *Computer Science Education*, 25, 351–370. doi:10.1080/08993408.2015.1130952

Wing, J. M. (March 2006). Computational thinking. *Communications of the ACM, 49* (3), 33–35. doi:10.1145/1118178.1118215

CHAPTER 10

BUILDING AND EXPANDING THE CAPACITY OF SCHOOLS OF EDUCATION TO PREPARE AND SUPPORT TEACHERS TO TEACH COMPUTER SCIENCE

Aman Yadav, Leigh Ann DeLyser, Yasmin Kafai,
Mark Guzdial, and Joanna Goode

To grow and establish computer science (CS) education into a sustainable primary and secondary school subject, traditional teacher preparation programs in schools and colleges of education in the United States will need to include CS education into their teacher preparation and professional development efforts. In this chapter, we outline recommendation areas for both general CS topics for all teachers as well as for building programs specifically designed to create teachers whose focus is exclusively on CS content. These recommendation areas outline action items and pathways for schools of education to develop strategic partnerships with school districts and CS programs to scale up from in-service into pre-service programs and meets the CS education needs of students and schools in under-resourced communities.

Preparing Pre-Service Teachers to Teach Computer Science: Models, Practices, and Policies,
pages 191–203.
Copyright © 2021 by Information Age Publishing
All rights of reproduction in any form reserved.

Keywords: Schools of Education, Pre-Service Teachers, Teacher Preparation

INTRODUCTION

Around the world, computer science (CS) education is growing as an academic subject in primary and secondary schools (e.g., Hsu et al., 2019). Many countries, including the United States are requiring schools to teach about CS in their K–12 schools. In the United States, a number of states have passed standards that are paving the way for CS to become a regular school subject and graduation requirement. Teaching CS is not just limited to standalone programming courses but is also becoming an integral part of other subject areas in the K–12 curriculum. In order to meet the demands for this nationwide introduction of CS, we need to prepare not only current teachers but also new teachers.

The majority of the current efforts to educate teachers in CS have focused on in-service teachers through professional development. These professional development efforts are supported by colleges and universities through funding by the National Science Foundation, nonprofit organizations, as well as for-profit companies who provide curriculum or devices to schools (Menekse, 2015). Given the high attrition rate of K–12 teachers across subjects (Ingersoll, 2001), these in-service teacher professional development efforts are stop-gap measures because they draw upon an existing pool of teachers rather than expanding the base. A number of factors, including lack of content knowledge and insufficient support play a significant role in teachers leaving the profession within the first five years of starting to teach (Borman & Dowling, 2008). These factors have potential consequences for the sustainability for CS education initiatives that rely only on in-service teacher training. However, the current pre-service teacher education is limited because there are only a few programs in schools of education focused on preparing pre-service CS teachers, and even in those programs there are few enrolled students. Further in-service opportunities can be situated in university CS departments or provided by industry-sponsored groups (Century et al., 2013) but may not reach all who are interested in becoming CS teachers.

The current in-service CS teacher professional development programs are not sufficient to educate and develop a pipeline and ensure long-term viability of CS education in U.S. K–12 schools. Thus, there is a critical need to provide pre-service teacher education programs that focus on educating future teachers to meet the growing demand for professionals who are qualified to teach CS. Without the support of existing teacher preparation systems, such as schools or colleges of education, the CS education teaching force will be difficult to create at scale, and finding CS teachers will continue to be a challenge for K–12 schools and principals. To expand access to CS in K–12, we must treat the preparation of pre-service CS teachers (i.e., while they are still in initial teacher preparation) the same as other subjects.

In order to develop a sustainable pipeline of K–12 teachers who are prepared to teach rigorous stand-alone CS courses as well as integrate computing ideas within other subject areas, we need to (a) provide critical, foundational content and pedagogical knowledge in CS to teacher candidates; (b) have faculty who conduct research focused in CS education in order to develop a better understanding of what knowledge teachers need to teach CS; and (c) help early CS career teachers pursue additional learning that enables them to grow into master teachers. However, so far efforts that have focused on professional development for in-service teachers miss the crucial pre-service programmatic components that prepare incoming new teachers.

In this chapter, we outline previous efforts and describe the conditions in K–12 schools and teacher education programs at colleges and universities. In addition, we summarize a recent report (DeLyser et al., 2018) based on discussions of researchers, school of education faculty and leaders, and directors of nationwide organizations. We offer concrete recommendations for schools of education to include CS as a part of teacher preparation, professional development, and doctoral training programs. We also offer actionable steps that schools of education can take to build the foundation of CS education within their faculty, graduate students, and teacher education programs. These recommendations are not meant to be implemented all at once, but the expectation is that schools of education will find synergy with other departments, regional, or state efforts to expand CS education and research.

BACKGROUND

Situating CS Education Within K–12 Landscape

CS education has emerged as a bipartisan issue. Former President Obama called for a *CS for All* initiative, including $4 billion in the proposed 2016 budget for states and cities to offer computing education. Subsequently, President Trump directed the Secretary of Education to allocate up to $200 million in grants for computing initiatives in schools. Bolstering these efforts has been an equally strong call to promote computational thinking throughout K–12 education. Computational thinking is defined as "taking an approach to solving problems, designing systems and understanding human behaviour that draws on concepts fundamental to computing" (Wing, 2006, p. 33).

Currently, there are number of CS education initiatives in the United States led by non-profit organizations, as well as more local efforts. National level efforts include CS for All, Code.org, and Exploring Computer Science. As an example at the local level, New York City has mandated every school to provide computing education to all students by 2025. Similarly, the city of Chicago and the state of

Virginia are making education in "coding" a requirement. The state of Arkansas has mandated computing education in every high school. Furthermore, the recently passed federal education legislation notably includes CS in the list of "well-rounded" and critically enriching subjects. States are rapidly developing certification and supplemental/endorsement credentials for CS teachers.

With the expansion of computing education in K–12 schools, the current approach of professional development for in-service teachers will fall short of having a sustainable pipeline of CS teachers for the scale many cities and states have committed to. Current methods of preparing teachers often rely on in-service teachers. Current teachers who hold a teaching position in a school are identified, and then provided with professional development in a specific program or curricula that the school commits to offering. If CS is going to become a core subject in K–12 education, the education community needs to engage with current methods of teacher preparation to produce CS teachers at scale, and also to update the technological preparation of K–8 teachers to include CS topics and computational thinking. Furthermore, current and incoming CS teachers need to be prepared to develop teaching strategies to deal with significant diversity issues (Margolis et al., 2017).

A Computer Science Teachers Association (CSTA) report found that CS teacher certification in the United States was deeply flawed (Lang et al., 2013). A review of how CS teachers get licensed in all 50 states suggested that teachers lacked adequate pathways to be certified to teach CS. The report found that only 2 out of 50 states and the District of Columbia (4%) required CS licensure to teach any CS course, and only 7 states (14%) required it to teach AP Computer Science. More recently, a report from Expanding Computing Education Pathways (ECEP), indicated that 27 states and the District of Columbia offer CS teacher certification and 12 states have approved pre-service CS teacher preparation programs at institutions of higher education (Stanton et al., 2017).

Teacher education programs at colleges and universities now face several questions regarding the implementation of CS education: Where does computing education fit into existing curricula and organizations? Is computing education more like science education or mathematics education? Does it fit more naturally in educational technology or educational psychology? In which courses should we teach all pre-service teachers about computer science and about teaching computer science? How do we prepare teachers to engage with computing and students from underrepresented groups?

In order to address these critical questions, the authors of this chapter received a National Science Foundation grant to convene CS education researchers, leaders from large departments of education, teacher education researchers, and computer scientists in a workshop held in April 2017 to help answer the above questions and more. This report shares the discussion outcomes and recommendations from the workshop group members. Additionally, the workshop talks and panels were recorded and are available at https://www.computingteacher.org/

NEXT STEPS

Moving K–12 Computer Science Education into Schools of Education

The starting point for our recommendations for setting up and expanding CS teacher education in the US are schools and colleges of education rather than CS departments for two reasons: historically, CS departments have been reluctant to create full standing faculty focused on CS education while schools and colleges of education have been the home of teacher pre- and in-service teacher education programs. In order to have sustainable CS in K–12 schools, we need schools of education to prepare new CS teachers, to research how to effectively teach CS, and provide broad and equitable access to CS teaching and learning (Yadav & Korb, 2012). Schools of education typically host teacher education programs charged with providing pre-service teachers the necessary coursework, practicum, and student teaching to be prepared to teach an increasingly racially and linguistically diverse student population. This design provides the following advantages:

- Pre-service coursework typically includes a course of study in learning sciences, multicultural education, and teaching methodology classes for particular subjects and grade bands.
- Pre-service observations and student teaching experience, likewise, arranged in collaboration with local schools, is also intended to be aligned with particular subjects and grade bands of certification.
- Non-traditional preparation programs allow teachers to work in the classroom while they complete coursework through school/provider collaborations, and account for approximately 12% of teacher preparation.
- Programs work with state agencies to ensure that pre-service teacher candidates successfully pass all state credentialing requirements.
- In-service programs are often housed in schools of education and provide teachers with the continued necessary professional development.

Teacher education programs primarily prepare new teachers across subject areas, and faculty in those programs have expertise in the scholarship of teaching. Few U.S. teacher preparation programs have created or sustained pathways for future teachers to get certified to teach CS (Lang, et al., 2013). A number of roadblocks prevent more certified CS teachers, which include lack of CS teaching methodology classes, lack of access to CS classrooms for student teaching, and lack of a state teaching certificate in CS. Given their insights on teacher preparation and knowledge of these unique challenges, schools of education are uniquely suited to discuss and explore opportunities to prepare CS teachers.

Schools of education do more than pre-service and in-service teacher education and certification. They provide programmatic research on teacher development efforts, curriculum design, teaching practices, classroom implementations, and assessment. They also examine administrative leadership and policy issues connected to introducing new initiatives in classrooms and districts. Educational researchers housed in schools of education have the expertise not only to conduct formative and summative evaluations but also to pay close attention to diversity and equity issues that have been and continue to be a critical issue in the field of computing. Students and teachers in under-resourced school districts make up the communities most lacking access to introductory and AP CS courses. They need the school of education support the most.

Developing Pedagogies for Computer Science Education Teachers

If we want to provide high-quality and accessible CS education for all, we need more CS teachers. An important question for any teacher development program is what these teachers need to know to be effective. The first focus area is defining what teachers need to know about computing. There are competing definitions and priorities for the integration of CS education into K–12 education. In recent years, the *K–12 Computer Science Education Framework,* the *ISTE Standards for Computer Science Teachers,* and the *Computer Science Teachers Association K–12 Standards* have all been released to offer a national definition of age-appropriate CS for all students in the United States. Many states have followed the lead of these national effort and are now updating or creating state-defined standards for CS education. Although national teacher standards do not yet exist, teacher preparation programs should look to the student-facing standards for clear definitions of CS content that teachers will need to teach to students.

A successful model of teacher preparation would involve both the definition of the relevant concepts, skills, and practices for the discipline of CS, as well as pedagogical approaches for teaching these concepts in K–12. Teachers would have access to preparation programs that would prepare them with what they need to be successful, highly capable CS teachers. We are far from this goal now. Currently, most of the preparation for teachers of CS is in short in-service professional development sessions, with little assessment about their success (e.g., if teachers retain the knowledge, use it, and can apply it in the classroom). More critically, we have not yet defined the CS concepts, skills, or practices teachers need to know.

As in other disciplines, the definition of what content knowledge teachers need to have is defined by the grade band and specific content area focus of each teacher. The appropriate CS minimum content knowledge will look different for an elementary school teacher, a high school Mathematics teacher, or a high school Social Studies teacher. The CS knowledge that a first grade teacher needs to teach is different from what a high school teacher needs to teach Advanced Placement CS Principles.

In addition to CS content knowledge, teachers should also have opportunities to develop pedagogical content knowledge. Pedagogical content knowledge is knowledge that a teacher has about how to teach a subject successfully. One part are *pedagogical methods*, e.g., knowing best practices for helping early elementary school students understand the sequentiality of computer programs. Another part is *knowledge of misconceptions*. Highly-capable teachers know the challenges that learners face when presented with difficult concepts or skills, can identify when students are not successfully meeting those challenges, and know how to help the students to overcome these difficulties (Sadler et al., 2013). In order to examine whether teachers are prepared to teach CS, we need to go beyond measuring CS content knowledge and also assess their pedagogical content knowledge. A recent study by Yadav and Berges (2019) designed and measured an instrument that characterized CS pedagogical content knowledge (CS-PCK) for teachers. The study used teaching vignettes of misconceptions students face and how teachers could respond to them. The authors recommended that the instrument is a good starting point for others to build upon and add other dimensions of CS.

Furthermore, teachers will need an understanding of the diversity issues in CS and learn equity-based teaching strategies. Given the historical, pervasive educational inequities in CS (Margolis et al., 2017), it is essential to prepare teachers with the knowledge and skills necessary to broaden access and enact welcoming and inclusive pedagogical practices that support diverse students (Goode, 2007; Margolis et al., 2014). The attention to equity issues in CS education should not be relegated to a separate course but should be authentically infused and supported across content and methodology coursework. Given the complexities of developing teacher knowledge around these issues, what can schools of education do to support teachers? Below are some key strategic actions that schools of education could take to move this work forward.

- Schools of education should include content, teaching methods, and state standards for CS in any preparation programs for teachers who may have responsibility for those standards.
- Faculty designing new courses or programs should partner with practitioners to make sure coursework aligns with any relevant offerings in regional schools.
- Faculty in schools of education should regularly connect with the CS teacher community of practice events and CS education research publications in order to include current best practices in coursework.

However, few models exist in the United States for the development of highly-effective computing education teachers, especially focused on CS or computational thinking, within schools of education. As the definition of appropriate CS content for K–12 students is becoming clear though state and national frameworks and standards, teacher preparation programs need to align to these. Early CS courses in college often focus on the programming aspect of CS, yet K–12 standards and frameworks also include networks and the internet, systems, data, and the impacts of computing. Teachers will need a broad introduction to all of these concepts if they are to be expected to teach them to students. As such, there needs to be clear alignment between student standards and teacher content preparation.

Another way forward is to embed CS education within teacher education, so all pre-service teachers are introduced to computing ideas. This is particularly relevant to elementary grades. Elementary teachers focus solely on the primary subjects which are tested without having a strong knowledge base of any one particular subject. In primary schools, math and literacy are the two areas that are heavily tested at the state level to measure the proficiency of K–5 students. As a result, CS as a standalone subject might not be a realistic expectation for all primary schools; however, incorporating the basic concepts of computational thinking into classrooms and preparing teachers to teach computational content are realistic. Computational content around problem solving, creative thinking, algorithms, computer programming, and general principles from CS are examples of programmatic aspects which could be taught by primary school teachers. The main hurdle in primary schools is around preparing teachers to incorporate these ideas into their classroom activities. How are we going to get teachers to focus on CS when they are already so pressured on teaching their kids to be proficient in so many other subjects?

The best way for CS is to be integrated it into other subject areas, such as mathematics, science, and literacy. But the challenge there becomes that we need to educate preservice teachers to embed CS and computational thinking within those content areas. This requires elementary teacher education faculty to be trained to themselves understand computing ideas and how they could be integrated within teacher education courses. We believe that preservice teachers can be exposed to computing ideas as a part of introductory educational technology courses, which the majority of preservice teachers take during their program (see Chapter 9). Then, they could learn to apply those ideas within the context of a subject areas as a part of their methods courses (Yadav et al., 2017). However, this would require ongoing collaborations between elementary teacher education and CS educators to compensate for the faculty turnover in teaching these courses. Schools of education can take the following strategic actions to move this work forward.

- Schools of education should ensure through programmatic requirements that K–8 teachers receive basic literacy instruction in CS as well as foundational CS education pedagogical instruction.
- Faculty of education can connect with members of the department of CS who are running professional development or in-service teacher preparation to identify needs and best practices.
- Faculty in schools of education should have opportunities to familiarize themselves with relevant K–12 CS education standards for integration into core pedagogical coursework.
- Faculty preparing courses for future teachers should review example syllabi or program outlines from other institutions for common practices.

- Schools of education should make sure teacher candidates have content preparation aligned with national and relevant state standards for CS education.

Building Education Leadership for Computer Science Education

As we think about educational leaders, we recognize there are several ways to be a CS leader in education. For example, CS leaders can be classroom teachers, district superintendents, school system leaders, and principals. Since the important role of teachers and teacher education are discussed elsewhere, this section will focus on those considered to be serving in formal educational leadership positions as school, district, and state-level administration.

There is urgency around preparing administrators and other educational leaders with the knowledge and skills needed to support CS teaching and learning for all students. Recent data indicate that CS is not a priority to administrators, despite strong support from school communities, students, and teachers (Wang et al., 2016). Additionally, many administrators may not understand the difference between traditional technology education which include word processing, spreadsheets, presentation software and keyboarding, and CS education which include the design and analysis of software, algorithms, or digital artifacts, often with code.

Administrators and other educational leaders must not only have an understanding of what content constitutes CS education (and what does not), they must also be aware of the trade-offs between stand-alone CS education, integrated CS education, and how to create rigorous pathways for students across multiple grades, both for general student CS literacy and for college preparation for students who would like to explore STEM disciplines with more rigor.

To successfully do this, CS education must be fully established within the complex and multi-layered United States school system. Building a robust and cohesive CS Education ecosystem for students requires the support of all stakeholders within this complex system of educational leaders, such as policymakers, superintendents, and principals. Many schools of education have educational leadership programs for mid-career professionals that include such information in their courses. Currently, there are few—if any—options for administrators to learn about CS education pathways.

Additionally, administrators often are part of the teacher feedback and evaluation cycle and need an understanding of what quality CS pedagogy looks like for teacher feedback purposes. The most common option now are the state-level convenings offered by many state working groups for CS education (Guzdial, 2016). In these convenings speakers share best practices, offer resources, and provide important information for both educational leaders and teachers.

Among educational leaders, superintendents are especially critical, because they can influence district-level strategic plans in a powerful way. For example, superintendents have the autonomy to draft and push forward strategic plans that will ultimately advance technology throughout their districts. Winning the support of superintendents would be imperative as they can leverage their decision-making power to impact practices adopted throughout the rest of their district. According to a recent Google poll (Wang et al., 2016), only 30% of superintendents think CS education is important, compared to 50% of teachers and building principals. This statistic highlights the opportunity to improve the overall sentiment and acceptance of superintendents to drive forward district-level adoption of CS preparation. While there is already greater approval among teachers, invoking buy-in of superintendents will create a strong combination of a bottom-up and top-down approach to driving forward CS preparation across districts. Reaching in-service educational administrators will require that professional convenings of regional educators include programming on CS education.

In schools of education, educational administration licensure and degree programs are often separated from the teacher education and curriculum and instruction programs. Many administrative programs offer a common set of classes required to become an administrator: school law, finance, leadership, and others that are particularly targeted towards the skill-set required of administrators. There is often little room in the curriculum for administrators to consider particular content-specific support of teaching and learning for any subject, including CS. Yet, many of these programs offer opportunities for educators to examine "problems of practice" from an administrative perspective as part of a doctoral thesis, and there are already emerging examples of how CS learning opportunities can be infused as possible areas of study for administrative licensure and degree programs. Below are some strategic actions that a school of education could take to move this work forward:

- Faculty in educational leadership programs should use case studies with problems of practice for CS education implementation. There are numerous examples from Chicago Public Schools, the New York City public schools, and many smaller city or rural schools with CS education implementation plans.
- CS educational leaders should participate in conferences and gatherings of educational leadership communities (including superintendents, principals, etc.). Having CS educators and researchers in these conferences will bring visibility to practicing educational leaders who are often mentors for new administrators.

Building Strategic and Innovative Relationships with School Districts

In order to successfully build a home for CS education, programs situated in schools of education need to build and expand strategic relationships with school districts as they innovate and integrate a new discipline into their existing programs, professional development, and research initiatives. Two existing successful efforts in the largest school districts in the U.S.—New York City and Los Angeles—provide examples of how these efforts can be rolled out on a larger scale.

Los Angeles

The *Exploring Computer Science* (ECS) curriculum and professional development program began in Los Angeles Unified School District (LAUSD), the nation's second largest school district. ECS has over a decade worth of experience preparing teachers for CS classrooms. The ECS course was created in collaboration with educational researchers, school district curriculum leaders, and high school teacher practitioners, and has been successful in reaching hundreds of thousands of students over the last decade through the focus on the development of a vibrant and well-prepared professional teacher community. The enrollment demographics of the ECS course in Los Angeles school district reflect the racial and gender demographics of school district enrollment.

Designed intentionally to reach diverse student populations who have traditionally not participated in computing courses, the ECS professional development program encourages teachers to build their inquiry-based pedagogy, equity-based teaching practices, and content knowledge to successfully teach the course to all students (Goode et al., 2014). Since many of these ECS teachers do not have an extensive background in either computing or this type of active pedagogy shown in educational research to be effective for teaching minoritized students, and girls, the professional development program takes place over two years. Over 3,500 teachers have completed the professional development program, and the ECS course has been adopted in the top seven major school districts and in several states across the nation reaching over 50,000 high school students each year.

New York City

The CS4All in New York City has secured CS education as a focus area in the nation's largest school system. The CS4All initiative, which mandates that each of the city's 1700+ schools offer CS to every student at least once within a grade band, is primarily supporting in-service teacher professional development with the funds committed by the public/private partnership. Complementary to this effort is an emerging strategy to provide pre-service or in-service education through the network of public and private colleges and universities in the NYC area.

Working with colleges and universities in the area, CSNYC has helped facilitate the creation of proposals to the NY State Department of Education as programs that would lead to teacher certification. One early partner is Queen's College, the nation's third largest pre-service teacher preparation program with over 7,000 students enrolled. The potential partners include a wide variety of models such as an *elementary school model* where CS is a choice for students' area of concentration within currently approved programs, a *5th-year master's program* designed to help students earn a certification in Computer Technology, *an extension model* where teachers certified in another discipline are able to complete 12–18 credits in both CS content and pedagogy to extend a current teaching certificate, and *an "update" model* where current educational technology courses are revisited to remove extraneous content and provide foundations for integrating CS education where appropriate.

These strategic relationships within school districts provide examples of the variety of ways CS education, teacher education programs and professional development can be infused into the current work and connections many schools of education have already established with public and private school districts.

SUMMARY

In summary, we have outlined a set of recommendations for schools of education, which are critical to setting up and expanding CS education in K–12 schools across the nation. For preparing future K–12 teachers who are ready to bring computing ideas to their classrooms to the next generation of CS education researchers who examine teaching and learning issues in CS, we see schools of education as an important component of the CS education landscape. The recommendations outlined here are meant to jump start the conversation about the critical role schools of education play in this effort, but we also see CS departments as important partners as well. CS departments bring expertise in computing discipline, which is invaluable to school of education faculty as they begin to develop CS education programs. Future work should examine how faculty from education and CS departments could collaborate and develop shared understanding of what it means to engage in teaching, learning, and researching issues relevant to CS education for all.

REFERENCES

Borman, G. D., & Dowling, N. M. (2008). Teacher attrition and retention: A meta-analytic and narrative review of the research. *Review of educational research, 78*(3), 367–409.

Century, J., Lach, M., King, H., Rand, S., Heppner, C., Franke, B., & Westrick, J. (2013). *Building an operating system for computer science.* Retrieved March 23, 2013, 2015. https://outlier.uchicago.edu/computerscience/OS4CS/

Delyser, L., Goode, J., Guzdial, M., Kafai, Y., & Yadav, A. (2018). *Priming the computer science teacher pump: Integrating computer science education into schools of education.* CSforAll.

Goode, J. (2007). If you build teachers, will students come? Professional development for broadening computer science learning for urban youth. *Journal of Educational Computing Research, 36*(1), 65–88.

Goode, J., Margolis, J., & Chapman, G. (2014). Curriculum is not enough: The educational theory and research foundation of the exploring computer science professional development model. In *Proceedings of the 45th ACM technical symposium on Computer science education* (pp. 493–498). ACM.

Guzdial, M. (2016). Bringing computer science to U.S. schools, state by state. *Communications of the ACM, 59*(5), 24–25. DOI: https://doi.org/10.1145/2898963

Hsu, Y.-C., Irie, N. R., & Ching, Y-H. (2019). Computational thinking educational policy initiatives across the globe. *TechTrends, 63*(3), 260–270.

Ingersoll, R. (2001). Teacher turnover and teacher shortages: An organizational analysis. *American Educational Research Journal, 38*(3), 499–534.

Lang, K., Galanos, R., Goode, J., Seehorn, D., Trees, F., Phillips, P., & Stephenson, C. (2013). *Bugs in the system: Computer science teacher certification in the US.* The Computer Science Teachers Association and The Association for Computing Machinery.

Margolis, J., Estrella, R., Goode, J., Holme, J., & Nao, K. (2017). *Stuck in the shallow end: Education, race, & computing. Revised edition.* MIT Press.

Margolis, J., Goode, J., Chapman, G., & Ryoo, J. J. (2014). That classroom 'magic.' *Communications of the ACM, 57*(7), 31–33.

Menekse, M. (2015). Computer science teacher professional development in the United States: A review of studies published between 2004 and 2014. *Computer Science Education, 25*(4), 325–350, DOI:10.1080/08993408.2015.1111645

Sadler, P. M., Sonnert, G., Coyle, H. P., Cook-Smith, N., & Miller, J. L. (2013). The influence of teachers' knowledge on student learning in middle school physical science classrooms. *American Educational Research Journal, 50*(5), 1020–1049.

Stanton, J., Goldsmith, L., Adrion, W. R., Dunton, S., Hendrickson, K., Peterfreund, P., Yongpradit, P., Zarch, R., & Zinth, J. D. (2017). *State of the states landscape report: State-level policies supporting equitable k–12 computer science education.* https://www.ecs.org/wp-content/uploads/MassCAN-Full-Report-v10.pdf.

Wang, J., Hong, H., Ravitz, J., & Hejazi Moghadam, S. (2016, February). Landscape of K–12 computer science education in the US: Perceptions, access, and barriers. In *Proceedings of the 47th ACM Technical Symposium on Computing Science Education* (pp. 645–650). ACM.

Wing, J. (2006). Computational thinking. *Communications of the ACM, 49*(3), 33–35.

Yadav, A., & Korb, J. T. (2012). Learning to teach computer science: The need for a methods course. *Communications of the ACM, 55*(11), 31–33.

Yadav, A., & Berges, M. (2019). Computer science pedagogical content knowledge: Characterizing teacher performance. *ACM Transactions on Computing Education, 19*(3). DOI: 10.1145/3303770

Yadav, A., Stephenson, C., & Hong, H. (2017). Computational thinking for teacher education. *Communications of the ACM, 60*(4), 55–62. DOI:10.1145/2994591

CHAPTER 11

UNDERSTANDING K–12 COMPUTER SCIENCE EDUCATION AT THE STATE LEVEL

Jeffrey Xavier, Rebecca Zarch, Sarah T. Dunton,
Anne T. Ottenbreit-Leftwich, and Michael Karlin

The importance of computer science (CS) education for U.S. students has become increasingly apparent over the past decade. Stakeholders at the state and national levels agree that CS education should be made available to all students, which has created considerable demand for new, well-trained CS teachers. The National Science Foundation (NSF)-funded Expanding Computing Education Pathways (ECEP) Alliance, which includes teams of education and policy experts from 23 U.S. states and territories, focuses on examining state change around CS education and has been examining issues around teacher training (both in-service and pre-service). This chapter describes the circumstances under which pre-service teacher training becomes a priority for state teams and what other state-level considerations (e.g., CS education standards) should be understood before pre-service teacher education programs can be fully implemented. As this is still an emerging area in many states, we also provide information on next steps for expanding understanding around how to scale pre-service CS teacher education.

Preparing Pre-Service Teachers to Teach Computer Science: Models, Practices, and Policies, pages 205–229.

Keywords: Pre-service CS Teacher Education, State Education Policy, National Science Foundation, Computing Education Alliances, Broadening Participation in Computing.

INTRODUCTION

Computer science (CS) education is increasingly viewed as an important subject in the U.S and, as a result, many stakeholders have made the argument that it should become an integrated part of K–12 education (Code.org Advocacy Coalition & Computer Science Teachers Association [CSTA], 2018; National Science Foundation [NSF], 2018). Despite the ubiquity of technology and the growth of CS education (e.g., Code.org, 2018), we still lack enough quantity and diversity of students in K–12 CS pathways (NSF, 2018; Wang et al., 2016). This chapter describes the evolution of CS education priorities, specifically the rise of pre-service needs, among members of a national CS education alliance comprised of state-based teams.

Over the last decade, there have been many local, state, and national initiatives designed to support CS education (Guzdial, 2016; Stanton et al., 2017). For example, in the U.S, the last two presidents have made national announcements and commitments to CS education (e.g., The White House, 2016, 2017). Also, support for CS in K–12 schools led to the development of a new Advanced Placement Computer Science Principles (CSP) course, which launched with over 44,300 students taking the AP exam during the 2016–2017 academic year.

Within the U.S, most educational policy takes place at the state-level (U.S. Department of Education, 2017). Therefore, to support state-level change in CS education, in 2012 NSF supported the Expanding Computer Education Pathways (ECEP) Alliance, a nationally funded alliance specifically focused on broadening participation in computing (BPC). ECEP focuses on state-level computing education reform efforts by helping states develop leadership teams and build strategic plans. The ultimate goal is to launch sustainable computing education efforts by engaging stakeholders, understanding the local K–16 education context, and bringing together broad-based groups that can lead state-level reform. ECEP has onboarded states in four cohorts over a 6-year period, and is currently comprised of 22 states plus the territory of Puerto Rico, each with unique K–16 educational ecosystems. These states collaboratively examine the issues associated with state-level reform in computing education, united in their efforts to collectively share model practices for BPC and understand how to support systemic change. In 2015, the ECEP PIs and the project evaluators from SageFox collaboratively developed a diagram illustrating the complex web of relationships that exist among state systems to produce educational change in CS education (see Figure 11.1).

State-level computing education policy reform efforts have focused on initiatives such as the development and adoption of curriculum standards, development of curriculum, making CS "count" or be required for high school graduation, and

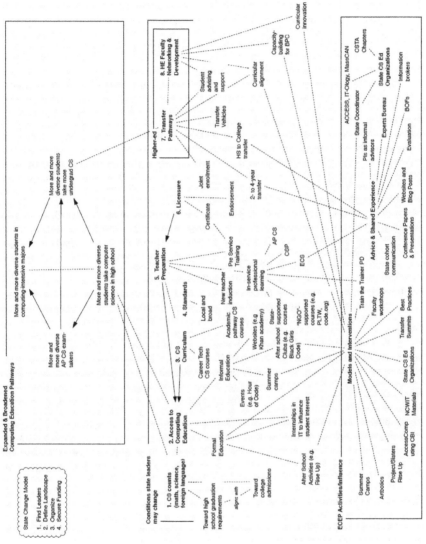

FIGURE 11.1. ECEP Diagram of Relationships Among State Systems to Produce Educational Change

instituting teacher credentialing for teaching CS (Stanton et al., 2017). One of the most impactful strategies has been the adoption of CS standards that span from Kindergarten to 12th grade. Currently, 35 states have either adopted state-level standards or are in the process of adopting standards, with three more actively developing standards (Code.org, 2018). In addition, many states have proposed requirements for high schools to offer at least one CS elective each year (e.g., Indiana General Assembly, 2018).

Even with these state-level efforts, we are not meeting the CS education needs of our students, our communities, and our economy. More than half of U.S high school students lack the opportunity to take CS. The 2016 Google Trends in the *State of Computer Science in U.S. K–12 Schools* report showed that only 40% of U.S. schools reported offering computer science (Google Inc. & Gallup, 2016). The report also suggested this number may be a high estimate due to confusion surrounding what counts as CS. In other words, the principals completing the survey may have conflated computer applications and even keyboarding courses with CS courses (Google Inc. & Gallup, 2016). A 2018 report from Code.org, reported even lower availability of CS courses being offered than reported by Google, with only 35% percent of high schools in 24 states offering CS (Code.org, 2018). Additionally, for those high schools where CS is being offered, the CS curriculum is not always high-quality (Nager & Atkinson, 2016). This may be due to the fact that CS teachers are often recruited from other subject areas, and do not possess adequate CS content and pedagogical knowledge to become highly qualified CS teachers (Nager & Atkinson, 2016; Phillips & Stephenson, 2013). Finally, in addition to the questionable quality of the CS curriculum, the number and diversity of students taking CS is low (Code.org, 2018; NSF, 2018). For example, the *NSF's 2018 Science and Engineering Indicators* report showed that only 23% of AP Computer Science A exams were taken by female students. Furthermore, the *Education Commission of the States* reported that Black, American Indian, rural, and low-income students also have less access to CS than their peers (Education Commission of the States, 2016). In short, there is a lack of CS courses available to U.S high school students, and where those courses are available, the curriculum may not be high quality and often lacks a diverse student population.

In-Service CS Teacher Training

There is also a shortage of highly qualified teachers to offer K–12 CS education (Phillips & Stephenson, 2013). There have been initiatives to train in-service teachers to teach CS including efforts to prepare teachers to offer CS classes (e.g., Guzdial & Morrison, 2016). Many of these efforts trained current in-service teachers (often with credentials to teach Math, Science, or Business) to offer a single CS course (Phillips & Stephenson, 2013). The NSF's investment in the CS10K program aimed to have 10,000 well trained CS teachers in 10,000 schools (NSF Program Solicitation 15-537). Over 7 years, the CS10K program trained approximately 3,500 high school teachers to offer either the Exploring Computer

Science (ECS) course or the Computer Science Principles (CSP) course (Zarch et al., 2018). ECS is an introductory CS course for high school students and is designed to be implemented with high fidelity to the curriculum to ensure a cohesive scope and sequence and to support inclusive teaching practices (http://www.exploringcs.org/). The AP Computer Science Principles Curriculum Framework provides information about the Big Ideas and Computational Thinking Practices that are to be covered in the course, the two through-course assessments, and the end-of-year assessment (https://apcentral.collegeboard.org/courses/ap-computer-science-principles/course). Other initiatives have also helped provide CS training to in-service teachers. For example, Code.org has provided workshops to over 87,000 teachers (Code.org, 2018), and Google's investment in CS4HS (now known as the Educator Grants Program) provided professional development (PD) to over 50,000 teachers (Davis et al., 2018).

Despite the investment in teacher development, the need for more teachers, and the burst of teacher PD offerings, the enrollment in the in-service teacher PD programs was not scaling quickly enough to meet the demand for CS teachers. Data from the CS10K program suggested that enrollment in many of the local-level teacher PD programs had stabilized and would not be sufficient to meet the teacher need (see Figure 11.2). As shown in Figure 11.2, ECS teacher training had a capacity of around 180 teachers per year and have stabilized by 2017–2018 (Zarch et al., 2018). Some PD programs offer national training efforts, bringing together in-service teachers for a week in the summer for residential PD. This led to collaborative efforts such as the CSPDWeek in Colorado and the Infosys Pathfinders program (for more information please visit http://www.infosys.org/infosys-foundation-usa/pathfinders/ and http://www.cspdweek.org/). These two collaborative efforts hosted PD programs such as Bootstrap, Exploring Computer Science, Code.org Discoveries & Principles, Everyday Computing, and Botball. Many of the CS PD courses are offered over one- to two-weeks periods, though several programs do use extended mentoring and coaching to support teachers beyond this point (Menekse, 2015).

Scholars have argued that although preparing in-service teachers to offer CS is valuable, it does not represent a sustainable model for closing the gap between available CS teachers and the growing demand (Yadav et al., 2016). Reaching pre-service teachers through schools of education ensures that future practitioners would have the foundational knowledge in CS and the skills necessary to effectively teach the material (e.g., DeLyser et al., 2018). However, pre-service teacher education varies based on state requirements. State-specific policy issues such as teacher credentialing and licensure requirements influence the models for the pre-service training process (see Figure 11.1). We need to consider how all the other factors interact to influence the pre-service process within the larger state system rather than viewing it as a set of individual training programs (Phillips & Stephenson, 2013). Therefore, we should investigate the evolution of state-level

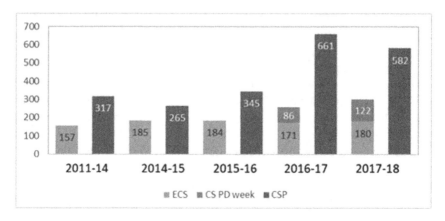

FIGURE 11.2.   Number of Teachers Trained Per Year Through CS10K-Funded PD

CS education reform as it relates to pre-service education, exploring how states are starting to address this issue.

BACKGROUND

This chapter follows trends in priorities of an alliance of state teams focused on CS education to identify when pre-service became an articulated priority.

Priorities of ECEP State Teams

ECEP state teams serve as leaders in computing education reform efforts at the K–12 level. One goal of the ECEP Alliance is to have state teams conduct a landscape report, gathering information on state-level reform related to K–12 computing education. Gathering information about state initiatives informs state strategies, as well as the overall work of the ECEP Alliance. States that have been invited to join ECEP indicate a level of readiness by (1) identifying the potential to form a leadership team, (2) describing efforts in CS change-making such as teacher PD offerings, and (3) sharing evidence of active CS education advocacy and research groups or coordinated CSTA chapters. ECEP states are led by broad-based leadership teams consisting of individuals representing several stakeholder groups.

It is critical to understand the member representation of each state team, because these individuals drive state priorities, strategies and can impact the success of change efforts. This overview of ECEP is included because this is crucial to understanding how state teams set goals and define state strategies. For example, if there is a heavy industry presence, there is the potential for strategies to be guided by more work-force principles. Broad-based teams of diverse stakeholders, including K–12 and higher education representatives, are well positioned to

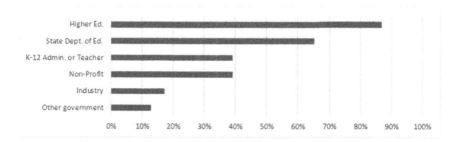

FIGURE 11.3. Percentage of ECEP Teams with Representation from Each Stakeholder Group

both champion multiple facets of CS education reform and develop the capacity within the state to make progress on CS education objectives. Figure 11.3 provides information on the percentage of ECEP teams with a representation from common stakeholder groups.

As shown in Figure 11.3, higher-education faculty are the most well-represented with 86% of ECEP team leaders being from higher-education. This is likely due to grant funding that allows faculty to focus on CS education issues. In fact, for the states that joined between 2012 and 2015, most were led by individuals with NSF grants related to teacher PD for in-service teachers. Seven of the eight states that joined ECEP in 2015 were led by faculty who had already developed strong PD models in their states, typically through CS10K funding. Project evaluation reports, developed from surveys and interviews with state team members found that teacher PD issues were consistently rated as the most highly prioritized and most likely to be worked on. Therefore, state leadership teams could have an impact on which CS issues are prioritized. Priorities could also be led by funding streams available to state teams, with NSF funding for PD clearly prioritized between 2012 and 2015.

Landscape of CS Education Advocacy

As ECEP continued to grow, Code.org, CSTA, and CSforALL emerged to address similar CS education challenges, creating a national conversation about the importance of, and urgency for, CS education. The focus on CS education received greater attention when President Obama announced the CS For All Initiative in 2016 (The White House, 2016). By fall 2018, the ECEP community grew to 22 states plus the territory of Puerto Rico. The ECEP model of state change (see Figure 11.1, above) was initially framed by ECEP PI Mark Guzdial during a workshop flashtalk at the 2014 National Center for Women & Information Technology (NCWIT) Summit (Guzdial, 2014). New and seasoned states both began using a four-stage version of this plan, while the additional "new" stage was added to reflect ECEP's commitment to data as a strategic driver (see Figure 11.4).

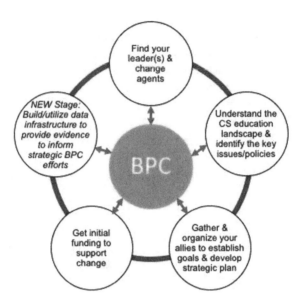

FIGURE 11.4.   ECEP 5 Step Model of State Change

States had begun to develop a common language and framework for BPC that was flexible enough to meet the unique political and educational structures of each state. Teacher PD was still critical to the broadening participation approaches of states, but the conversation shifted away from prioritizing the preparation of high school teachers to offer specific elective courses towards preparing teachers in pre-service programs. With six new state teams added in 2018, the ECEP summit, an annual convening of 3–5 leaders from each Alliance state, was an opportunity for the Alliance to facilitate cross-team discussions of what state teams had accomplished, goals to achieve state-level reform, and what support they needed to achieve these goals.

METHODS AND DATA COLLECTION

The purpose of this study was to examine how pre-service education emerged as a priority for ECEP states. The primary data source were posters collected at the 2018 ECEP summit. As secondary data sources, we also examined findings from ECEP state team surveys and interviews, conducted between 2015 and 2017, to identify the evolution of the pre-service education focus.

Posters

In the fall of 2018, the ECEP Alliance held its sixth summit where all 23 state teams met to discuss state-level BPC efforts. The summit was attended by approxi-

Texas	Indiana	Maryland

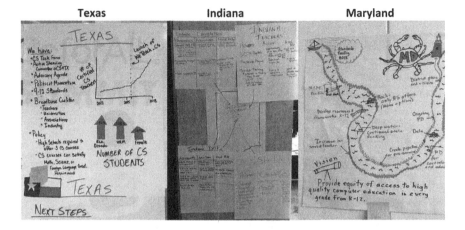

FIGURE 11.5.   Examples of ECEP Posters Created at Summit

mately 100 individuals, including members from state teams, the ECEP leadership team, and ECEP evaluators. During the summit, state teams were asked to construct posters to describe teams' CS education state-level reform work, focusing primarily on 3 areas in their states: (1) Accomplishments related to K–12 CS education, (2) Goals and next steps related to K–12 CS education, and (3) Areas in which they needed guidance or support. The posters were used in a "gallery walk" where participants reviewed the posters from other states and exchanged ideas. Each team's poster varied in visual layout and response to the prompts (see Figure 11.5).

Annual Surveys

Beginning in 2015, ECEP states were annually surveyed and interviewed to identify key change areas around CS education in their states, specifically the current status of efforts and priorities for CS education. Teams were asked to collectively answer an online survey. Follow-up interviews were conducted with team leads to resolve questions and address nuances in their responses. The survey was administered in fall 2015, spring, 2016, and spring 2017.

Each iteration of the online survey evolved to include more questions that captured the changing nature of state-level CS education reform. Surveys were built empirically drawing upon the original, four-stage model of state change (see Figure 11.4 for the current model) and observations of the ECEP teams' priorities through regular webinars and annual summits. The categories identified were vetted by the PI team as representative of what component of CS educational change the teams were addressing at the time. As the focus of state team efforts evolved, the survey was revised to respond to the shifts in priorities to better explain and capture the activity of the ECEP state teams. Each component included two close-

TABLE 11.1. Example of Format of State Survey Questions

	What is Happening in the Area Within Your State to Advance CS Education?					To What Extent do You Think This is a Priority Area for Your ECEP State Team?				
	Do Not Know	Little or None	Being Worked On	Good Enough	Good Enough to Be a Model	Not at All a Priority (1)	(2)	(3)	(4)	High Priority (5)
1) Statewide high school graduation requirements for CS	☐	☐	☐	☐	☐	☐	☐	☐	☐	☐
Open response/elaboration on above										

ended questions to document current status and priorities moving forward (see Table 11.1). There were 15 component areas included on the 2015 and 2016 surveys; the survey was revised in 2017 with 17 component areas (see Table 11.2). The open response for each theme allowed state teams to explain their responses in detail (see Table 11.1 for an example of how each question was structured).

Although the first two survey iterations did not ask directly about pre-service teacher training, they did ask about the tangentially related topic of teacher induction. "Teacher induction" proved to be a confusing term for both the teams and evaluators, which in itself could be interpreted as a shift in the understanding of pre-service as a priority. The survey defined it as "the state-specific processes of support and guidance provided to novice CS teachers." The third iteration specifically asked about pre-service training (see Table 11.2). Re-examining the results of this work helped us contextualize how pre-service education emerged as a priority in the spectrum of state-level reform.

TABLE 11.2. CS Education Areas Asked About on 2015–2017 ECEP State Surveys

	2015 & 2016	2017
Statewide high school graduation requirements for CS	✓	✓
Statewide CS curriculum*	✓	✓
Statewide CS teacher credential/endorsement	✓	✓
Statewide guidelines governing assignment of K–12 CS teachers	✓	✓
Statewide guidelines governing K–12 CS teacher induction	✓	✓
Pre-service professional development in CS		✓
Statewide efforts to offer K–12 CS teacher PD	✓	✓
Making K–12 CS teacher PD more accessible	✓	✓
Making K–12 CS teacher PD more relevant	✓	
Statewide efforts to enhance participation of underrepresented students in K–12 CS courses	✓	✓
Statewide efforts to improve student performance on the AP CS exam	✓	✓
K–12 informal/out-of-school CS education opportunities	✓	✓
Allow CS to count for admission to institutions of higher education		✓
Establishing transfer pathways from 2 to 4 year public colleges/universities in CS	✓	✓
Post Secondary student retention in CS	✓	✓
CS Ed. outreach/recruitment activities among colleges/universities	✓	✓
Industry support to K–12 and higher education CS programs	✓	✓
Industry engagement in CS ed. Policy and advocacy at the state level		✓

*Called "statewide framework or standards" in 2017 version

Data Analysis

The data from the posters were categorized into one of three areas (1) *accomplishments* related to K–12 CS education, (2) goals or *next steps* related to K–12 CS education, and (3) areas in which state teams *needed* guidance or support. All teams' poster statements were thematically coded. A description of the categories into which responses were condensed are included below (see Table 11.3).

TABLE 11.3.   Themes, Definitions, and Examples from ECEP Team Posters*

Theme	Definition	Example
Foundational Efforts		
Leadership—related	Issues associated with ECEP team leaders or general development of leadership around CS education advocacy in state.	**Accomplishment:** Growing division CS leads **Next Steps:** Raise funding for CS specialist **Needs:** Lack of state-level CS position
Understanding landscape	Gaining a greater understanding of the issues and context around CS education and its status and challenges within a given state.	**Accomplishment:** Strategic CS plan **Next Steps:** Expand measurement efforts **Needs:** What do districts need?
Summit stakeholders	Bringing together important stakeholder groups in formal or semi-formal settings to help devise a common understanding of the problem and create a plan.	**Accomplishment:** 1st statewide CS summit **Next Steps:** Finalize draft of CS endorsement proposal and build consensus among stakeholders **Needs:** Effort in state not coordinated
Broader awareness/buy-in	Related to gaining greater recognition of issues around CS education or establishing credibility with important groups.	**Accomplishment:** Recognition as leader in CS ed **Next Steps:** Advocacy materials and elevator pitch **Needs:** To get more to be involved
Implementation Efforts		
Policy/legislation	Issues around creating formal structure and rules at the state level to shape the landscape of CS education (e.g. standards, legislative bodies, credentials).	**Accomplishment:** K–8 standards developed and approved **Next Steps:** Revise K–8 Tech standards to include comp. thinking **Needs:** HQ teacher certification
District-level implementation	Referring to descriptions or specific efforts at the district level, such as student diversity or specific professional development efforts.	**Accomplishment:** CS course in 78% of high schools **Next Steps:** Focus on rural **Needs:** Sustainable funding to RPDPs? Districts?
Infrastructure/training	Comments associated with broad training initiatives or the creation/modification of organizations that help to advance CS education in the state.	**Accomplishment:** PD for 800+ teachers **Next Steps:** Where will the teachers come from **Needs:** Providing support and PD to build CS teacher base without state funding

TABLE 11.3. Continued

Theme	Definition	Example
	Implementation Efforts	
Pre-service	Efforts specifically aimed at enhancing or developing pre-service teacher programs or training.	**Accomplishment:** Pre-service program **Next Steps:** Finalize draft of proposal of pre-service teacher program and build consensus among stakeholders **Needs:** Model pre-service...teacher programs
Funding-related	Obtaining funding, especially for team sustainability but also for specific activities or individuals.	**Accomplishment:** State funding for CS and PD **Next Steps:** Raise funding for district CS Coaches **Needs:** Legislation funding excluded some key players: i.e. NDE representative, RPDPs, (training programs)

*AC = "accomplishments," NS = "next steps," SU = "need support"

We classified the first four categories as **foundational** efforts, which typically involved planning. The second five categories (5–9) were classified as **implementation** efforts, which typically involved taking action, creating products, and/or planning for long-term sustainability.

The analysis of the final surveys involved the examination of both quantitative and qualitative data. Quantitative data mostly included the scaled responses regarding (1) the extent to which certain items were being worked on in a state, and (2) the extent to which the team prioritized working on a given item. These items were presented using descriptive frequency counts, illustrating what percentage of teams provided each response. Qualitative data for each item were examined for common themes and to explore commonalities and differences. Each item was divided based on whether it fell into the "accomplishments," "needs support" or "next steps" bin. Items were then listed in a spreadsheet and codes were developed that noted which of the "foundational" or "implementation" categories it fell into. Key findings that represented the typical representation of ECEP teams as well as notable exceptions were described.

Limitations

There were some limitations associated with the poster data. First, the poster session was not designed as a data collection activity. Rather it was intended to serve as a tool for facilitating community discussion. This may have influenced how teams designed their posters. Second, not all poster elements were easily analyzed and classified into 3 areas (accomplishments, next steps, and need support). Classification of the poster content and use of the posters as a data collection tool were an exercise retroactive to the summit. Therefore, it was not always clear how to classify where various poster elements belonged. This required some additional interpretation and inference. Third, some poster elements contained only a small amount of detail and may not have been interpreted as originally intended by the state team. For example, Mississippi wrote "consensus" on the poster (see Figure 11.6). It was interpreted as "convening stakeholders" as an area of needing support.

To account for these limitations, we presented the tables and figures below during a monthly ECEP community call to examine the accuracy of our emergent themes. In order to mitigate some of the uncertainty brought about by these limitations, we also used previously known information about the state teams gathered from prior state survey efforts and monthly ECEP calls. Finally, it is important to note that the absence of component of change on a team's poster did not necessarily mean that the state team did not have an accomplishment or need. Given the limited amount of time and space available for the posters, it could mean that certain areas may not have been prioritized or deemed recent enough to mention for the purpose of the gallery walk.

FIGURE 11.6. Mississippi State Poster

RESULTS AND DISCUSSION

We sought to examine how and when pre-service teacher training factored in as a priority for state teams. Therefore, we first present survey and interview data from 2015, 2016, and 2017. Poster data from 2018 provides an update. Together these data provide a picture of the evolution of when and how pre-service teacher preparation emerged as a priority. Finally, we share ECEP's current focus in supporting pre-service efforts with the newly launched pre-service community of practice.

Surveys and Interviews

In the fall of 2015 and 2016, ECEP state teams were asked to describe the status of teacher induction in their state. When asked, "What is happening in this area [teacher induction] within your state to advance CS education," state teams could respond as (a) Do not know, (b) Little or none, (c) Being worked on, (d) Good enough, and (e) Good enough to be a model. Most state teams indicated that teacher induction was not an active focus area, with 10 out of 11 saying that there was little or no activity in this area in 2015 and 2016 and all teams saying this in 2017. However, many identified it as a moderately high priority with an average ranking of 3.5 out of 5 in 2015 and 2016. States were provided an open space to elaborate on their responses. Teams reported that teacher induction was highly dependent on other policy and structural supports in the state. For example, since many states did not have a license specifically for "computer science" teachers, this required prerequisite work to establish a license or endorsement, which further dependent on standards and/or credentialing to be in place before this could be pursued. Examples of responses to this item include:

- Nothing going on. This would follow the standards and then credentialing.
- The area of adding a credential is another huge project; think we need to start with developing more CS curriculum and teachers interested in it, we'll be able to affect something at credentialing level once there's interest and demand. A lot of the teachers interested in a credential are pre-service, want a STEM background and are aware of lack of CS preparation.
- [We have] fought for in-service teachers to obtain a graduate certificate for recognizing CS knowledge and practices that they've gained through graduate work. Working toward creating change in this area. Don't have a state-level certification process, but leaders and administrators do see the value and would like to see teachers having some kind of certification that they can rely upon.
- [Our state] has very specific guidelines regarding teacher induction, which are no different for computer science.
- Bigger focus on in-service, which relates back to certification. Pre-service know they can't get a CS teacher certification right now, so it's not part of

core studies at any level. Have someone who's a CS major who wants to go
into education, she can't get certified in CS to teach so has to get certified
somewhere else, like math.

Although during this time period preparing pre-service teachers felt daunting,
the teams described in-service teacher PD as an area of high-activity. PD was
recognized as a high priority for nearly everyone, with eight of the eleven ECEP
teams active in the Alliance at the time[1] rating this as the highest priority level
to strategically address. However, in the interviews, state teams described that
although there was considerable state-level work dedicated to in-service PD, this
work was often being conducted by multiple providers, often in uncoordinated
ways. For example, PD was offered on a variety of topics (some were duplicated
or conflicted with other efforts), varied in terms of duration (ranging from short
day-long workshops to more sustained efforts), and varied in funding sources (local, federal and private dollars). This disjointed approach to providing in-service
PD, while important for quickly expanding CS opportunities for students was
insufficient to meet growing state-level demand, which would require systemic
change.

By early 2017, ECEP state teams were beginning to identify pre-service teacher education as a focus area. As the demand for K–12 CS education increased,
states were trying to identify how to meet and support these demands. As in-
service teacher PD programs saturated the local areas, states were looking for
additional ways to prepare enough teachers to meet growing demand for CS education. Pre-service teacher education was identified as a potential solution, but
also created a significant challenge for many states. Several states mentioned having pre-service preparation programs; however, most were not system-wide nor
well-utilized. In some cases, states expressed that there were financial barriers to
creating and implementing programs. For example, in the 2017 State Survey, a
state team described that one of their major universities needed to pursue a grant
focused specifically on CS pre-service teacher education to establish a pre-service
program. In other cases, the issue of pre-service teacher PD was linked closely
with certification and standards. For example, in an interview/survey response,
another team described their rationale for focusing on CS standards first: once
their state CS standards were adopted, the state would immediately recognize a
serious shortage of CS teachers as very few teachers would be properly certified.
This would prompt calls for certifying large numbers of teachers, likely including
pre-service education.

Regardless of the specific ecosystem of a state, pre-service teacher education
was beginning to emerge as a potential consideration. These examples illustrated

---

[1] ECEP states joined the alliance in multiple phases over time, beginning with two origin states and
progressing to 4 in cohort 1 (in 2013), 11 in cohort 2 (2014) and 17 in cohort 3 (2016). Cohort 4
(bringing the total number of states/territories to 23) came on board as phase 2 of the grant began
in 2018.

the complex set of state systems and how pre-service teacher education needs to fit differently in relation to other elements within this system. Though there was little cited as happening in ECEP states during this data collection period (14 of 17 teams said there was little or no activity), pre-service preparation was cited as a moderately high priority (it ranked exactly in the middle of all of the areas asked about and had an average of 3.3 out of 5).

In the 2017 state survey, scaled responses about team priorities indicated that most state teams identified pre-service teacher education as an emerging area of focus. This included exploring possible avenues for certification (e.g., extra courses for math or science teachers, dedicated CS minor program) and selecting teacher education programs that could educate CS pre-service teachers. Some state teams found that the need for CS pre-service teachers was well-established at the state level through a top-down call for actions, as was the case in a member state in which the governor was directly making a push for CS education. Other state teams, such as Connecticut, were in the early stages of creating pre-service teacher education programs and described the importance of obtaining grants and additional funding possibilities to support these developments. In Rhode Island, the team also explored different pathways within their state. In another ECEP state, an institution of higher education was working on a CS certificate while another was working on a CS minor for educators. In another example, South Carolina had one institution working on a middle-school pre-service program while another was working on a high-school level pre-service program. Other state teams described looking at elementary level programs with Massachusetts, working on infusing computational thinking into the general K–5 licensure. Given the variety of pathways for pre-service preparation described both in open-ended comments and interview follow-ups, these findings reinforce the importance of having mechanisms in place, such as certification and standards that can help frame the knowledge and skills needed in pre-service teacher education programs.

Posters and Summit

Data from the posters at the October 2018 summit provided insights into the current priorities of the teams. Figure 11.7 illustrates the percentage of state teams that described focusing on accomplishments, next steps, and needs for *foundational* efforts (described above) while Figure 11.8 illustrates the percentage of teams that focused on accomplishments, next steps, and needs for *implementation* efforts. By examining these two figures, it becomes clear that many teams have experience in an array of areas necessary to enact change in CS education at the state level. Pre-service emerged as an area where most teams have less experience, but it suggests that teams need to have developed abilities and knowledge in other areas prior to beginning work on this specific area.

It was also critical for us to examine state teams' themes and accomplishments, next steps, and needs. Therefore, we created two additional figures that illustrated the foundational and implementation work themes (see Figures 11.9 and 11.10).

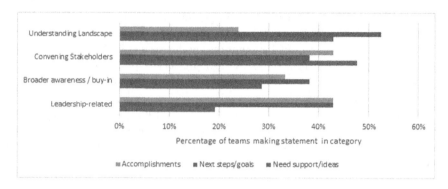

FIGURE 11.7.   Percentage of Teams Citing Accomplishments, Next Steps, and Needs (foundational work)

Within each figure, each category of response has been divided based on whether the state team referred to it as an accomplishment, next step, or area in which they need support. Accomplishments are presented in shades of green, next steps in shades of blue, and support areas in shades of red. The shades deepen depending on the number of times a team cited an item in a given area. At the bottom of the figure, the percentage of teams who cited something in a given area is provided.

These findings demonstrated, particularly among the first 3 ECEP cohorts, that state teams seemed to prioritize certain accomplishments (e.g., summit stakeholders, policy/legislation-related) before embarking on other work related to the implementation of K–12 CS education at the local level. For example, the first 3 cohorts had 44 accomplishments in the prioritized areas, as opposed to the 4th cohort of states which only had 4 accomplishments across all 5 states. It could be inferred that these prior accomplishments laid the groundwork for additional

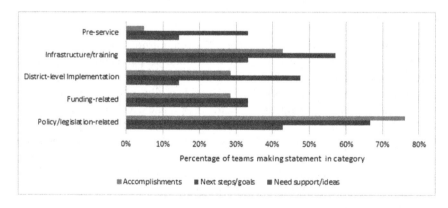

FIGURE 11.8.   Percentage of Teams Citing Accomplishments, Next Steps and Needs (implementation work)

		Foundational Work											
		Leadership - related			Understand Landscape			Convening Stakeholders			Broader awareness / buy-in		
		AC	NS	Su	AC	NS	Su	AC	NS	Su	AC	NS	Su
Cohort 1	MA		1			1							
	GA		1			1			1			1	
	CA	1	1		1			1	1		1		
	SC					1						1	
Cohort 2	AL		1	2				2		1	1		
	CT				2	1			1	1		1	
	IN		1		2	3				1	1	1	2
	MD		1			1	1			1			
	UT	1					1	1	1	2			1
	NH												
	TX	1			1	1	2	5			2		1
Cohort 3	NC	1	2			2	1				1	1	
	AR							1	1			1	
	NV	2			1		1	2	1	1			1
	RI		1					1	1				1
	VA	3		1	1	1		1		1	1		
Cohort 4	HI	1				1		3					
	MN		1			2						1	
	MS	1		1	1					2			
	OH	1		1						1	1	1	
	OR						1			1			1
% States		43%	43%	19%	24%	52%	43%	43%	38%	48%	33%	38%	29%

AC = Accomplishments
NS = Next steps / goals
Su = Need support / ideas

LEGEND	0	1	2	3	4+
Accomplishments					
Next Steps					
Need support / ideas					

FIGURE 11.9.   Foundational Work Cited by Teams

work to develop new infrastructure and promote teacher training. For some of the more experienced teams, it may have shown pre-service teacher training as an area they need to focus on. Ten of the 21[2] states included pre-service teacher education in their posters, with 7 specifically mentioning it as a next step. This shows that CS teacher pre-service teacher education has recently emerged as a priority for ECEP state teams.

The decision to focus on CS pre-service teacher education illustrates an important shift in thinking about CS education at the state level. This shift could indicate that the state teams have progressed from identifying quick fixes to recruit

---

[2] Two teams did not have members available to participate in the poster session

		Implementation Work														
		Policy / legislation - related			District-level Implement.			Infrastructure / training			Pre-service			Funding - related		
		AC	NS	Su	AC	NS	Su	AC	NS	Su	AC	NS	Su	AC	NS	Su
Cohort 1	MA	2	4			2		2	2						1	
	GA		3			2			1		1					
	CA	1	1	1												1
	SC	4		1					1	2			1		1	
Cohort 2	AL	1	1		1			1		1		1		1		1
	CT					2										
	IN	6	1	2	1			4	2	2	1			2	4	
	MD	1	2			1		1	3			1		1	1	
	UT	2		3	1		2		1				1			1
	NH	2		1	1					1	1					
	TX	3	1		1				1						2	1
Cohort 3	NC	1	2	2						2		1		1	1	
	AR	3	1		4	2		1	1					5		
	NV	4					2	1	2			2	1			2
	RI	3	1		2	2	1	2	1			1			2	2
	VA	2		2	1			2		1						
Cohort 4	HI	1	1	2				1								
	MN		2			1										
	MS		2						1					1		
	OH	1	1			2			2							2
	OR			2						2						
	% States	76%	67%	43%	29%	48%	14%	43%	57%	33%	5%	33%	14%	29%	33%	33%

AC = Accomplishments
NS = Next steps / goals
Su = Need support / ideas

LEGEND	0	1	2	3	4+
Accomplishments					
Next Steps					
Need support / ideas					

FIGURE 11.10. Implementation Work Cited by Teams

more in-service teachers to meet the increased demand for CS, toward thinking about how to meet this demand sustainably. This distinction, though subtle, perhaps indicates the beginning of the next phase of state teams' work.

Pre-Service Community of Practice

Every summit of ECEP state leaders offers insight into the changing landscape of CS education reform efforts. While reform efforts are unique within each state and depend on a variety of factors (e.g., Ericson et al., 2016), we observed some consistency among the selected priorities that ECEP state leadership teams choose. ECEP project goals allow for fluidity of focus, meaning that when multiple states identify one area, like pre-service teacher education, we can revise our summit and meeting agendas to provide assistance in these new areas.

Pre-service teacher education was identified as a core area of focus in the NSF proposal to extend the work of ECEP beyond the original funding cycle (NSF, 2019). The PI, Co-PIs, and Alliance Director had observed more state-level discussions among ECEP state leaders regarding the need for CS pre-service teacher education programs. As discussed in this chapter, this assumption was confirmed in the conversations among state teams at the 2018 ECEP summit.

To address this call to action, the ECEP leadership devised the formation of a community of practice (e.g., Wenger, 1999) to address the need for sustainable pre-service preparation programs with the intention of broadening participation in computing. Within this space, state teams could meet and discuss CS pre-service teacher education programs. During the 2018 summit, state team members could attend different workshop sessions to focus on areas of need (e.g., BPC professional development, community college, pre-service teacher education). As part of the pre-service teacher education workshop, state team members could express areas of concern or questions. These concerns included the following shown in Table 11.4.

In the first official meeting in February 2019, we had 12 individuals from state teams participate in an online, synchronous meeting. To establish cultural norms for our community of practice, we first sought to identify the key terms to agree upon (Figure 11.11). Therefore, the leaders of the community of practice have started to create a working document that has these key terms, definitions, and examples.

Another item of focus during the first pre-service community of practice call, was to develop priorities. The 12 state team members were provided with 7 choices to focus on over the next year. The state team members ranked those choices in order of importance (see Figure 11.12). Therefore, over the next year, our community of practice will focus on two priorities: (1) identifying methods to educate enough teachers to teach quality CS education at every grade level, and (2) preparing teacher educators to develop programs.

NEXT STEPS

Working with leadership teams in 22 states and the territory of Puerto Rico provides a loop of continuous feedback for both ECEP leadership and the state leadership teams. The ECEP PI, Co-PIs, director, and evaluation team are continuously monitoring for shifts in state-level trends. With annual ECEP summits, and other opportunities to meet at state and national events, we are able to document the evolution of state-level CS education reform efforts. The regular monthly virtual meetings provide another source for input and reflection. As patterns continue to emerge from meetings, convenings, and Alliance member dialogue, ECEP is well positioned to share our collective knowledge with the CS education reform community and CS education advocates. We plan on working to support state-level teams as they move forward with pre-service teacher education.

TABLE 11.4.   Concerns and Questions Related to CS Pre-service Teacher Education

1.   Licenses and certifications

– How can we get states to adopt CS teacher licenses?

– How can we facilitate discussions and connections between DOE and Schools of Ed?

– What comes first? Certification or pre-service programs?

– How do the certification exam compare (Praxis versus Pearson)?

– How do in-service teachers become certified?

2.   Optional Structures

– What are the agile structures for meeting needs of multiple tracks of licensures/entry?

– How could we use micro-credentials for pre-service teachers towards licensure?

– How can we use competencies or micro-competencies to assess GAPS in pre-service knowledges?

– How can we support those leaving the workforce that have the technical knowledge and want to teach?

– What do undergraduate and graduate models look like?

3.   Getting Schools of Education Programs Committed

– Can we create a resource or playbook of how to create a healthy ecosystem connecting CS departments, local teachers, and Schools of Ed?

– How can we get higher education to make this commitment when money is such a deciding factor?

– How can we help Schools of Education recruit and provide examples of incentives to drive enrollment in pre-service programs (grants, stipends)?

– How can we convince university administration to take faculty off current courses to teach/ create these new CS-ED courses?

– What are some examples of program structures and the required resources?

– What other pathways are available to teachers, especially elementary?

4.   Best Practices

– What does good CS teaching look like in the context of coaching and observing pre-service teachers?

– What are CS content recommendations for elementary pre-service teachers?

– How can we support field experiences and facilitating placements?

– How do we infuse equity throughout CS teacher education program designs, not just an add-on?

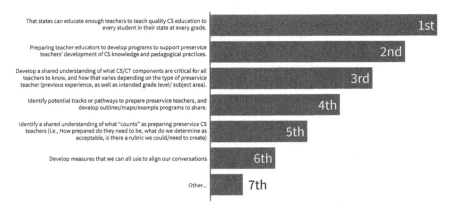

FIGURE 11.11.   Key Terms for the CS Pre-service Teacher Education Community of Practice

That states can educate enough teachers to teach quality CS education to every student in their state at every grade.	1st
Preparing teacher educators to develop programs to support preservice teachers' development of CS knowledge and pedagogical practices.	2nd
Develop a shared understanding of what CS/CT components are critical for all teachers to know, and how that varies depending on the type of preservice teacher (previous experience, as well as intended grade level/ subject area).	3rd
Identify potential tracks or pathways to prepare preservice teachers, and develop outlines/maps/example programs to share.	4th
Identify a shared understanding of what "counts" as preparing preservice CS teachers (i.e., How prepared do they need to be, what do we determine as acceptable, is there a rubric we could/need to create)	5th
Develop measures that we can all use to align our conversations	6th
Other...	7th

FIGURE 11.12.   Priorities for ECEP CS Pre-service Teacher Education Programs Community of Practice

REFERENCES

Code.org. (2018). *Code.org 2018 annual report.* https://code.org/files/annual-report-2018. pdf

Code.org Advocacy Coalition & Computer Science Teachers Association. (2018). *2018 state of computer science education.* https://code.org/files/2018_state_of_cs.pdf

Davis, S., Ravitz, J., & Blazevski, J. (2018, February). Evaluating computer science professional development models and educator outcomes to ensure equity. In *2018 Research on Equity and Sustained Participation in Engineering, Computing, and Technology (RESPECT)* (pp. 1–4). IEEE. doi: 10.1109/RESPECT.2018.8491716

DeLyser, L. A., Goode, J., Guzdial, M., Kafai, Y. B., & Yadav, A. (2018, April). *Priming the computer science teacher pump: Integrating computer science education into schools of education.* CSforALL. https://www.computingteacher.org

Education Commission of the States. (2016, August). *Bridging the computer science access gap.* http://ecs.force.com/studies/rstempg?id=a0r0g000009TLeI

Ericson, B., Adrion, W. R., Fall, R., & Guzdial, M. (2016). State-based progress towards computer science for all. *ACM Inroads, 7*(4), 57–60. doi: 10.1145/2994607

Google Inc. & Gallup Inc. (2016). *Trends in the State of computer science in U.S. K–12 schools.* http://services.google.com/fh/files/misc/trends-in-the-state-of-computer-science-report.pdf

Guzdial, M. (2014, May). *How to change a state: Making computing education fit into public education.* Workshop presented at the 2014 National Center for Women & Information Technology Summit, Tucson, Arizona.

Guzdial, M. (2016). Bringing computer science to US schools, state by state. *Communications of the ACM, 59*(5), 24–25. doi: 10.1145/2898963

Guzdial, M., & Morrison, B. (2016). Growing computer science education into a STEM education discipline. *Communications of the ACM, 59*(11), 31–33. doi: 10.1145/3000612

Menekse, M. (2015). Computer science teacher professional development in the United States: A review of studies published between 2004 and 2014. *Computer Science Education, 25*(4), 325–350.

Nager, A., & Atkinson, R. D. (2016). *The case for improving US computer science education.* Information Technology and Innovation Foundation. http://www2.itif. org/2016-computer-science-education.pdf

National Science Foundation. (2016). *STEM + computing partnerships (STEM+C). program solicitation: NSF 16-527.* https://www.nsf.gov/pubs/2016/nsf16527/nsf16527. htm

National Science Foundation. (2018). *Science and engineering indicators 2018.* Author. https://www.nsf.gov/statistics/2018/nsb20181/assets/nsb20181.pdf

National Science Foundation. (2019). *NSF award search: Award#1822011—Expanding computing education pathways 2.0.* Retrieved on September 1, 2019 from https:// www.nsf.gov/awardsearch/showAward?AWD_ID=1822011&HistoricalAwards=fa lse.

Phillips, P., & Stephenson, C. (2013). *Bugs in the system: Computer science teacher certification in the U.S.* Computer Science Teachers Association.

Stanton, J., Goldsmith, L., Adrion, W. R., Dunton, D., Hendrickson, K. A., Peterfreund, A. Yongpradit, P., Zarch R., & Zinth, J.D. (2017). *State of the states landscape report:*

State-level policies supporting equitable K–12 computer science education. https://www.ecs.org/ec-content/uploads/MassCAN-Full-Report-v10.pdf

The White House. (2016). *FACT SHEET: President Obama announces computer science for all initiative.* https://obamawhitehouse.archives.gov/the-press-office/2016/01/30/fact-sheet-president-obama-announces-computer-science-all-initiative-0

The White House. (2017). *Presidential memorandum for the Secretary of Education.* https://www.whitehouse.gov/presidential-actions/presidential-memorandum-secretary-education/

U.S. Department of Education. (2017). *The federal role in education.* https://www2.ed.gov/about/overview/fed/role.html

Wang, J., Hong, H., Ravitz, J., & Hejazi Moghadam, S. (2016). Landscape of K–12 computer science education in the US: Perceptions, access, and barriers. In *Proceedings of the 47th ACM technical symposium on computing science education* (pp. 645–650). ACM. doi: 10.1145/2839509.2844628

Wenger, E. (1999). *Communities of practice: Learning, meaning, and identity.* Cambridge University Press.

Yadav, A., Gretter, S., Hambrusch, S., & Sands, P. (2016). Expanding computer science education in schools: Understanding teacher experiences and challenges. *Computer Science Education, 26*(4), 235–254. doi: 10.1080/08993408.2016.1257418

Zarch, R., Haynie, K., McKlin, T., Ong, C., Peterfreund, A., Silverstein, G., Xavier, J., & Dunton, S. (2018). *CS10K common data elements. Evaluation working group. year 3 common data collection report. 2016-107. Award #1228355.* Sagefox Consulting Group. http://sagefoxgroup.com/dev/wp-content/uploads/2018/02/Combined-CS10K-Year-3-Report-2018.pdf

CHAPTER 12

TEACHER-FOCUSED POLICIES TO BROADEN PARTICIPATION IN K–12 COMPUTER SCIENCE EDUCATION IN THE UNITED STATES

Megean Garvin, Katie A. Hendrickson,
Sarah T. Dunton, Jennifer Zinth, and Lynn T. Goldsmith

In the United States, each state retains the authority to enact education policies to promote high quality K–12 computer science (CS) education. These efforts include an intentional focus on engaging underrepresented students in order to broaden participation in computing. CS education advocates have organized efforts, focused on policy reform, and learned valuable lessons in the process. Increasingly, state policy reform efforts have focused on preparing teachers to teach CS. Three comprehensive state cases (Arkansas, Maryland, and Massachusetts) provide an overview of state policies which govern pre-service teacher preparation programs, teacher licensure, and in-service teacher professional development. The chapter concludes with state policy recommendations which reflect upon what has occurred since the 2013 report

Preparing Pre-Service Teachers to Teach Computer Science: Models, Practices, and Policies, pages 231–255.
Copyright © 2021 by Information Age Publishing
231

Bugs in the System as well as policy approaches beyond traditional methods that states can use to address CS teacher shortages.

Keywords: State Education Policy, Broadening Participation in Computing, K–12 Computer Science, Teacher Licensure, Pre-Service Teacher Preparation Programs, Professional Development

INTRODUCTION

The push to expand high-quality K–12 computer science (CS) has gained momentum over the past decade. Initiatives from federal agencies, such as the White House and the National Science Foundation (NSF), have dedicated funding to support K–12 CS education. National organizations, such as the Code.org Advocacy Coalition, the Computer Science Teachers Association (CSTA), CSforALL, and the Expanding Computing Education Pathways (ECEP) Alliance, have focused on state and federal policy reform efforts, including efforts specifically aimed at increasing the number of qualified CS teachers. These initiatives have generated more momentum in some states than others, but as a nation, the United States is making progress at providing CS education for all students. As of 2020, approximately 47% of high schools in the United States taught at least one foundational CS course (Code.org, CSTA, & ECEP, 2020). In addition, the number of students taking AP CS exams has increased dramatically over the past five years (Code. org et al., 2020), with AP CS Principles exams doubling between 2017 and 2019 (College Board, 2019). Despite this growth, CS has yet to become an established and required content discipline within all K–12 classrooms. A Google and Gallup (2015) survey of 11,558 U.S. principals and school administrators found that two of the biggest barriers to offering CS courses were the lack of qualified teachers and a lack of funding to hire or train new CS teachers. The lack of universal K–12 student access to CS has resulted in inequities in students' access to educational opportunities and preparation for the future workforce and global citizenry (Code. org, CSTA, & ECEP, 2019).

In efforts to increase CS offerings and promote both equitable access to CS courses and equitable enrollment in them, advocates from industry, non-profit organizations, and institutions of higher education (IHE) have learned valuable lessons that inform current and future advocacy and policy efforts (Code.org et al., 2019). This chapter highlights teacher-focused state policies related to in-service teacher professional development (PD), teacher licensure (including certifications, endorsements, and micro-credentialing), and pre-service teacher preparation programs. These teacher-focused state policy efforts are essential to reach all students and ensure future diversity in the CS workforce.

Each state retains the authority to set education policy. At the district and school levels, administrators tend to have substantial influence in decisions related to how and when CS courses are taught and which students are able to take them. This policy structure hinders the ability of federal or state policymakers to design potential solutions to equity issues related to the lack of CS teachers and complicates efforts to increase the number of qualified CS teachers.

The process for the development of prospective teachers of more established content areas generally follows the same sequence: pre-service preparation, licensure, and in-service PD. However, as CS is a fairly new K–12 subject, the CS teacher development process has not followed this sequence. This section describes the three categories in the order in which the policy efforts have generally evolved over the past few decades: in-service PD, licensure, and pre-service preparation.

STATE POLICES FOR IN-SERVICE
TEACHER PROFESSIONAL DEVELOPMENT

With a dearth of credentialled CS teachers, CS education advocates, industry leaders, and non-profit organizations have provided PD for in-service teachers of other subjects as a scalable way to increase K–12 CS course offerings (Yadav et al., 2013). Typically, CS PD is designed to prepare teachers to implement specific curricula such as Beauty and Joy in Computing (BJC), Bootstrap, Exploring Computer Science (ECS), or Mobile Computer Science Principles (Mobile CSP). Twenty-five states have dedicated funds for in-service PD as a solution to increase qualified CS teachers (Code.org et al., 2019).

Over the past five years, some of these 25 states have implemented on-going PD funding models. For example, the Rhode Island legislature has funded the CS-4RI initiative at $210,000 per year since 2016 (Code.org et al., 2019). Similarly, Utah and Idaho each have funded a CS grant program through the state STEM Action Center each year [2019 Idaho Laws Ch. 118 (H.B. 215); U.C.A. § 9-22-113]. The Pennsylvania General Assembly has funded a state initiative since 2018 which included a $20 million per year grant program for CS and STEM education. The Pennsylvania Department of Education (PDE) created two funding tiers: larger *Advancing Grants* for scaling large programs, and smaller *Targeted Grants* for school systems and schools that have few or no CS programs. The application for the *Targeted Grants* was short and accessible to first-time grant applicants, making it more likely that small and under-resourced schools could successfully apply (PDE, n.d.). By the end of the second year of the program, PDE had reached almost every district in the state.

Even though PD has increased the number of CS teachers, state policies need to address more long-term and sustainable methods to prepare and maintain CS content knowledge and skills for the CS teaching workforce, including credentialing for existing teachers and the development of pre-service pathways.

State Policies for Teacher Licensure

Requirements for a CS-specific certification are in place in 40 states (Code.org et al., 2020). From the authors' conversations with state leaders, we know anecdotally that relatively few CS teachers have earned a standalone full licensure in CS education, possibly due to the relatively short time period that these licenses have been available in most states or the relative lack of interest CS majors have in teaching (Velez et al., 2019). In the 2013 *Bugs in the System* report, Florida's CS certification process was highlighted as one that was challenging for teachers to earn, mainly due to confusion around the process. Similar confusion continues in other states launching certification plans, often leading to years-long periods of system testing and system refinement before reaching a strong, functional process. In recognition of the various challenges of implementing initial full licensure programs, policy changes over the past few years have focused on increasing the number of credentialed CS teachers through add-on certifications or endorsements and, more recently, micro-credentialing (Code.org, 2019; DeMonte, 2017).

As a result of the challenges to obtaining a CS credential, many CS teachers have been teaching without CS certification or licensure. These teachers typically taught other content areas before attending PD to teach a specific CS course. Even if a CS certification exists in the state, in most states, teachers with any licensure can teach CS courses as long as it is not the primary subject being taught; in other states, teachers with a mathematics or science licensure can teach CS (Code.org, 2018). For example, Maryland allows teachers to teach out of licensure content area via an exemption or waiver if the teacher's course load is primarily in their licensed content area (COMAR 13A.12.02.02) or if they have a license that is accepted for CS courses (MSDE, 2020).

Endorsements

As the demand for K–12 CS has increased, states have been challenged to quickly increase the number of qualified CS teachers. Immediate implementation of a required full licensure could result in no credentialed CS teachers, whereas allowing teachers with any licensure to teach CS could result in inadequately taught CS courses. Endorsements, on the other hand, leverage the existing teacher workforce, because they can be added on to an existing standalone licensure while also ensuring that teachers have CS content knowledge. These CS endorsements attempt to acknowledge teachers' previous experience, balance rigor with accessibility, and provide multiple pathways to CS teaching.

In the past few years, many states have made policy changes around CS endorsements; states that did not have any CS licensure created CS endorsements and states with existing CS licensure modified their policy to include endorsements (Code.org et al., 2020). However, some states, such as Michigan, have reacted to this need by discontinuing CS endorsements. Effective with the 2017–2018 school year, this policy change allowed school districts to staff CS courses with any teacher who demonstrated documentation of CS content knowledge and skills (Michigan Department of Education, 2019).

Some states include a ramping-up period of one to five years before requiring CS teachers to hold the endorsement. For example, the New Jersey endorsement created in 2018 will not be required until the state board determines that there is a sufficient number of teachers holding the endorsement (N.J.S.A. 18A:26-2.26 and N.J.S.A. 18A:26-2.27). Once a critical mass is reached, teachers must earn the endorsement, but teachers can do so by submitting evidence of recent successful teaching experience. In New York, rules that went into effect in 2018 allow any teacher in the state who taught CS between 2017 and 2022 to continue to teach CS for 10 years in the same school district (8 NYCRR 80-3.14). Further, the state added CS as a "special subject tenure area" (8 NYCRR 30-1.8) and allowed current CS teachers to be exempt from licensure requirements for CS. In Iowa's first year of implementation of the CS and Career and Technical Education (CTE) Information Technology endorsements, the board of educational examiners established criteria to waive course requirements for teachers who demonstrated a combination of content knowledge mastery and successful teaching experience in CS or CTE Information Technology [Iowa Admin. Code 282-13.28(272)]. In 2018, Nevada passed changes in requirements for CS endorsements but exempted teachers who held the previous endorsements in CS or computer literacy. Legislation in Ohio created a CS endorsement in 2017 (R.C. § 3319.236), but the FY 2020–21 budget (2019 Ohio Laws File 10 [Am. Sub. H.B. 166], Section 733.61) created a temporary exemption for teachers who attend PD. This exemption will expire with the budget in summer 2021, unless another temporary exemption is granted. Upon expiration, all CS teachers will be required to hold the endorsement.

Some states have created levels of endorsements. For example, Nevada's regulation changes in 2018 established two endorsements related to CS: one to teach "computer technology-based applications and computational thinking" that requires nine semester hours of coursework (NAC 391.202), and another to teach "advanced CS" that requires either 12 semester hours or a passing score on the Praxis II CS content exam (NAC 391.196). The recent Iowa CS endorsements require 12 semester hours of CS content for teachers who already hold licensure in another area, and 24 semester hours for those who do not currently hold a state teaching license [Iowa Admin. Code 282-13.28(272)]. Utah has six CS and IT endorsements that allow the educator to teach varying levels of courses: for example, the Intro to Computer Science endorsement requirements include a set of online courses and completed CSP training and allows teachers to teach eight introductory CS courses; the Programming and Software Development endorsement requirements include 30 credit hours or successful passage of the CS Praxis exam and allows the teaching of both introductory and advanced CS courses, including AP CS (Utah State Board of Education, n.d.).

States have also created multiple pathways for teachers to obtain a CS endorsement that include exams or experiences. For example, certification in Nevada can be earned via coursework or exam (NAC 391.196 and NAC 391.202). New York has approved four pathways: an approved bachelor's or master's degree program, an individual evaluation pathway, industry experience, or an additional certificate pathway. New York also allows teachers seeking an initial certification in CS to complete a minimum of 12 semester hours of coursework in CS, even though all other initial certifications require 30 semester hours of coursework in the content area (8 NYCRR 80-3.7).

Micro-Credentialing

Micro-credentialing, also called competency- or mastery-based credentialing, is a relatively modern approach to teacher PD that has the potential to provide an efficient and effective means for teachers to demonstrate acquisition of specific skills or sets of skills. These skills are components of the complex disciplinary knowledge and pedagogical practices that comprise high-quality teaching. Over time, teachers can earn multiple micro-credentials for a variety of skills that, taken together or "stacked," indicate an advanced mastery of professional knowledge for a given discipline (Code.org, 2019). In education, micro-credentials have the ability to focus on skills relevant to classroom instruction and the development of teacher competencies that are important for practice (rather than a teacher's demonstration of pure content knowledge which may not always transfer to quality instruction).

Micro-credential providers typically offer online resources to support teacher learning in the selected area. Teachers are free to decide how they will learn the targeted skills. Micro-credentials can be earned through a variety of modalities such as workshops, academic coursework, individual study, or participation in professional learning communities. Teachers submit evidence of their knowledge and skill such as lesson plans, analyses of student work samples, videos of classroom interactions, and/or reflections on aspects of classroom practice. The rubrics used to score submissions are available online, so teachers can prepare their submission materials with the rubric criteria in mind. Some micro-credentials can be earned at little or no cost, and teachers can submit materials for consideration at their convenience (Code.org, 2019).

Because the demand for certified CS teachers exceeds the supply from IHE teacher preparation pathways or alternative pathways, micro-credentialing may offer a scalable approach to increasing the number of CS teachers. Micro-credentials focus on the development of targeted skills and can be individualized based on the need of the teacher. For example, teachers currently certified in other disciplines can build CS-specific competencies, and career changers (CS professionals who are interested in entering the teaching profession) can develop their pedagogical practices (Code.org, 2019).

Although micro-credentials offer a promising avenue for developing and certifying abilities related to CS instruction, this approach is new enough that we do not have data about their effectiveness in promoting and assessing high-quality instruction (DeMonte, 2017). Currently, several states are exploring how micro-credentials might play a role in increasing the number of CS teachers. In Massachusetts, teachers seeking licensure in Digital Literacy and Computer Science (DLCS) must demonstrate knowledge of all 12 subject matter areas in the DLCS standards. Teachers can demonstrate this knowledge via successful accumulation of state-approved micro-credentials that collectively address all 12 knowledge areas. The University of Rhode Island is working with BloomBoard, a large micro-credential provider, to create a series of CS micro-credentials (Code.org, 2019). BloomBoard has developed partnerships with 16 states to create opportunities to earn micro-credentials toward CS certification, and other states appear to also be exploring ways to use micro-credentials to demonstrate professional learning and competency (Code.org, 2019; DeMonte, 2017).

State Policies Governing Pre-service Teacher Preparation Programs

Although states retain the authority to set their teacher licensure requirements,[1] the process teacher candidates must follow is similar across the country. Typically, teachers obtain a bachelor's degree from an IHE which includes a specified amount of time of mentorship in the classroom. Some states require teachers to take national exams in pedagogy and content to demonstrate competency, although each state sets the passing score for teachers in their state. Other states such as Texas and California create and administer state-specific teacher competency exams. The length of time and additional training required to progress through the teaching profession and licensure process is also set by individual state policy (Zinth, 2017).

In the United States, there are over 26,000 teacher preparation programs. Of these programs, 70% are traditional schools of education located within IHEs, 20% are alternative pathways located at IHEs, and 10% are alternative pathways in other locations (Kuenzi, 2018). Without specific policy and clear state strategies to clarify how CS will be included in teacher preparation, IHEs are reluctant to invest in the development of CS teacher preparation programs. State policies that facilitate change in teacher preparation programs include adding CS content to teacher standards, creating requirements for state approval of CS teacher preparation programs, or state funding to develop these programs (Code.org et al., 2020).

CS Content or Standards

State policy can require that CS content be incorporated into teacher preparation programs in various ways. Recent state legislation in Connecticut and Ne-

---

[1] Generally licensure refers to the initial full licensure process, certification refers to teacher credentials broadly, and endorsement refers to an add-on or supplemental credential that is earned by an already licensed teacher. The terms licensure and certification are often used interchangeably. Endorsements generally require coursework in subject content knowledge and pedagogical content knowledge, but not general pedagogy.

vada has required teacher preparation programs to include instruction in CS for all pre-service teachers [2019 Conn. Legis. Serv. P.A. 19-128 (S.B. 957); 2019 Nevada Laws Ch. 434 (S.B. 313)]. Arkansas has also required teacher preparation programs to include CS instruction for elementary teachers for the past few years. At the early childhood and elementary levels, programs for generalist educators can incorporate CS content and methods into existing course requirements, including integration into other core subjects. Similarly, programs for technology specialists, such as education technology or library/media specialists, should be updated to include more CS and computational thinking.

At the secondary level, teachers typically specialize in one subject area. Generally, full pre-service teacher preparation programs require teachers to complete coursework for a major in the content area (e.g., CS) and in education. However, CS majors are less likely to prepare for teaching, consider teaching, or ultimately teach K–12 in comparison to other content area majors (Velez et al., 2019). At the same time, CS departments across the country are already overburdened and struggling to keep up with CS student demand (NASEM, 2018). This complicates matters for teacher preparation programs that want to create a CS teacher pathway or a requirement for education majors to take CS courses but are limited in support from their CS departments. Some IHEs are turning to dual certification—adding CS to a pre-service teacher's coursework plan—to more quickly produce qualified CS teachers. One such program at the University of Alabama (See Chapter 8, this Volume) requires secondary mathematics education majors to take one CS course and provides a second optional course with a stipend (Gray, 2017).

State Approval of Programs

A systematic approach to addressing the shortage of teachers with CS credentials requires state support for the development of accredited teacher preparation programs within IHEs, and institutional commitment and support to maintain them. In the past, most IHE CS teacher development programs have been created for in-service teachers to add a CS qualification to their license or earn a graduate degree. However, to create a sustainable pipeline of CS teachers, more IHEs are turning their focus to *pre-service* or initial teacher preparation, and states are preparing to approve these programs (Code.org et al., 2020). For example, in 2018 the Pennsylvania Department of Education (PDE, 2018) developed a content-specific framework for the development and approval of grade 7–12 CS teacher preparation programs.

Teacher preparation programs in each state must be approved or accredited by the state department of education or an independent professional educator standards board (Chamberlin, 2017). In addition, many states require programs to be accredited by the Council for the Accreditation of Educator Preparation (CAEP, 2018). Thirteen states still lack a comprehensive set of K–12 CS standards, which are vital for the accreditation of teacher preparation programs (Code.org et al., 2020). Until 2018, CAEP accreditation for CS programs required the use of the technology education standards from the International Society for Technology in Education (ISTE). CAEP now allows state flexibility for CS education program accreditation and ISTE recently collaborated with the CSTA on the development of standards for CS educators. However, until these are adopted or adapted by states, IHEs will not have motivation to launch CS teacher preparation programs. Both Praxis and Pearson developed content exams for CS education, which can drive statewide adoption and teacher standards (ETS, n.d.; National Evaluation Series, n.d.).

State Funding

Integrating CS into teacher preparation programs requires institutional motivation, time, and funding. Institutions have found developing robust and sustainable programs to be challenging. Dedicated state-level funding can support IHEs in the initial development of CS teacher preparation programs, but thus far, only Maryland, Nevada, and Washington have allocated funds for this purpose (Code. org et al., 2020). 2019 legislation in Nevada allows the Board of Regents to apply for a state grant to develop curriculum and standards for pre-service teacher preparation in CS (N.R.S. 396.5199). The Washington Opportunity Expansion Fund program was created by legislation in 2011 and is an example of a program which allowed companies to donate tax credits to a fund that could be used by colleges and universities in the state to expand high-demand programs. Central Washington University and Western Washington University were awarded grants in 2016 to develop CS teaching endorsements (WSOS, 2016).

Another approach to the funding of teacher preparation in CS is the initiative by individual IHE faculty to secure NSF funding or other research grants to develop programs. For example, the Computer Educator License program (which can be added by pre-service teachers working towards another licensure area in elementary or secondary education) at Indiana University Bloomington includes CS and computational thinking embedded into the coursework (Ozogul et al., 2018). However, relying on relatively stand-alone programs and individual faculty is not a sustainable solution. In the past, CS teacher preparation programs have lapsed with the departure of the faculty leader.

EXEMPLARS: COMPREHENSIVE STATE CASES

Over the past decade, several states rapidly enacted state policies around K–12 CS teaching, including Arkansas, Maryland, and Massachusetts. These three states all follow the same educational governance model: the electorate elects a governor, the governor appoints the state board of education, and the state board of education appoints the chief state school officer (Railey, 2017). However, they differ in terms of size, student demographics, and education funding (see Table 12.1). CS advocates in each of these states have also approached reform efforts in different ways. This section offers case studies of how each of these states structured CS education policy with respect to teacher-focused state policies.

TABLE 12.1. Geographic and Demographic Data from the National Assessment of Educational Progress (National Center for Education Statistics, 2017).

State	Geographical Location	# Districts/LEAs	# Public Schools	# Charter Schools	# Students Enrolled, K–12	# FTE Teachers	Pupil/Teacher Ratio	$ per Pupil Expenditure	% Free/Reduced Lunch	Student Racial/Ethnic Background						
										% White	%Black	% Hispanic	% Asian/Pacific Islander	% Amer. Indian/Alaskan Native	%Native Hawaiian/Other Pacific Islander	% Two or More Races
AR	South	292	1090	75	493,447	73,599	13.81	9,900	34.53	61.33	20.57	12.72	1.63	<1	<1	<3
MD	Mid-Atlantic	25	1424	49	886,221	117,750	14.84	14,523	46.67	38.19	34.05	16.45	6.44	<1	<1	<5
MA	East	431	1856	78	964,514	130,732	13.32	16,986	N/A	61.38	8.91	19.33	6.64	<1	<1	<5

Arkansas

The CS education initiative in Arkansas follows a top-down model. Governor Asa Hutchinson established the initiative in one of the first Acts he signed into law as Governor: Act 187 of the 90th General Assembly (2015 Arkansas Laws Act 187) required each public high school and public charter high school to offer at least one CS course starting in the 2015–16 school year. To complement and support this requirement, the state also: (a) brought together a working group to develop a comprehensive strategic plan, (b) established a State Director of CS Education position, and (c) dedicated funding to prepare CS teachers and support course implementation.

Act 187 established the Arkansas CS and Technology in Public School Task Force. Members of the task force were appointed by Governor Hutchinson and met six times in 2015. The task force's 2016 report, posted publicly on the Arkansas Department of Education (ADE) website, contained a summary of the group's activities, findings, general recommendations, and recommendations from five subcommittees: Awareness, Curriculum, Metrics, PD and Training, and Resources (ADE, 2016b). The resulting comprehensive state strategic plan, including tasks, start dates, and end dates, was posted publicly on the ADE website and has been regularly updated with the completion of tasks (ADE, 2019b).

The ADE State Director of CS Education was tasked with coordinating and completing many of the items in the strategic plan, including bringing together a framework development committee, petitioning the state board of education for specific policy changes, and collaborating with other offices and roles within the department. Funding has been a critical component of the sustainability of CS education in the state, and the governor and legislature have funded the initiative at $2.5 million per year since 2015 for a total investment of $15 million. Together, these elements supported a multi-pronged approach to increase the CS teaching force in the state, addressing issues of in-service PD, certification and endorsement, and pre-service teacher preparation.

In-Service

A variety of initiatives have been coordinated by the State Director of CS Education to ensure that the existing teaching force is well prepared and supported in implementation of the CS requirement. In addition to providing grant funding for teacher PD and reimbursing assessment fees to teachers who pass the CS certification exam, a statewide system of support has been created to ensure quality continuing education in CS teaching. This includes an annual CS educators conference, a statewide network of full-time CS specialists, part-time CS trainers, and a K–8 CS lead teacher program. Each of these initiatives are well funded and provide stipend incentives to teachers.

Certification

The CS endorsement in Arkansas is unique in that it can be added by teachers of any academic subject or CTE (ADE, 2019a). The state also developed a CS approval code, which can be earned by any teacher regardless of their initial licensure areas. The approval code can be obtained via a variety of pathways: prior experience teaching CS during four of the past seven years; a CS minor; a CS certification; industry-recognized certification and college coursework in CS; or prior experience teaching advanced CS courses and PD for teaching an IB or AP CS course approved by either the International Baccalaureate Organisation or College Board, respectively (ADE, 2019a).

Pre-Service

Arkansas's policies ensure that every new elementary teacher will be teaching CS and has appropriate pre-service preparation to do so. The state teaching standards for elementary education majors in the state include CS content knowledge (ADE, 2018). This ensures that new graduates entering the teaching profession have a baseline knowledge of CS education. For secondary education majors, the state has approved the CS Education for Teacher Licensure program at Arkansas Tech University, Henderson State University, and University of Arkansas Fayetteville (ADE, 2020). At the University of Arkansas, a partnership of the Arkansas State Board of Education, the Winthrop Rockefeller Foundation, and the Walton Family Foundation (called ForwARd) provided funding for scholarships to incentivize pre-service teachers to study CS education (University of Arkansas, 2019). The ADE established a two-year provisional license for candidates interested in non-traditional routes to educator licensure in CS, and funded tuition for the first 50 candidates (ADE, 2016a).

Maryland

Maryland CS education reform efforts took both a grassroots-up and top-down approach beginning in 2011. The initial movement began at the grassroots level, focused on broadening participation in computing by raising awareness about CS education and providing PD for in-service teachers. In 2011, only 28% of the school systems reported that more than 10% of their graduates had taken at least one computing course; in 2016, this increased to 72% of the school systems (Garvin et al., 2018). This dramatic increase shows the success of the grassroots effort to increase teacher capacity through PD and expand CS courses across the state.

After this initial grassroots and teacher-focused effort, a steering committee with 45 interested stakeholders from government, education, industry, and non-profit organizations worked from the top down to enact state policy and funding to support schools and school systems. In 2016, the steering committee agreed to create a central location for the CS education efforts in the state. In 2018, legislation signed into law by Governor Larry Hogan established the Maryland Center for Computing Education (MCCE) and provided $7 million in state funding over three fiscal years for both in-service CS teacher PD and pre-service teacher preparation reform (MD Code, Education, § 4-111.4; MD Code, Education, § 12-118).

The 2018 legislation also required that each Maryland public high school must offer a high-quality CS course by the 2021–22 school year, and county boards must make efforts to incorporate CS instruction in each middle and elementary school while broadening participation to increase enrollment of "female, students with disabilities, students of ethnic, racial, and other demographic groups that are underrepresented in the field of computer science" (MD Code, Education, § 4-111.4). This held school systems accountable at the school level. By the end of the 2017–18 school year, 67% of the diploma granting high schools offered at least one high quality CS course. Within one year, this increased to 81% of the high schools. The school systems are on track to meet the policy conditions by the 2021–22 school year.

In-Service

The existing certification policy in Maryland allows any teacher to teach up to two classes in another content area. This policy was leveraged by the grassroots PD effort to quickly scale CS teacher capacity and enable schools to offer CS courses across the state (Garvin et al., 2019). The effort is continued by the MCCE, which was directed to "provide PD and programs to broaden and sustain the pool of teachers" (MD Code, Education, § 12-118). The bulk of the state funding is intended to provide PD for in-service teachers to be able to teach CS and to meet the requirement for all high schools to offer a high-quality CS course.

Certification

Teachers who already hold a certification in another content area in Maryland can add a CS certification by taking 30 credit hours (15 in CS and 15 in CS-related courses) from an IHE or taking the Praxis II CS exam. This certification is not required for teachers who teach only one or two CS classes per year. Non-CS certified teachers who teach more than two CS classes are required to earn six credits toward the CS certification each year (COMAR 13A.12.02.02).

For individuals who do not yet hold any teaching certification, there are four distinct pathways to become a certified CS teacher in Maryland: (a) those with a CS bachelor's degree must complete 21 credits of education coursework and one year of teaching; (b) career-changers with industry experience can teach CS in CTE departments by meeting the education or occupational requirements for CTE along with the required education coursework; (c) those who hold a bachelor's degree in any area must meet school system requirements and pass content and pedagogy exams; and (d) those who hold a bachelor's degree in any area can complete a master's degree in teaching from an IHE. All pathways require the passage of the Praxis basic skills exam.

Pre-Service

A portion of the state funding is designated for traditional pre-service teacher preparation programs to develop plans to incorporate CS into their programs. The first round of MCCE grants were awarded to 13 public and private IHEs across the state in 2019. Proposals submitted by teams of education and CS faculty described how the IHE will incorporate CS into their teacher education programs. In general, awardees plan to increase CS content knowledge in accordance with Maryland's K–12 CS Standards as well as CS pedagogy and teaching methods with a focus on equity, inclusion, and diversity.

Massachusetts

Massachusetts was an early leader of many CS education policies that have since been adopted across the United States. The initial state CS coordinating entities, the Commonwealth Alliance for Information Technology Education (CAITE), and the Massachusetts Computing Attainment Network (MassCAN)[2] are often referenced by other states as successful models for advancing CS education reform. CAITE was the foundation for ECEP, which has scaled the CS education policy reform coordinating model across 22 states and the territory of Puerto Rico.

Coordinated CS education work in Massachusetts began with the creation of MassCAN (2014 Massachusetts H.B. 4377, Section 102). The organization was charged with coordinating the major CS education stakeholders in the state and provided with $1.5 million in 1:1 matching funds to promote CS education advocacy and policy efforts. Combined leadership from MassCAN, higher education, government, the Massachusetts Department of Elementary and Secondary Education (DESE), local education agencies, and non-profits facilitated the adoption of CS initiatives.

DESE, the State Board of Education, former Massachusetts Governor Deval Patrick, MassCAN, and NSF-funded projects such as CAITE and Broadening Advanced Technological Education Connections (BATEC) developed a set of seven policy support initiatives that would support the growth of CS in the state while developing the teacher workforce and would be carried out by MassCAN (Vinter et al., 2015). These seven policies were outlined at the 2014 Massachusetts STEM Summit by DESE, MassCAN, and Wellesley College: voluntary state K–12 CS standards, CS curriculum frameworks, CS PD counting towards math and science re-certification, CS counting as a math/science graduation credit, CS counting for math/science admission in higher education, CS in-service licensure endorsement, and pre-service CS courses for dual certification (Massachusetts Department of Elementary and Secondary Education, 2019a). These teacher-focused policies continue to be refined and adjusted to meet the needs of K–12 students and teachers.

---

[2] MassCAN ceased operations in 2018.

In-Service

Prior to the existence of national PD offerings, CAITE, in partnership with BATEC, the Commonwealth Information Technology Initiative (CITI), ECEP, and Education Development Center (EDC), tracked and offered a wide range of in-service PD in Massachusetts. Industry, NSF, and other state and national programs like Code.org, Mobile CSP, Bootstrap, and ECS funded the PD or offered teacher stipends for attendance. As initiatives have matured and grants have run their cycle, there is a lack of funding and fewer PD offerings than in prior years. This reduction in the number of PD offerings suggests that the current in-service CS PD plan in Massachusetts, like plans in other states, is not a stable or sustainable model.

Certification

DESE, with support from the Board of Education and MassCAN, has been the driver of the certification plan in the state. Teachers of grades 5–12 who apply for DLCS licensure must demonstrate subject matter knowledge in 12 specific areas[3] of CS, grouped into three major strands—Computing and Society, Digital Tools & Collaboration and Computing Systems, and Computational Thinking (Massachusetts Department of Elementary and Secondary Education, 2019b). The competency review process allows teachers to demonstrate this knowledge via documentation of teaching experience or at least 10 hours of professional learning in each area. Alternatively, a pre-service educator can complete the performance-based Structured Guidance and Supports process with 150 hours of field-based experience. There is no Massachusetts test for the DLCS license; however, this is currently in development with an anticipated launch date of September, 2021.

Pre-Service

Pre-service education policy efforts began in earnest after the Digital Literacy and Computer Science (DLCS) Standards were approved by the Board of Elementary and Secondary Education in 2016 and DESE formed the DLCS Implementation Panel in 2017. The DLCS Implementation Panel, led by DESE, Mass-CAN, and the Massachusetts Computer Using Educators (MassCUE), consisted of a group of 30–35 diverse stakeholders and was charged with developing recommendations for:

- Licensing DLCS teachers through a Competency Review (CR) process;
- Synthesizing public comment on proposals related to DLCS licensure and subject matter knowledge requirements;
- Identifying DLCS PD needs of in-service teachers; and
- Cultivating a communication plan to support DLCS Framework implementation and credentialing (Peske, 2017).

---

[3] http://www.doe.mass.edu/stem/dlcs/?section=512smk#512smk

With emerging teacher certification pathways, IHEs began to develop CS teacher preparation programs. Lesley University and Gordon College are currently the only in-state CS teacher preparation providers; however, there has been discussion from leaders in the University of Massachusetts system and other state and private institutions.

The State Board of Education is currently revising general elementary and early childhood teaching licenses. Once approved, all new elementary and early childhood teachers will graduate from pre-service programs with the required DLCS content and pedagogy knowledge. By the time of publication, there may be additional approved teacher preparation programs, as well as elementary and early childhood teachers graduating with DLCS content knowledge.

NEXT STEPS

The 2013 report *Bugs in the System*, published by the CSTA just before the groundswell of state CS policy activity, proposed a call to action with eight recommendations for future state and federal policy (Lang et al., 2013). We close this chapter by (a) juxtaposing the *Bugs in the System* report's recommendations against the current landscape of state-level CS teacher-focused policy, and (b) suggesting alternatives beyond the traditional approaches to meet the need for more CS educators.

The Current Landscape in Response to the Bugs in the System Recommendations

> Establish a system of certification/licensure that ensures that all CS teachers have appropriate knowledge of and are prepared to teach the discipline content. Establish a system of certification/licensure that accounts for teachers coming to the discipline from multiple pathways with appropriate requirements geared to those pathways (Lang et al., 2013, p. 26).

As of September 2019, 38 states have adopted a certification, endorsement, licensure, or authorization that allows a teacher to teach CS courses (Code.org et al., 2019). States have varied in their approach to credentialing, with some states creating both a licensure and add-on endorsement, and other states creating only one of these options. States diverge in the grade levels authorized by CS certifications and endorsements as well as the orientation of these authorizations to traditional academic CS courses, CTE courses, or both. Ongoing debates about increasing the rigor of teacher certification requirements are colored by teacher shortages that plague many states (Darling-Hammond & Podolsky, 2019; Dee & Goldhaber, 2017).

> Require teacher preparation institutions and organizations (especially those purporting to support STEM education) to include programs to prepare CS teachers (Lang et al., 2013, p. 26).

Of the policy areas discussed in this chapter, states made the least progress developing CS teacher preparation programs. Only 19 states have approved pre-service teacher preparation programs in CS even though 38 states have CS teacher licensures or endorsements (Code.org et al., 2019). The shortage of pre-service teacher preparation programs is a major barrier to increasing the number of credentialed CS teachers. The creation of the programs, in turn, is hampered by a lack of faculty with the qualifications to prepare pre-service CS teachers; a lack of curricula, assessment tools, and other instructional resources; and the absence in some states of K–12 CS state standards to align program content (Stanton et al., 2017).

In order to create a truly sustainable CS teaching workforce, all elementary teachers need CS and computational thinking knowledge, and pre-service secondary teachers need pathways to work towards CS certification. State leadership can serve a critical role in the development of teacher preparation programs. For example, the state educator standards of required knowledge and skills for elementary generalists and educational technology specialists should include CS content. To help drive the development of programs preparing secondary CS teachers, states can provide financial support in the form of grants to IHEs and stipends for teacher candidates. Stipends for teacher candidates can lower candidates' financial hurdles to pursuing a CS credential, while grants can reduce or eliminate financial challenges IHEs might otherwise face in recruiting and hiring faculty and establishing the new programs.

> Establish a system of certification/licensure that accounts for previous teaching experience ("grandfathering") for teachers with at least two years of experience teaching CS courses that are aligned to grade-level CSTA K–12 Computer Science standards (Lang et al., 2013, p. 26).

Some states have adopted policies allowing teachers to earn CS certification by substituting CS teaching experience for traditional coursework requirements; in some cases only during a transitional period when a new CS credential is implemented [e.g., New York, Iowa] (8 NYCRR 80-3.14; Iowa Admin. Code 282-13.28(272)). However, this approach is more prevalent in the 13 states with comprehensive K–12 CS education strategic plans (Code.org et al., 2019). Further, some states do not permit teaching experience to substitute for coursework requirements (either in CS, or across subject areas) based on the belief that course completion and licensure exam performance are the only means to ensure a candidate's mastery of requisite knowledge and skills.

Micro-credentialing, a competency-based credentialing approach of growing state interest, may eliminate the need for policies that allow substitution of teaching experience for other requirements. A micro-credentials system could allow CS teachers to demonstrate mastery of rigorous content and pedagogy during classroom practice. Looking forward, state systems of licensure and credentialing will need to be flexible in order to add CS to the K–12 education of all students. As more states develop flexible systems, state data on student achievement in CS courses and the qualifications of teachers who teach those courses may build support for novel CS credentialing approaches.

> Provide a certification/licensure pathway that includes both content and pedagogical knowledge for those transitioning into teaching from industry (Lang et.al., 2013, p.26).

Although alternative teacher licensure pathways have existed since the early 1980s (Walsh & Jacobs, 2007), the convergence of growing student interest in CS coursework—both academic and career/technical—and the lack of qualified teachers has made alternative certification pathways an attractive option for states seeking to grow the CS teacher workforce. States vary on the amounts of pedagogical training required for individuals transitioning from industry to education, although a trend to streamline entry into the teaching profession has reduced pedagogical requirements (Woods, 2016). In some states, career-changers can meet those requirements during their first year to two years of teaching. Some states—including those with acute teacher shortages in high-demand careers, technical fields, or STEM disciplines—allow the certification of part-time "adjunct" educators who demonstrate subject-area competency but are required to complete little if any pedagogical training before entering the classroom. For example, Florida issues adjunct teaching certificates to individuals who pass a subject area test and meet other minimum qualifications. These certificates can be annually renewed for up to three years provided the teacher is rated effective or highly effective each academic year (F.S.A. § 1012.57).

> Establish a CS Praxis exam that assesses teacher knowledge of Computer Science concepts and pedagogy (Lang, et al., 2013, p. 26).

Since 2013, Praxis and Pearson have each developed CS exams that evaluate candidates' knowledge of CS concepts and pedagogy (ETS, n.d.; National Evaluation Series, n.d.). Not all states use national examinations for teacher certification, but some states have contracted with Pearson to create a version of the national exam specific to that state (e.g.,Pearson Education, 2021).

> Provide comprehensive PD for teachers to enable them to achieve or maintain a certification/license or endorsement in CS (Lang, et al., 2013, p. 26).

In-service teacher PD has thus far focused almost exclusively on preparing teachers to teach CS for the first time or to earn a CS credential. A few states have developed PD programs and pathways for CS teachers to expand their knowledge. However, as more teachers across the U.S. gain initial skills in teaching CS courses and earn licensure credentials, there will be a need for a system of continuing education and educator support. One potential area for advancement would be the creation of a National Board Certification in CS to allow CS educators to demonstrate mastery of advanced knowledge and skills. Micro-credentials, as discussed earlier in this chapter, likewise provide structured professional learning opportunities for teachers to advance their CS teaching knowledge or earn an endorsement in CS.

> Incentivize school level administrators to offer rigorous CS courses offered by qualified CS teachers (Lang et al., 2013, p. 26).

Few states today provide incentives for building-level leaders to offer rigorous CS coursework. Oklahoma provides school systems with an opportunity to proudly display their robust CS programs with a Champions of Excellence designation next to their school report cards. One of the criteria for achieving the designation is that the school "employs certified or credentialed computer science teachers in all computer science classrooms" (Oklahoma State Department of Education, 2019, p. 5).

School administrators' authority to dictate course offerings, curricula, or teaching assignments within their building varies by state, school system, and school. Further, federal and state accountability systems created in response to the Every Student Succeeds Act (ESSA) do not provide incentives for school leaders to offer CS courses as they do for other types of coursework (ESSA, 2015). That said, rather than incentivizing local decision makers to offer rigorous CS courses, states are increasingly moving to mandates, either to require high schools to offer CS (19 states; Code.org et al., 2019), or to require all students to complete CS coursework to earn a high school diploma (Mississippi and South Carolina; Mississippi Department of Education, 2019; S.C. Code of Regulations R. 43-234(I)(A)).

Shedding light on local disparities in the availability of CS course offerings and demographics of students enrolled in and completing those courses may drive incentives or mandates for high schools to offer, or students to take, CS coursework. Legislation enacted in Washington State in 2019 codified a requirement that districts annually report the total number of CS courses offered in each school, the number and percentage of students who enrolled in a CS program disaggregated by various enumerated student academic and demographic characteristics, and the number of CS instructors at each school, disaggregated by certification (if applicable), gender, and highest academic degree (2019 Wash. Legis. Serv. Ch. 27 (S.H.B. 1577), RCWA 28A.300.587).

Alternatively, grant programs that support school system development of K–12 CS programs (e.g., Pennsylvania's *Targeted Grants*) can eliminate local financial barriers and incentivize the offering of CS courses taught by a credentialed instructor. In 2019, Colorado enacted legislation that created the Computer Science Education Grant Program "in order to increase enrollment or participation of traditionally underrepresented students in computer science education" (C.R.S.A. § 22-97-203). In awarding grants, the state board of education must give priority to applications that (1) will serve high-poverty, rural, or a high percentage of minority or female students; (2) expose students to diverse professionals in CS;

or (3) indicate a low number of CS activities in the school or district (C.R.S.A. § 22-97-203).

State Policies Beyond Traditional Approaches

Addressing CS teacher shortages may require policy approaches in addition to those around traditional preparation, credentialing, and PD. A broader set of policy approaches might include: (a) expanded offering of AP CS Principles (CSP), (b) broader offering of CS dual enrollment, (c) co-teaching models, and (d) summer teacher externships.

Expanded Offering of AP CS Principles (CSP) Courses

AP CSP teaches programming skills in an interactive approach in which students work individually and in teams to solve problems (College Board, n.d.a.). Unlike other rigorous CS courses that can be taught only by an CS-certified instructor, the College Board authorizes teachers from across disciplinary backgrounds (including those who do not hold a CS teaching credential) to teach AP CSP by participating in course-specific PD (College Board, n.d.b.), including online mentoring (College Board, n.d.c.). With this approach, the College Board is helping address the CS teacher shortage by broadening the pool of educators who are authorized to deliver AP CSP.

Broader Offering of CS Dual Enrollment

Dual enrollment courses are postsecondary courses offered to high school students, often for both high school and postsecondary credit. They may be taught by a postsecondary faculty member or approved high school teacher, at the college campus, high school, a third-party location, or online. While relatively few high school CS teachers will possess the qualifications to teach college-level CS coursework, CS faculty may be an under-tapped resource for offering rigorous CS courses that can spark student interest in pursuing a CS credential or degree. Alternatively, states may consider models such as Colorado's CS education grants (C.R.S.A. § 22-97-102) and Indiana's STEM Teach III (STEM Teach, n.d.), that provide resources for secondary teachers interested in becoming qualified to teach postsecondary CS coursework.

Co-Teaching Models

Under the co-teaching model, a certified classroom teacher collaborates with another individual—often an industry-embedded professional—to co-deliver course content. For example, Microsoft's TEALS model pairs a trained volunteer CS professional with a high school teacher to co-teach CS (TEALS, n.d.). TEALS and other co-teaching models address the CS teacher shortage by allowing schools lacking a CS instructor to offer CS coursework while potentially providing the high school teacher with PD to be able to teach CS alone in the future. Additionally, if well-executed, co-teaching models provide real-world, problem-based and project-based experiences for students to apply CS knowledge and skills with the guidance of the industry-embedded professional.

Summer Teacher Externships

Some states require CTE teachers to have recent work experience or hold a current industry credential in the area in which they wish to teach (e.g., Virginia; VA Code Ann. § 22.1-298.1). In such states, an absence of recent CS or IT work experience can prevent teachers from earning a CTE CS certification and teaching CS courses. Summer teacher externships can address this barrier. Missouri has a definition for "local business externship" and requires that externship hours count as contact hours of PD (V.A.M.S. 168.024). Iowa's externship program provides secondary math, science, and technology teachers paid full-time six-week summer externships in local businesses and agencies as well as one graduate credit via the University of Northern Iowa's Continuing Education program (Iowa Governor's STEM Advisory Council, n.d.).

REFERENCES

8 NYCRR 30-1.8

8 NYCRR 80-3.7

8 NYCRR 80-3.14

2014 Massachusetts H.B. 4377

2015 Arkansas Laws Act 187 (H.B. 1183)

2018 Maryland Laws Ch. 358 (H.B. 281)

2019 Conn. Legis. Serv. P.A. 19-128 (S.B. 957)

2019 Idaho Laws Ch. 118 (H.B. 215)

2019 Nevada Laws Ch. 434 (S.B. 313)

2019 Ohio Laws File 10 (Am. Sub. H.B. 166)

2019 Wash. Legis. Serv. Ch. 27 (S.H.B. 1577)

Arkansas Department of Education. (2016a). *Arkansas professional pathway to educator licensure (APPEL): FAQ's computer science option.* http://dese.ade.arkansas.gov/public/userfiles/HR_and_Educator_Effectiveness/APPEL/APPEL_Computer_Science_FAQ_s2017-2018_Updated_December_2016_.pdf

Arkansas Department of Education. (2016b). *Computer Science and Technology in Public School Task Force: Report of activities, findings, and recommendations.* http://dese.ade.arkansas.gov/public/userfiles/Learning_Services/Curriculum%20and%20Instruction/Resource%20Mat/Computer%20Science/taskforce/CSTF_12_16_Report.pdf

Arkansas Department of Education. (2018). *Competencies for elementary teachers, grades K–6.* http://dese.ade.arkansas.gov/public/userfiles/Educator_Effectiveness/Becoming_a_Teacher_or_School_Leader/AR_Educator_Competencies/K–6_All_Competencies_6-15-18.pdf

Arkansas Department of Education. (2019a). *Arkansas computer science: Approval code requirements.* https://docs.google.com/document/d/11qCJG_1Q21wfZUXQLm0_IVniicvE- 1pRsDSjR4lFd_Q/edit

Arkansas Department of Education. (2019b). *Arkansas K–12 computer science: A comprehensive plan for the development and implementation of Arkansas's K–12 computer science standards.* https://docs.google.com/document/d/1irX746sAaXCBvqneUstU d2measwftjaW8JpKBiyBzVM/edit

Arkansas Department of Education. (2020). *Approved IHE programs for educator licensure.* https://dese.ade.arkansas.gov/Files/20201106142459_IHE_Approved_Programs_Matrix_May_2020.pdf

CAEP. (2018). *ISTE discontinuing SPA program review with national recognition.* www.ncate.org/accreditation/caep-accreditation/spa-standards-and-report-forms/iste

Code.org. (2018). *Everyone and no one can teach CS: Certifications eligible to teach CS (by state).* http://bit.ly/cscertification

Code.org. (2019). *Micro-credentials: Building computer science teacher capacity.* https://advocacy.code.org/micro-credentials.pdf

Code.org, CSTA, and ECEP. (2019). *2019 state of computer science education.* https://advocacy.code.org/

Code.org, CSTA, and ECEP (2020). *2020 state of computer science education.* https://advocacy.code.org/stateofcs

College Board. (n.d.a). *AP computer science principles.* https://apcentral.collegeboard.org/courses/ap-computer-science-principles?course=ap-computer-science-principles

College Board. (n.d.b). *AP computer science principles frequently asked questions, Do I need specific experience to teach AP Computer Science Principles?* https://apcentral.collegeboard.org/courses/ap-computer-scienceprinciples/course/frequently-asked-questions/do-i-need-specific-experience-teach-ap-computer-scienceprinciples

College Board. (n.d.c). *Enroll in AP Mentoring.* https://apcentral.collegeboard.org/professional-development/enroll-in-ap-mentoring

College Board. (2019, July 31). *Participation in AP computer science principles more than doubles 3 years after launch.* https://www.collegeboard.org/releases/2019/participation-csp-nearly-doubles

COMAR 13A.12.02.02

C.R.S.A. § 22-97-102

C.R.S.A. § 22-97-203

Darling-Hammond, L., & Podolsky, A. (2019). Breaking the cycle of teacher shortages: What kind of policies can make a difference? *Education Policy Analysis Archives, 27,* 34.

Dee, T. S., & Goldhaber, D. (2017). *Understanding and addressing teacher shortages in the United States.* The Hamilton Project.

DeMonte, J. (2017). *Micro-credentials for teachers: What three early adopter states have learned. So far.* American Institutes for Research. Retrieved from: https://www.air.org/sites/default/files/downloads/report/Micro-Creditials-for-Teachers-September-2017.pdf

ESSA. (2015). *Every Student Succeeds Act of 2015,* Pub. L. No. 114-95 § 114 Stat. 1177.

ETS. (n.d.). *Praxis: Computer science.* https://www.ets.org/praxis/prepare/materials/5652

F.S.A. § 1012.57

Garvin, M., Neary, M., Carrigan, K., & desJardins, M. (2018). Maryland computing education growth from 2011–2016. In *Proceedings of the third annual respect conference.* IEEE.

Garvin, M., Neary, M., & Desjardins, M. (2019). State case study of computing education governance. *ACM Transactions on Computing Education (TOCE)*, *19*(4), 1–21.

Google, Inc., & Gallup, Inc. (2015). *Searching for computer science: Access and barriers in U.S. K–12 education*. https://services.google.com/fh/files/misc/searching-for-computer-science_report.pdf

Gray, J. (2017). *UA receives funding for math, computer science teacher pathway*. https://www.ua.edu/news/2017/08/ua-receives-funding-for-math-computer-science-teacher-pathway/

Indiana University Bloomington. (2019). *Computer educator undergraduate license addition*. https://education.indiana.edu/licensing/initial-licensure.html

Iowa Admin. Code 282-13.28(272).

Iowa Governor's STEM Advisory Council. (n.d.). *Iowa STEM teacher externships program*. https://iowastem.org/externships

Kuenzi, J. J. (2018). *Teacher preparation policies and issues in the Higher Education Act* (Rep.No. R45407). Congressional Research Service.

Lang, K., Galanos, R., Goode, J., Seehorn, D., Trees, F., Phillips, P., & Stephenson, C. (2013). *Bugs in the system: Computer science teacher certification in the US*. The Computer Science Teachers Association and The Association for Computing Machinery.

Maryland State Department of Education (MSDE). (2020). *Adding an endorsement: Credit count*. http://www.marylandpublicschools.org/about/Pages/DEE/Certification/Endorsements.aspx

Massachusetts Department of Elementary and Secondary Education. (n.d.). https://gateway.edu.state.ma.us/elar/licensurehelp/LicenseRequirementsCriteriaPageControl.ser

Massachusetts Department of Elementary and Secondary Education. (2019a). *Digital literacy and computer science (DLCS)*. http://www.doe.mass.edu/stem/dlcs/?section=512

Massachusetts Department of Elementary and Secondary Education. (2019b). *Digital literacy and computer science DLCS instructional resources*. https://www.doe.mass.edu/stem/dlcs/?section=512#resources

MD Code, Education, § 4-111.4

MD Code, Education, § 12-118

Michigan Department of Education, Office of Educator Excellence. (2019, April 16). *Quick reference: Courses that can be taught*. https://www.michigan.gov/documents/mde/courses_taught_by_endorsement_523203_7.pdf

Mississippi Department of Education. (2019). *Mississippi public school accountability standards*. https://www.mdek12.org/sites/default/files/mississippi_public_ school_ accountability_standards_2019.pdf

NAC 391.196

NAC 391.202

National Academies of Sciences, Engineering, and Medicine (NASEM). (2018). *Assessing and responding to the growth of computer science undergraduate enrollments*. The National Academies Press. https://doi.org/10.17226/24926

National Assessment of Educational Progress (NAEP). (2017). *The nation's report card: State profiles*. https://www.nationsreportcard.gov/profiles/stateprofile?chort= 1&sub=MAT&sj=&sfj=NP&st=MN&year=2017R3

National Center for Education Statistics. (2009). *National Assessment of Educational Progress: An overview of NAEP.* National Center for Education Statistics, Institute of Education Sciences, U.S. Dept. of Education.

National Evaluation Series. (n.d.). *Computer science.* https://www.nestest.com/TestView.aspx?f=HTML_FRAG/NT315_TestPage.html

N.J.S.A. 18A:26-2.26

N.J.S.A. 18A:26-2.27

N.R.S. 396.5199

Oklahoma State Department of Education. (2019). *Program of excellence: Computer science.* https://sde.ok.gov/sites/default/files/documents/files/POE-CS.pdf

Ozogul, G., Karlin, M., & Ottenbreit-Leftwich, A. (2018). Preservice teacher computer science preparation: A case study of an undergraduate computer education licensure program. *Journal of Technology and Teacher Education, 26*(3), 375–409.

Pearson Education. (2021). *Indiana CORE assessments for educator licensure.* http://www.in.nesinc.com/PageView.aspx?f=GEN_Tests.html

Pennsylvania Department of Education. (2018). *The framework for computer science: 7–12 program guidelines.* https://www.education.pa.gov/Documents/Teachers-Administrators/Certification%20Preparation%20Programs/Specific%20Program%20Guidelines/Computer%20Science%207-12%20Program%20Guidelines.pdf

Pennsylvania Department of Education. (n.d.). *FAQs for the PAsmart computer science and STEm education grants.* https://www.education.pa.gov/Policy-Funding/SchoolGrants/PAsmart/Pages/faqs.aspx

Pennsylvania Department of Labor and Industry. (n.d.). *PAsmart grants.* https://www.dli.pa.gov/Businesses/Workforce-Development/grants/Pages/pasmart.aspx

Peske, H. (March 6, 2017). *Application solicitation for the 2016 Massachusetts Digital Literacy and Computer Science (DLCS) Framework Implementation Panel.* [Memorandum]. Center for Instructional Support: Massachusetts Department of Elementary and Secondary Education.

Railey, H. (2017). State education governance structures: 2017 update. 50-state review. *Education Commission of the States.* https://www.ecs.org/state-education-governance-structures-2017-update/

R.C. § 3319.236

S.C. Code of Regulations R. 43-234(I)(A)

Stanton, J., Goldsmith, L., Adrion, W. R., Dunton, S., Hendrickson, K. A., Peterfreund, A., Yongpradit, P., Zarch, R., & Zinth, J. D. (2017). *State of the states landscape report: State level policies supporting equitable K–12 computer science education.* Waltham, MA:

STEM Teach. (n.d.). *About STEM Teach.* www.stemteachindiana.org/about-stem-teach

TEALS. (n.d.). *About.* https://www.tealsk12.org/about/

U.C.A. § 9-22-113

University of Arkansas. (2019). *ForwARd arkansas computer science education scholarship.* https://teach.uark.edu/forward-arkansas-computer-science-scholarship.php

Utah State Board of Education. (n.d.). *Educator endorsements.* https://schools.utah.gov/cte/computer/educatorendorsements

VA Code Ann. § 22.1-298.1

V.A.M.S. 168.024

Velez, E. D., Lew, T., Thomsen, E., Johnson, K., Wine, J., & Cooney, J. (2019). *Baccalaureate and beyond (B&B:16/17): A first look at the employment and educational experiences of college graduates, 1 year later* (NCES 2019-241). U.S. Department of Education. National Center for Education Statistics. https://nces.ed.gov/pubsearch/pubsinfo.asp?pubid=2019241

Vinter, S., Stanton, J., & Jones, J. (2015). *MassCAN Strategic Plan 2015-2018*. http://masscan.edc.org/documents/annual_reports/MassCAN_Strategic_Plan_2015-2018.pdf

Washington State Opportunity Scholarship. (2016.) *2016 legislative report*. Olympia, WA: Washington State Opportunity Scholarship & College Success Foundation.

Walsh, K., & Jacobs, S. (2007). *Alternative certification isn't alternative*. https://www.nctq.org/nctq/images/Alternative_Certification_Isnt_Alternative.pdf

Woods, J. R. (2016). *Mitigating teacher shortages: Alternative teacher certification*. https://www.ecs.org/wp-content/uploads/Mitigating-Teacher-Shortages-Alternative- Certification.pdf

Yadav, A., Hambrusch, S., Korb, T., & Gretter, S. (2013). Professional development for CS teachers: A framework and its implementation. In *Future directions in computing education summit*. http://web.stanford.edu.proxy-bc.researchport.umd.edu/~coopers/2013Summit/attendees.html

Zinth, J. (2017, April). *States' teacher certification policies for computer science* [Memorandum]. Education Commission of the States. https://www.ecs.org/wp-content/uploads/State-Information-Request_Computer-Science-Certification.pdf

AUTHOR/EDITOR BIOGRAPHIES

Dr. Chrystalla Mouza is Distinguished Professor and Director of the School of Education at the University of University. Her research focuses on teacher learning and professional development, applications of emerging technologies in K–12 classrooms, and computer science education. She directed several projects aimed at improving teaching and learning with technology in high-need schools, preparing in-service and pre-service teachers in computer science, and broadening participation in computing. Dr. Mouza's work has been published in key outlets including the Journal of Research on Technology in Education and Teachers College Record. She is the recipient of the 2010 Distinguished Research in Teacher Education Award from the Association of Teacher Educators and current Editor-in-Chief of the journal of Contemporary Issues in Technology and Teacher Education.

Dr. Aman Yadav is a Professor of Educational Psychology and Educational Technology at Michigan State University with extensive experience in research, evaluation, and teacher professional development. His research and teaching focuses on improving student experiences and outcomes in computer science and engineering classrooms at the K–16 level. Within this line of inquiry, he studies: (1) how to prepare pre-service and in-service teachers to teach computer science and

Preparing Pre-Service Teachers to Teach Computer Science: Models, Practices, and Policies, pages 257–266.

integrate computational thinking ideas within subject areas; and (2) how to implement active learning approaches to improve student outcomes in undergraduate computer science and engineering. His work has been published in a number of leading journals, including ACM Transactions on Computing Education, Journal of Research in Science Teaching, Journal of Engineering Education, and Communications of the ACM. Twitter (@yadavaman), website (http://www.amanyadav.org)

Dr. Anne Ottenbreit-Leftwich is the Barbara B. Jacobs Chair in Education and Technology and Associate Professor of Instructional Systems Technology within the School of Education and an Adjunct Professor of Computer Science at Indiana University—Bloomington. Dr. Leftwich's expertise lies in the areas of the design of curriculum resources, the use of technology to support pre-service teacher training, and development/implementation of professional development for teachers and teacher educators. Dr. Leftwich investigates ways to teach computer science and expand these offerings at the preservice and in-service levels. She is Indiana's co-lead for the Expanding Computing Education Pathways (ECEP) alliance and working with CSforIN to increase computer science access opportunities for all K–12 Indiana students. Her research focuses on teachers' value beliefs related to technology and computer science, as well as how those beliefs influence teachers' adoption and implementation.

CONTRIBUTOR BIOGRAPHIES

Heather Benedict is a learner experience designer and has consulted with organizations to leverage technology as a creative platform. In her collaborations, she brings over 15 years of experience creating and delivering learning experiences for children and educators in both the formal and informal space. She has a BFA in Drama (Design) from Carnegie Mellon University and an M.Ed in Learning Technologies from the University of Minnesota. She has a passion for engaging learners with STE[A]M+C content through computational thinking and the maker movement in education. She is currently an instructional designer for an online public high school in Minnesota.

Dr. Lisa Benson is a Professor of Engineering and Science Education at Clemson University, and the Editor-in-Chief of the *Journal of Engineering Education.* Her research focuses on the interactions between student motivation and their learning experiences. Her projects include studies of student attitudes towards becoming engineers and scientists, and their development of problem solving skills, self-regulated learning practices, and beliefs about knowledge in their field. She earned a B.S. in Bioengineering (1978) from the University of Vermont, and M.S. (1986) and Ph.D. (2002) degrees in Bioengineering from Clemson University.

Dr. Leigh Ann DeLyser has spent her career building the K-12 computer science (CS) field. As an Executive Director of CSforALL (csforall.org), she oversees programs and strategic planning and supervises research to build support for high quality CS education at all levels. A former high school and university CS educator, Dr. DeLyser understands challenges faced by teachers, administrators, and students developing their competency in the field and accessing high-quality learning opportunities and resources. Her influential "Running on Empty" report guides policies and research that support high-quality program implementation. Previously, Dr. DeLyser was Director of Research and Education at CSNYC, which built a foundation for CS in New York City public schools. She received a Ph.D in Computer Science and Cognitive Psychology, with a focus on CS education, from Carnegie Mellon University.

Sarah T. Dunton is the Director of Expanding Computing Education Pathways (ECEP) Alliance, a National Science Foundation Broadening Participation in Computing Alliance. Ms. Dunton holds a degree in Women's Studies and a M.Ed. in Teacher & Curriculum Studies with a concentration in Learning, Media & Technology from the University of Massachusetts Amherst. She works with broad based leadership teams from K-12, higher education, research, government, and industry in 22 states and the territory of Puerto Rico to develop strategies that will increase the number and diversity of students in K-16 computer science education and career pathways. As a seasoned leader in STEM education and advocacy, Ms. Dunton has launched multiple programs and developed strategic plans to address the persistent inequities in STEM.

Dr. Nikleia Eteokleous holds a Ph.D in Educational Administration with emphasis in Educational Technology, M. Ed in Instructional Systems, and M. Ed in Educational Administration from Pennsylvania State University and a B.A in Public and Business Administration from the University of Cyprus. She works as an Associate Professor in Educational Technology at the Educational Sciences Department, School of Educational and Social Sciences at Frederick University (Cyprus). She is also the Head of the Distance Learning Committee (responsible for policy development, strategic planning, and professional development training) and co-founder of the Robotics Academy. Her research interests focus on technology integration in educational practice, teacher education and technology, technology-enhanced learning environments and online learning. She is currently involved in research activities related to open and online distance learning, and the integration of robotics in educational practice.

Dr. Michelle Friend is an Assistant Professor in the Teacher Education Department at the University of Nebraska Omaha. Her research focuses on equity in computer science and on interdisciplinary connections between computer science and other disciplines to enhance learning in each. She received her Ph.D. from the Stanford University Graduate School of Education in Learning Science and Technology Design, and holds a Master of Information Science and Bachelors of Biochemistry and Science Education degrees from Indiana University. She previously taught computer science at The Girls Middle School in Mountain View, CA, and was the first female president of the Computer Science Teachers Association.

Dr. Megean Garvin is the Director of Research and Assessment at the Maryland Center for Computing Education (MCCE), University System of Maryland. She oversees MCCE's publications, grants, and reports. She also monitors state education policy and regulation changes. She is focused on strengthening the computing knowledge, skills, and pedagogy of the Maryland teaching workforce and monitoring progress towards providing equitable access and participation in computing for all Maryland public school students. Dr. Garvin earned her doctorate in Science Education Curriculum and Instruction from the University of Maryland, College Park and master's degree in Environmental Science and Policy from Johns Hopkins University.

Dr. Lynn Goldsmith, Distinguished Scholar at Education Development Center, Inc., has explored central issues in STEM education from a variety of perspectives, including student learning, teacher professional development, and educative curriculum materials. Over the past five years she resurrected the memory of exploring her high school's PDP-9 and turned her attention to issues related to computer science education. This work includes exploring states' progress toward equitable K–12 computer science education and developing elementary science and mathematics curriculum materials that are rich in opportunities for computational thinking.

Dr. Joanna Goode is the Sommerville Knight Professor in the College of Education at the University of Oregon. She began her career in education as a high school computer science teacher in a large, diverse urban school, and she builds on this experience to research how educational policies and practices can foster equity, access, and inclusion in K-12 computer science education. Joanna has directed multiple National Science Foundation-sponsored research projects, developed the equity-focused *Exploring Computer Science* high school course, and is the co-author of the book, *Stuck in the Shallow End: Education, Race, and Computing* (MIT Press, 2008/2017).

Dr. Jeff Gray is a Professor in the Department of Computer Science at the University of Alabama. Dr. Gray received a B.S and M.S in Computer Science from West Virginia University and a Ph.D. in Computer Science from Vanderbilt University. His research interests are in the areas of software engineering and computer science education. He has served as the Principal Investigator on several National Science Foundation and U.S Department of Education projects that are focused on teacher professional development for computer science, with a focus on broadening participation in computing. He also organizes summer camps and various competitions for K-12 students, including mentoring of high school science fair projects. Dr. Gray was one of the original members of the Code.org Advisory Council and serves as the coordinator for the North Alabama NCWIT Aspirations award. He is the co-Chair of Alabama Governor Kay Ivey's Computer Science Advisory Council.

Dr. Mark Guzdial is a Professor in Computer Science & Engineering and Engineering Education Research at the University of Michigan, after spending 25 years in the College of Computing at Georgia Tech. He studies how people come to understand computing and how to make that more effective. He is an ACM Fellow and received the 2019 ACM SIGCSE Outstanding Contributions to Education award.

Dr. Katie A. Hendrickson leads government affairs efforts across multiple states for Code.org, supporting state coalitions and policymakers in expanding access to computer science education. She manages national and state-level data analysis on computer science education metrics, including the annual State of Computer Science Education report. Dr. Hendrickson holds a doctorate in Curriculum and Instruction from Ohio University, a master's degree in Cultural Studies in Education, and a bachelor's degree in Mathematics Education. She is a former secondary mathematics teacher and Albert Einstein Distinguished Educator Fellow.

Dr. Aleata Hubbard is a Senior Research Associate in the Learning and Technology program at WestEd. Her research focuses on understanding and documenting the knowledge educators develop around how to teach computing, particularly at the secondary school level. She also conducts external program evaluations for organizations in the areas of informal and alternative pathways into computing and professional learning for high school and community college instructors. She received a B.S in Computer Science and French & Francophone Studies from Carnegie Mellon University and an M.A and Ph.D in Learning Sciences from Northwestern University.

Dr. Jung Won Hur is an Associate Professor in the department of Educational Foundations, Leadership and Technology at Auburn University. She earned her doctorate at Indiana University in 2007 and received her M.Ed. and B.S. in Elementary Education from Seoul National University of Education, South Korea. Her research interests focus on technology integration in classrooms, online teacher professional development, computer science education, and global learning. She is interested in designing learning environments where every student is encouraged to achieve his/her potential.

Dr. Yasmin B. Kafai is Lori and Michael Milken President's Distinguished Professor at the Graduate School of Education at the University of Pennsylvania. She is a designer of online tools and communities to promote coding, crafting, and creativity across grades K–16. She helped develop with MIT colleagues the popular programming tool Scratch. Currently, she is developing a high school curriculum with electronic textiles that introduces students to computer science. She is also creating new fabrication tools and activities that bring biomaking into classrooms. She has written and edited books for MIT Press in addition to several national policy reports. Her work has received generous funding from the National Science Foundation, the Spencer Foundation, and the MacArthur Foundation.

Dr. Yvonne Kao is a Senior Research Associate in the Learning and Technology group at WestEd. Her work focuses on curriculum and assessment in K-12 mathematics and computer science education and the design and use of educational technology. Her research uses a range of approaches from nationwide cluster-randomized trials to smaller behavioral studies. She also leads user experience research, program evaluation, and provides technical assistance on instructional design and student assessment. She received a B.S in Computer Science, Mathematics, and Psychology from the University of Wisconsin--Madison and a Ph.D in Psychology from Carnegie Mellon University.

Dr. Mike Karlin is a former K-12 teacher and current adjunct faculty member in Indiana University's Instructional Systems Technology program, as well as an instructor for in-service teachers in ISTE's Computational Thinking course. Dr. Karlin's research has focused on exploring best-practices in instructional design related to technology professional development, educational technology interventions, and how to best prepare preservice teachers to be future computer educators. Dr. Karlin is also deeply passionate about leveraging technology in support of efforts to broaden participation in computing. His doctoral dissertation and current research agenda focus on strategies and recommendations for broadening participation in computer science. He received his B.S and M.S in education from the University of Kansas and his Ph.D in Instructional Systems Technology from Indiana University.

Dr. Cazembe Kennedy is a Teaching Consultant for Clemson University's Office of Teaching Effectiveness and Innovation and a Lecturer in Clemson's Honors College. His research focuses on Science, Technology, Engineering, and Mathematics education, particularly evidence-based practices, misconceptions, curriculum design, and policies relating to diversity, equity, and inclusion in learning environments both in-person and virtual. His projects include identifying factors across institutions that impact retention and graduation rates of Black computer science majors, evaluating institutional high-impact practices to improve equity, and analyzing instructor pedagogy shifts when moving from in-person to virtual or blended learning environments. He earned a B.S. degree in Computer Science from Morehouse College (2014) and his Ph.D. in Human-Centered Computing from Clemson University (2020).

Dr. Eileen Kraemer is a Professor in the School of Computing at Clemson University and the graduate coordinator of the Ph.D program in Human-Centered Computing. Prior to her time at Clemson, she served as Professor of Computer Science and Associate Dean of the Franklin College of Arts & Sciences at the University of Georgia. Dr. Kraemer received a B.A in Biology from Hofstra University(1980), an M.S in Computer Science from Polytechnic University (now the Tandon School of Engineering at NYU) (1985), and a Ph.D in Computer Science from Georgia Institute of Technology (1995). Her current research focuses on CS education at the undergraduate and 7-12 levels. She serves as a Co-PI on the NSF-funded CRōCS (Culturally Responsive * Computer Science) project at Clemson University, which seeks to broaden participation in computing in South Carolina by preparing computer science teachers to effectively use culturally responsive, inclusive pedagogies.

Dr. Jill Long holds an Ed.D in Educational Leadership from Hamline University, M.A. in Curriculum and Instruction from the University of St. Thomas, and a B.A in Elementary Education from The College of St. Scholastica. She is an Assistant Professor and Director of the Elementary Degree Completion Program in the School of Education and Social Work at The College of St. Scholastica. Her work includes teaching and curriculum writing with a focus on equity and social justice, developing effective teacher dispositions, and collaborating with the National Center for Computer Science Education at St. Scholastica. She has presented nationally and internationally on a curriculum model infusing computational thinking and computer science in a teacher licensure program.

Dr. Chery Lucarelli is Professor and Chair of Doctoral and Graduate Education Studies at The College of St. Scholastica and a former elementary teacher. She has facilitated the design of several online graduate programs, including the Doctorate in Educational Leadership, the nationally-ranked Master of Education, and Certificate in Computer Science Education. Recently, she served as PI on the TeachCS@CSS grant funded by Google and Co-PI on a National Science Foundation grant to scale computer science teacher professional development by leveraging online communities of practice. Her research interests focus on inclusive innovation in education, online learning, and educational technology. She holds a Ph.D in Education with an emphasis in Educational Technology, an M.Ed in Math and Science Education, and a B.S in Elementary Education.

Dr. Chrystalla Mouza is Distinguished Professor and Director of the School of Education at the University of University. Her research focuses on teacher learning and professional development, applications of emerging technologies in K–12 classrooms, and computer science education. She directed several projects aimed at improving teaching and learning with technology in high-need schools, preparing in-service and pre-service teachers in computer science, and broadening participation in computing. Dr. Mouza is the recipient of the 2010 Distinguished Research in Teacher Education Award from the Association of Teacher Educators and current Editor-in- Chief of the *Journal of Contemporary Issues in Technology and Teacher Education.*

Dr. Raphaela Neophytou holds B.A in Primary Education (Frederick University), M.A in New Technologies for Communication and Learning (Cyprus University of Technology), and Ph.D. in Education (Frederick University). Since 2018 she has been working at the Frederick University Open and Distance Learning Center while since 2014 she has been a member of the Frederick University Robotics Academy Teaching Team. She has participated in various academic conferences and research programs in Cyprus and abroad, including the ERASMUS + (e.g., RoboScientists) which focuses on educational technology and robotics. She has also participated in a variety of social, cultural, and outreach events organized by the Robotics Academy. Her research interests focus on technology integration in educational practice.

Dr. Rebecca (Becky) Odom-Bartel holds a Ph.D from the University of Alabama. She is an Instructor in the Department of Computer Science (CS) at The University of Alabama (UA). Dr. Bartel is a founding member of the inaugural Women in STEM Experience (WISE) conference, a regional conference for empowerment in STEM. She teaches courses in CS Education Methods, CS Principles, Python, and Web Foundations and Design. Dr. Bartel is an active contributor with the Alabama State Department of Education Computer Science division where she works to increase training for in-service and pre-service teachers throughout the state.

Dr. Anne Ottenbreit-Leftwich is the Barbara B. Jacobs Chair in Education and Technology and Associate Professor of Instructional Systems Technology within the School of Education and an Adjunct Professor of Computer Science at Indiana University—Bloomington. Dr. Leftwich's expertise lies in the areas of the design of curriculum resources, the use of technology to support pre-service teacher training, and development/implementation of professional development for teachers and teacher educators. Dr. Leftwich investigates ways to teach computer science and expand these offerings at the preservice and in-service levels. She is Indiana's co-lead for the Expanding Computing Education Pathways (ECEP) alliance and working with CSforIN to increase computer science access opportunities for all K–12 Indiana students. Her research focuses on teachers' value beliefs related to technology and computer science, as well as how those beliefs influence teachers' adoption and implementation.

Jennifer Rosato is the Director of the National Center for Computer Science Education and an Assistant Professor in the Computer Information Systems department at the College of St. Scholastica. She has been the principal investigator on several national grants that advocate for and support K-12 teachers and teacher educators, including creating curriculum and professional development. She was a member of the CSTA Standards for CS Teachers writing team and led the development of the resources for Schools of Education. She holds an M.A in Information Systems Management from Carnegie Mellon University and a B.A. in Biochemistry from the College of St. Scholastica.

Dr. Christa Treichel, President of Cooperative Ventures, works as an independent consultant providing program evaluation and educational research services. Recent projects include working on an NSF-funded project to develop sustainable computer science pathways in rural and tribal schools in addition to documenting STEM program impacts, with an emphasis on underrepresented and under-resourced K-12 and post-secondary populations for a global corporate foundation. She holds a Ph.D in Educational Research and Program Evaluation, an M.A in Family Education, and a B.A in Psychology. Dr. Treichel enjoys partnering with clients to help them examine their work and use what they learn to positively impact others.

Jeffrey Xavier is a senior consultant at SageFox Consulting Group, based in Amherst, Massachusetts. He has a background in psychology and applied sociology. During his time at SageFox, he has worked on evaluation and research of many STEM and computer science focused grant-funded initiatives. This includes multiple initiatives focused on creating common metrics across a suite of computing education projects including early efforts on The NSF's Broadening Participation in Computing Alliances (BPC-A) as well as work on the NSF's CS10K suite of projects. His work is increasingly focused on CS education and understanding how to address issues around broadening participation in computing.

Dr. Aman Yadav is a Professor of Educational Psychology and Educational Technology at Michigan State University with extensive experience in research, evaluation, and teacher professional development. His research and teaching focus on improving student experiences and outcomes in computer science and engineering at the K-16 level. His work has been published in a number of leading journals, including *ACM Transactions on Computing Education, Journal of Research in Science Teaching, Journal of Engineering Education,* and *Communications of the ACM.*

Dr. Hui Yang is an education researcher (STEM & CS) at SRI International. Her research interests focus on the design of technology-rich learning environments that engage learners into meaningful experiences and teacher preparation in computer science education. Prior to joining SRI, Dr. Yang was a postdoctoral associate in the department of Information Science at Cornell University. Yang completed her doctoral training at the University of Delaware.

Rebecca Zarch is Director of SageFox Consulting Group, an independent organization specializing in computer science education, research and evaluation. Over the last decade Ms. Zarch has increased her focus on computer science education initiatives and has served as a PI on several National Science Foundation grants focused on broadening participation and capacity building efforts. Ms. Zarch holds a Masters of Business Administration from the Heller School of Social Policy at Brandeis and a Masters in Education from the Harvard Graduate School of Education, both of which inform her approach to managing complex change in support of equitable education.

Dr. Jeremy Zelkowski is professor of secondary mathematics education at The University of Alabama and a former high school mathematics teacher. His research focuses on mathematics teacher preparation program design, measurement in mathematics education, policy related to high school mathematics, and technology use for teaching mathematics. Dr. Zelkowski's teaching and leading is deeply invested in teacher preparation and professional development programs, focusing on delineating well-prepared teacher pathways as opposed to just-barely qualified pathways, with respect to teaching impact on student learning. He received his B.S in Mathematics and M.S in Mathematics/Curriculum & Instruction from West Virginia University and his Ph.D in Mathematics Education from Ohio University.

Jennifer Zinth is founder and principal at Zinth Consulting, LLC, a firm that provides states and the private sector with policy research, analysis and counsel on CS/STEM and high school to postsecondary transition issues. As a consultant and previously in a leadership role at Education Commission of the States, she has worked with numerous state leaders, nonprofit organizations, and philanthropies to develop a wide range of policy supports, including in-state and cross-state convenings, 50-state policy compilations, state policy gap analyses, recommendation reports, customized memos, presentations, and legislative testimony. Ms. Zinth's expertise includes (a) state legislative, statutory and regulatory tracking and analysis; (b) qualitative evaluation; (c) policy evaluation; (d) report development; and (e) in-person and virtual meeting development and execution.

Printed in the United States
by Baker & Taylor Publisher Services